How best to use the

Internet and e-mail

Jayant Neogy

UNICORN BOOKS Pvt. Ltd.

Publisher
UNICORN BOOKS
F-2/16, Ansari Road, Daryaganj, New Delhi-110002
☎ 011-23275434, 23262683, 23250704 • *Fax:* 011-23257790
E-mail: info@unicornbooks.in • *Website:* www.unicornbooks.in

Branch : Mumbai
23-25, Zaoba Wadi Thakurdwar, Mumbai-400002
☎ 022-22010941, 022-22053387
E-mail: rapidex@bom5.vsnl.net.in

Showroom :
★ **PM Publications,** New Delhi
- 10-B, Netaji Subhash Marg, Daryaganj
  New Delhi-110002
- 6686, Khari Baoli, Delhi-110006

Distributors :
★ **Pustak Mahal,** New Delhi
Delhi: ☎ 011-23276539
Bengaluru: ☎ 080-22234025
Patna: ☎ 0612-3294193

★ **V & S Publishers,** Hyderabad
☎ 040-24737290

ISBN 978-81-7806-036-1
How best to use the Internet & e-mail

Edition: 2012

***Printed at :** Unique Color Carton, Mayapuri, New Delhi-110064*

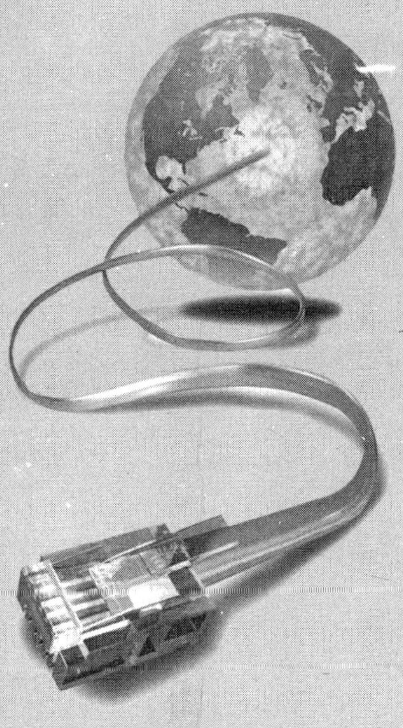

Acknowledgement

My sincere thanks are due to the entire editorial team and Unicorn Books for bringing out this third revised & enlarged edition of ***How best to use the Internet and e-mail***. Their advice and suggestions have been invaluable in updating information, verifying authenticity of the content and making important additions to cover newly emerged areas on the Internet such as Blogs, Social Networking and special chapter of resources on the Web, which will be of great value to students.

Contents

Preface

Welcome to the third edition of this book! Thank you for your support, enthusiasm and interest. It spurs us on to give you more for your money and we have done just that in this reprint. We have not only completely revised and rewritten 9 out of the 12 chapters in the current edition, but have added entirely new chapters on Social Networking, Student's Resources and a new section on Blogs.

In this era of Information Technology (IT), there has been breathtaking growth of applications, software and hardware. While the use of IT is all-pervasive, its rapid developments can easily make our current knowledge obsolete. To protect you from falling behind, the entire book has been given a complete makeover. What you hold in your hand now is the very latest information on all the subjects covered in this book.

If you have bought this book, the chances are that you already use a computer at work and perhaps at home, as well. You have already noticed how information has become the most valuable commodity in our rapidly changing society and how we have come to depend more and more on the Internet for information. And not just information, we turn to the Net to learn, to communicate, to do business, to be entertained and to form social groups. How successful we are in all these depends on two things — our computer-handling skills and our skills in using the Internet. These skills will rule our lives more and more in the times to come.

You, my readers, who have bought this book to sharpen your skills, please accept my congratulations! You have perhaps taken the most important step in your life to remain in step with the world! From now on, this book will be your friend and guide as you enter the exciting world of the Internet. Whether you are already an adept or just beginning to surf the Internet, by the time you finish you will become an Internet "Guru", no less! Together, we will walk this path towards new knowledge and power, and walk it safely!

One of the most exciting and the fastest growing segment of the Internet is social networking, a virtual meeting place in the cyber world where people meet, chat with each other, exchange videos, audio files, photographs and just plain gossip. While it is so very popular, especially amongst the young, it is also a dark place where cyber-stalking and other crimes take place. We deal with this new development in an entirely new chapter, *Chapter 9 – Social Networking*.

Today, you need not wait for a kind publisher to publish your thoughts for the whole wide world to read! You can set up your own personal Blog on the Internet in a special niche called the "Blogosphere" and air your views on current affairs, complain against persecution or give vent to very personal and intimate thoughts. Along with the rest of the world, Blogging is growing very rapidly in India as well. We have added a new section to *Chapter 7 – Beyond E-mails*, to tell you all about Blogs and how you can start your own.

We have thoroughly revised and updated *Chapter 11 – Virus, Spam and Other Perils* since we want all your Internet experiences to be pleasurable and safe. This chapter is a source for the latest information on protecting your computer from malicious attack and the means to remove viruses should any get through your defences.

For the students amongst you, there is a special bonus at the end of the book, an entirely new chapter titled *Chapter 12 – Student's Resources* devoted entirely to the needs of the student. No matter what your subjects are, you will find excellent Websites listed here for authoritative and up-to-date information on the subjects of your choice.

We wish you pleasurable reading, a great Internet experience and a safe journey through cyber-space!

— Jayant Neogy

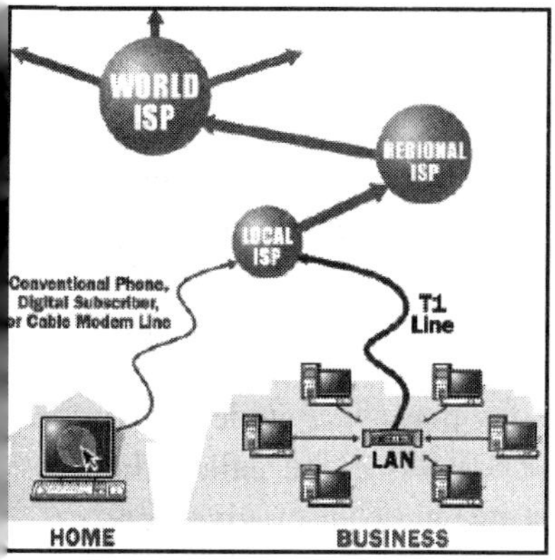

1. Introduction

In this chapter:

- You are introduced to the Internet and the World Wide Web. We look briefly at the history of the Internet and how it came into being.
- We look at how Internet has grown in India and how the growth has really accelerated in recent years.
- We look at the reason why the Internet has such a powerful influence on our lives. We look at the reasons why it is so important for us to develop computer literacy and Internet surfing skills.
- The structure and contents of this book is summarised for you. We give you suggestions on which chapter you may wish to read to learn about a specific topic.
- We explain the icons used to highlight the contents of the book so that you can easily locate tips, be warned by alerts and directed to useful information tagged as notes.

The Internet

The Internet is a worldwide series of interconnected computer networks that may be used by the public to send and receive data using a standard called the Internet Protocol (IP). The data may be in the form of e-mails or files containing pictures, video or audio clips. Data transfer between the user and Websites allow us to open Web pages and view the contents like news, stories, pictures and anything else that we can view in a newspaper or magazine. It is a "network of networks" that consists of millions of small and big news service, academic, business, and government networks, which together carry various information and services and the interlinked Web pages and other resources of the World Wide Web (WWW).

Growth

The basic applications and guidelines that make the Internet possible had existed for almost a decade before the Internet was opened to the public in the 1990s. On August 6, 1991, CERN, which straddles the border between France and Switzerland, went public with the new World Wide Web project. The Web was invented by English scientist Tim Berners-Lee in 1989.

Fig 1.01 – The Internet

Thereafter for a decade, the Internet grew at roughly 100% per year mainly by absorbing many of the already existing public computer networks in the United States and Europe. For a brief period between 1996 and 1997, the growth was even faster. This rapid growth is mainly due to lack of constricting central administration since no one person or country really owns the Internet. Networks operating in different countries could connect and talk to each other because open protocols were used much like the international networks for telephones.

By the end of 2007, over 1.2 billion people (the total population of India) use the Internet worldwide. It has been said that the Internet has already become a basic feature of global civilisation. As a result, traditional "civil society" the world over is being transformed into an Information Technology (IT) based society as a result of Internet use. It is sobering to think of this amazing power of transformation of the Internet when worldwide only 2% of the peoples of the world have regular access to the Internet.

Internet and India

The penetration of computers and the Internet is still very small when compared to the US, Europe, etc. But we are catching up rapidly. In 2007, India's annual Internet growth was 7.9% compared to the worldwide growth rate of 2.7%. Now with 18 million Internet users, India has become the ninth biggest country in terms of the total online population from its 10th position last year. The US still retains its top ranking with 153 million Internet users.

How Does It Affect You?

The Internet has profoundly influenced the way we communicate, do business, entertain ourselves and acquire information. It is already all-pervading and is going to increase its impact on our lives more and more. This is because all sources of information, entertainment and business are increasingly moving to the Internet to communicate with us. As an ordinary person, you will also find it increasingly easier to hook on to the vast network of the Internet with the help of a home computer, a modem and a telephone line. If you do not have a computer, you can go to the nearest Cyber cafe and be connected to the Internet for the cost of a cinema ticket.

Fig 1.02 – An E-mail

Since it is possible to send and receive electronic mails (e-mails) or surf the Internet for information or entertainment from any Cyber cafe without learning anything more than the most elementary Web browser commands, you may well ask, why read this book?

The reason is that since the Internet and the World Wide Web is going to have so profound an influence on us, it is only prudent to get to know it well. The purpose of this book is just that, to give you the understanding, the tools and the skills so that you too can get the most out of what will surely be the mover and shaker of the 21st century, the Internet. I promise you, this journey of discovery will be both entertaining and exciting.

What This Book Contains

The twelve chapters of the book are each quite self-contained. Here is a brief preview:

Chapter 1: Introduction

You can get some background about the Internet here. You are given some suggestions about the sequence for reading this book, depending on your experience and your needs. We explain the icons used and the liberal use of graphics.

Chapter 2: Windows Basics

Beginning with the hardware of a typical computer, you are familiarised with basic Windows operations. Skip this chapter if you know your Windows inside out. A must read for people new to computers.

Chapter 3: Connecting to the Internet

This chapter tells you how to install your modem and set up your own Internet connection. Step by step instructions to have you up and surfing the Web in no time!

Chapter 4: Web Surfing

The fun really begins for you now. You learn how to surf the World Wide Web like a champion. You learn all the time saving shortcuts and techniques here!

Chapter 5: Search Engines

You learn how to search the Internet to find the exact information you need in the least possible time. You learn where to find search engines and how to use them.

Chapter 6: E-mail

This chapter opens the doors to electronic communications. You learn all about sending and receiving e-mail. Techniques in this chapter show you how to read downloaded e-mail and compose replies without being connected to the Internet.

Chapter 7: Beyond E-mails and Surfing

This chapter takes you beyond e-mails, to newsgroups, Internet chats and video conferencing. You experience the latest methods of communication over the Internet, where you supplement the written word with sound and pictures. You are introduced to Blogs and Blogging, including how you can set up your own Blog.

Chapter 8: Entertainment on the Net

The Internet is not all information and business. You can listen to music, watch video and play games on the Internet. You are introduced to streaming media, the software you need to play music and movies, as well as Websites where you can find entertainment and games. Be warned, though, the charms of the Internet can be addictive!

Chapter 9: Social Networking

Social networking is a recent phenomenon that has taken young India by storm. You learn all about Internet communities that are both purely social and meant for business — where to find them on the Internet, how to join them and what you can do after you are registered.

Chapter 10: Sharks in the Ocean

The vast oceans of fun and games that is the Internet also have sharks in them! Unfortunately, many Websites have excessive violence, sex or racist content. They are unsuitable for most of us. Especially, you will want to protect children from exposure to such content. In this chapter, we discuss ways of controlling access to objectionable Websites.

Chapter 11: Virus, Spam and Other Perils

While we have met undesirable Internet content in *Chapter 10 – Sharks in the Ocean*, their threat is passive. You can easily block seeing what you do not want to see. Virus, worms, Trojans and spam are quite different however. They force their way into your computer, destroying data, flooding your e-mails and even crashing your computer. They take away your enjoyment of Internet surfing. To combat them, we have assembled together hints and tips, procedures and sources of software you can use to foil these invasive threats.

Chapter 12: Student's Resources

This chapter has been added keeping the students amongst you in mind. There is no shortage of information on the Internet on any subject. For education however, it is very important that the information you read on the Web is both authoritative and authentic. Sometimes, it may be dangerous to use unchecked information of doubtful accuracy. To protect you, the Websites we refer to are carefully selected to be the best and most reliable you can find.

How to Use this Book

To help you navigate this book, here are some suggestions:

- For those of you who would like a bit of "hand-holding" to become familiar with your computer, it will be a good idea to start with *Chapter 2 – Windows Basics*. Here you will get all the hints, tips, explanations you need to demystify your computer, and to tackle the Windows Operating System installed in your machine.
- For Internet basics, read *Chapter 3 – Connecting to the Internet*. It will be a good idea to first skim through *Chapter 2 – Windows Basics* as well.
- For a description of the equipment (hardware) that you need to be connected to the Internet, read *Chapter 3 – Connecting to the Internet*. Here you will learn the techniques for setting up hardware items such as your modem, and procedure for configuring your computer to connect to your Internet Service Provider (ISP).
- To search the Internet efficiently and to utilise the special features of your Web browser effectively, read *Chapter 4 – Web Surfing*. For finding, downloading and using special "search" software, read *Chapter 5 – Search Engines*.
- For a comprehensive briefing on e-mails, see *Chapter 6 – E-mails*. E-mails are perhaps the most popular means of written communication today, for business or for personal use.
- Read *Chapter 7 – Beyond E-mails and Surfing* to master the mysteries of Internet chat, newsgroups, file transfer protocols (FTP), etc. For information on Blogs, this is the right chapter to read.
- For people addicted to games, a new and exciting opportunity has opened up on the Internet. Read about it in *Chapter 8 – Entertainment on the Net*. You will find that there are many other forms of entertainment out there!

- For an insight into social networking, Websites to visit and networks to join, read *Chapter 9 – Social Networking.*
- Beware though, the Internet can be a shocking place as well, with content that may offend you. Learn all about protecting yourself and your children in *Chapter 10 – Sharks in the Ocean.*
- Not merely shocking, the Internet can be a really dangerous place. You can pick up a virus, a worm or a Trojan that will not only destroy your valuable data but may also render your computer unusable. Your inbox may be flooded with unwanted e-mail, choking it altogether. To avoid these perils and to recover from disaster, read *Chapter 11 – Virus, Spam and Other Perils.*
- The Internet is a rich source of authoritative text in almost all educational subjects along with lecture notes, tutorials and educational videos. Much of it is free. If this is what interests you, go directly to the newly added *Chapter 12 – Student's Resources.*

So, just plunge into whatever interests you – learn, have fun and be safe!

Graphics and Icons

We have designed this book for quick reference and easy reading. Graphics, such as screenshots, Web pages and illustrations have been used liberally in all the chapters. In addition, we have used special icons to highlight tips for your benefit, alerts about dangers that you must avoid and notes that you may wish to go over.

A tip contains smart ideas, shortcuts and other information that will make your work easy. Look for a TIP in each chapter that has valuable information for you on the subject covered in that chapter. A tip is the result of much experience in using computers and the Internet.

An alert warns you for danger. Like everything else in life, working with computers and on the Internet does have slips and pitfalls. You will want to avoid them to save yourself time and not to get frustrated. Look for the danger sign marked ALERT. It will tell you what to avoid and your journey through the Internet will be a safe one.

Each chapter contains useful information that you may wish to find quickly. To help you find them, we have marked the important paragraphs with a NOTE icon. Whenever you find this icon, do take the time to go over the marked paragraph carefully. They will give you useful insights.

2. Windows Basics

In this chapter:

- You are introduced to the Windows operating system. You learn about the Windows desktop, the start menu and the icons on your desktop. We show you how to start and shutdown Windows.
- We look back at the first operating system for the Personal Computer (PC). We trace the route that the "unfriendly" Disk Operating System (DOS) took to evolve into Windows.
- How do you communicate with your computer? We discuss how to set up and use the keyboard and mouse. We see how the computer answers your commands via writing on the computer's monitor screen.
- We look at basic tasks such as manipulating the windows that are opened on your monitor's screen, often referred to as your desktop. We get familiar with the Windows Explorer that you will use to manage files.
- We look at file operations in detail. Since all programmes and data on the hard disk(s) of your computer are organised as files, a good understanding of file structure and of file manipulations is essential for using your computer.
- We end this chapter with an understanding of the Recycle Bin.

A Typical Computer Set-up

What you can see in front of you when you are at your computer desk and what you can reach out and touch is hardware. Your computer will usually consist of:

- The computer itself, housed in a flat box on your desk or housed in a vertical tower, placed below your desk top
- The monitor, looking like a small TV set, placed on your desk top
- A keyboard, similar to the keyboard of a typewriter, but with many more keys
- A mouse with 2 or 3 buttons, or with two buttons and a central scrolling wheel, sitting on its mouse pad
- A printer
- A modem used to connect your computer to the Internet. The modem may be internal or external.

In addition, your computer may have additional attachments such as an external hard disk drive, a scanner and speakers for playback of multimedia files such as movies or music.

The items shown in Fig 2.01 are typical for many computer installations. The names are listed below:

1. Monitor
2. Motherboard
3. Central Processing Unit (CPU)
4. Memory Cards
5. Expansion cards such as video cards
6. Power Supply Unit (SMPS)
7. CD or DVD ROM drive
8. Hard Disk Drive
9. Keyboard
10. Mouse

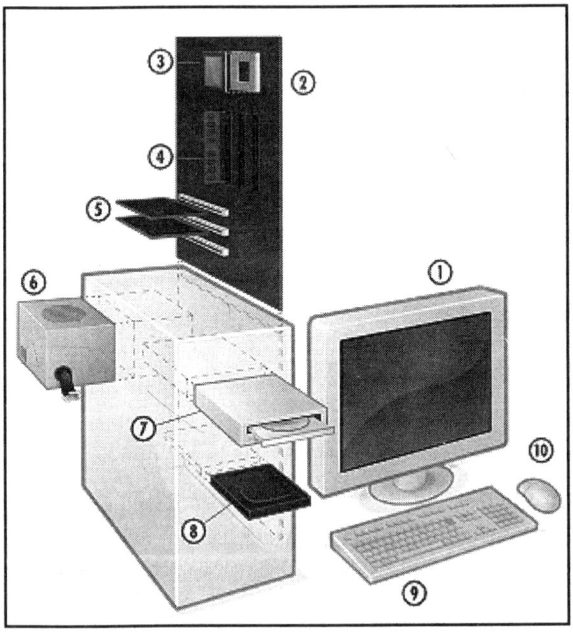

Fig 2.01 – A Typical Desk Top Computer

We will presume that you already have some knowledge of your computer's hardware and have some basic computer operation skills. The essential skills you will need include:

- Switching power on and switching the monitor, computer, modem, etc on and off
- Type commands on the keyboard

- Move the mouse cursor (or pointer) to different parts of the monitor's screen and then click the mouse buttons as required. If you have a mouse with a scroll wheel, you will use the wheel mainly to scroll the picture on the monitor's screen, up or down
- Operate other hardware devices you may have such as the printer, the scanner, etc.

Loading Instructions

Instructions for a computer are written in a language that the computer can understand. A set of instructions when taken together forms a computer programme. The operating system on your machine such as Windows XP is a programme. Word processing software such as Microsoft Office is a set of programmes including Microsoft WORD, EXCEL, etc.

A programme enables the computer to carry out your commands. You can send commands to your computer by typing commands on your keyboard or by pointing and clicking with your mouse. In turn, the computer responds by displaying its reply on the monitor's screen or by printing out the reply on the printer.

Operating Systems

The starting programme (or the set of instructions) that you load in your computer is the Operating System. When you power your computer on, this programme loads automatically. The operating system we are studying here is Microsoft Windows XP. Today, this is by far the most popular operating system in use in India, both in industry and by personal users. However, the comments of this chapter apply equally to all other operating systems of the Windows family such as Windows 98, Windows ME and Windows 2000, etc. The operating system is the fundamental programme that controls your computer. All other programmes that you may load and run on your computer such as the Microsoft "WORD" word processing programme will act on your computer through the operating system, which must be loaded first.

Discussions on other operating systems such as Linux or the Apple operating systems are outside the scope of this book.

A Little Bit of History

In this book, we will deal with the IBM PC and its clones that use the Windows operating system. They are generally referred to as personal computers. We do not discuss the Apple McIntosh which has a different system, and is relatively quite rare in India.

The Unfriendly DOS

When first introduced, personal computers used a rather unfriendly operating system called DOS (for Disk Operating System). The computer user had to type instructions at what was called the DOS Prompt that looked like "C>". The commands were cryptic and difficult to remember.

A Window Opens

Things became easier with the introduction of the "Windows" interface. Unlike DOS, Windows is pictorial or graphic in nature. Instead of having to type confusing commands, the user could now point with the mouse-driven pointer and click with the mouse button on little pictures on the screen called Icons, to make the computer to do things. The monitor screen, with several little icons is called the "Graphical User Interface" or GUI for short. While Apple computers were the first to introduce the GUI, Microsoft Windows followed shortly after.

The Current Avatar

Windows has now progressed all the way from Windows 1.0 to Windows Vista. Even within Windows XP and Vista, there are several versions meant for personal use, office use or use by a large enterprise. As of the time of writing of this edition, Windows Vista is still new. Most of the personal computer users continue to use some version of the Windows XP operating system. Therefore, discussions in this chapter will focus on Windows XP.

Since Windows 98 is no longer supported by Microsoft, you may want to upgrade your operating system soon.

Unless you have a very powerful computer preferably with a dual core processor, Windows Vista, the latest operating system from Microsoft, may not be the ideal operating system for you. Instead, you can use the tried and tested operating system Windows XP with Service Pack 2 included.

However, even for Windows XP, at least a Pentium 4 machine is recommended.

Starting and Shutting Down Windows

Starting Windows

To get some practice in starting Windows, you may follow the steps in the example below.

Switch on your computer. In a short while you will be prompted for your username and password. Once you have done so, you should see your opening screen. A typical opening screen (or desktop) is shown here. What you may see will depend both on your operating system and the programmes you

Fig 2.02 – Opening Screen

have loaded. The screen shown here has been specially compressed. In your case, it will occupy the entire screen of your monitor.

The Start button is at the bottom left of your screen and you can see icons on your Taskbar along the bottom of your screen. You can quickly launch a programme by clicking on its taskbar icon.

Fig 2.03 – Start Button and Taskbar

Opening the Start Menu

Point and click on the **Start** button to open the Start menu. You can use the arrow keys on your keyboard, or use the mouse to point at any of the options on the Start menu. A click on the selected option will open its associated sub-menu. Here the Programme option is shown highlighted and a portion of the programme sub-menu is shown open.

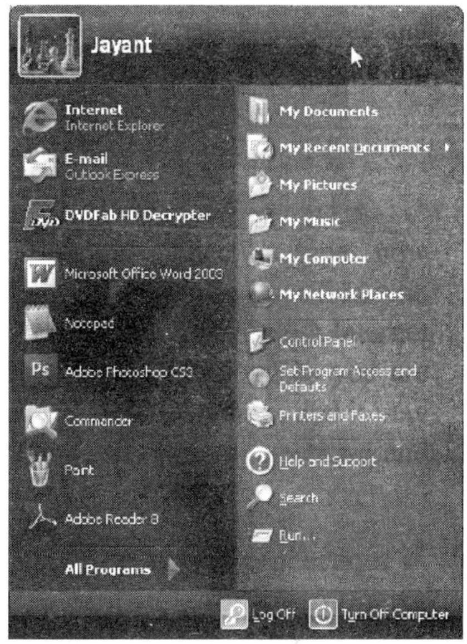

Fig 2.04 – Start Menu

In the programme sub-menu, point at a programme name and click on it to launch the programme. This is an alternative to clicking on the programme icon on the desktop that you may see along the left margin of the opening screen in Fig 2.02.

You can click on the **All Programs** button with the arrow mark ▶ to display all the programmes installed on your computer. Clicking on the programme will launch the software.

Commonly used programmes are listed along the left of the Start menu. The list is automatically updated by Windows to show recently used programmes.

Fig 2.05 – Splash Screen

Splash Screens

When a programme is launched, you will usually see its opening screen or Splash Screen. In Fig 2.05 – Splash Screen, you can see the splash screen of Microsoft Word, the popular word processing programme. The splash screen contains information on product identification, registration, copyright information, etc.

Shutting Down

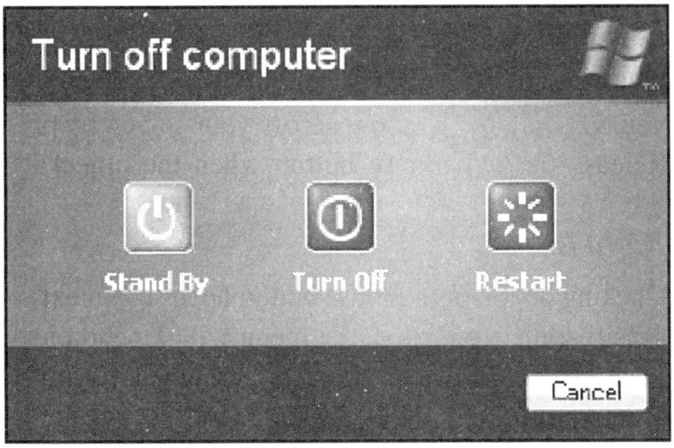

Fig 2.06 – Shut Down Dialogue Box

To shut down your computer, click on the **Start** button and then click on the **Turn off computer** option that appears at the very bottom of the Start menu. A dialogue box titled Turn off computer will appear. Click on the centrally placed **"Turn Off"** button and the computer will save your settings and then turn itself off. Other options on the dialogue box include "Stand By" and "Restart". There is also a button marked "Cancel" at the bottom right that you may click to close the dialogue box without taking any action. See Fig 2.06 – Shut Down Dialogue Box.

The Restart command is useful when you have made some setting changes to Windows that can only take effect after you have shut down and restarted Windows. To do so, you can click on the **Restart** button on the shutdown dialogue box. Note that all computers may not have the Stand By option on their machine.

Conversing With Your Computer

The Keyboard

Most common keyboards have 101 keys. Apart from the alphabet keys, there are numerical keys, navigation (arrow) keys, a keypad to enter numbers conveniently, special keys called function keys, etc. Since the keyboard is your primary means of communication with your computer, especially if you are typing out letters, reports or books like the one you are reading, it is a good idea for you to regularly practice using the keyboard.

The Mouse

You may have either a two-button or a three-button mouse. Today, the trend is to use a two-button mouse with a scroll wheel located at the centre of the two keys. The scroll wheel is mainly used to scroll whatever is on your monitor screen, up or down.

Left Button

Generally, clicking the left mouse button once will select an item and the second left button click will activate the item you have selected. In Windows XP, you can also configure your computer so that an item is both selected and activated by a single click of the left mouse button.

Left Button Drag

If the mouse pointer is on an object on your screen that can be moved, such as an open window, you can drag the window across your screen by pressing and holding down the left mouse button. Release the left mouse button when the object has reached its destination.

Right Button

Clicking on the right mouse button opens a context sensitive menu. That is, the menu will depend on what programme is running. For instance, if you point your mouse pointer to any empty part of the desktop and right click your mouse, a pop-up menu will open that lets you set the icons, the graphic properties and the display properties of the desktop. In Fig 2.07, you can see the pop-up menu with the icon properties sub-menu opened. Here you can select how the icons should be arranged on the desktop.

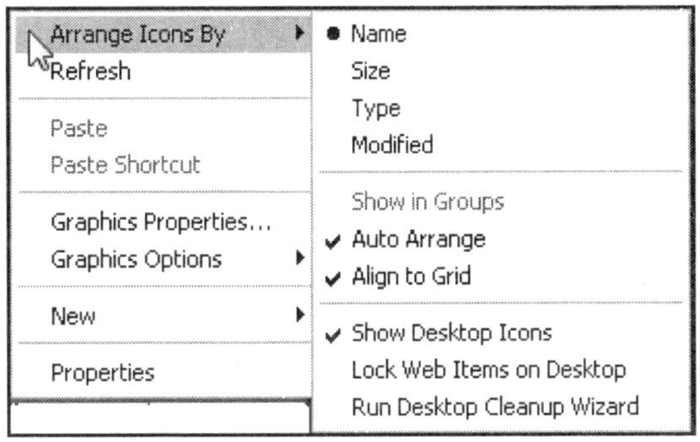

Fig 2.07 – Pop-up Menu and Icon Sub-Menu

Navigation Tools

Dialogue Boxes

Dialogue boxes permit you to hold a dialogue with your computer. For instance, you may open the Windows Help and Support centre by clicking **Start** ➔ **Help and Support** ➔ **Index** to display the dialogue box shown in Fig 2.08 – Help and Support. Type in your query in the box marked "Search" and click on the right arrow to search a new topic or type the query in the box marked "Index" and click on the button marked **Display** for Windows to respond to you.

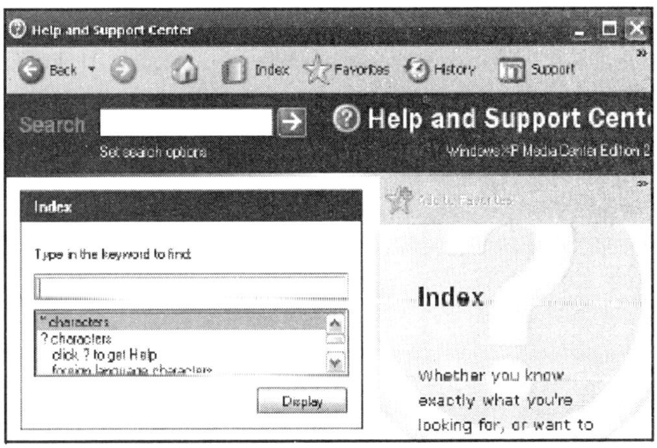

Fig 2.08 – Help and Support

Tabbed Dialogue Boxes

Tabbed dialogue boxes display a number of options in a convenient manner. A good example is the Folder Options dialogue box. You can open this box by clicking on **Start** ➔ **Settings** ➔ **Control Panel** ➔ **Folder Options** to display the dialogue box. Along the top edge, you will observe four tabs that read "General", "View", "File Types", "Offline Files". By clicking on the tab you want, you can display additional options.

Radio Buttons

Radio buttons are a convenient way to group several sets of options so that you can conveniently select the particular option you want in each set by clicking on it with your mouse. In Fig 2.09, if the General tab is open, you can observe three sets of selections titled “Tasks”, “Browse folders” and “Click items as follows”. Each set has two or more radio button that you may select.

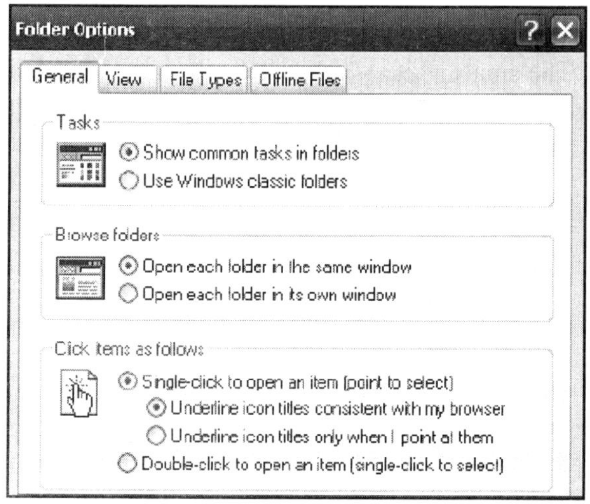

Fig 2.09 – File Types Tabbed Dialogue Box

Command Buttons

After you have responded to a dialogue box, you will want to ask Windows to execute the option you have selected, or cancel the dialogue box. If you have changed some settings, you may want to apply these changes and at other times, you may want some help from Windows regarding the dialogue box. To allow you to tell Windows exactly what you want, command buttons are provided, usually along the bottom of a dialogue box that read “OK”, “Cancel”, “Apply” and “Help”. Click on the appropriate command button for Windows to take the action you want. Note that command buttons are context sensitive too. Therefore, all the command buttons will not appear on all dialogue boxes.

Scroll Bars

Windows dialogue boxes or even full screens are not sufficient to display all the information at one time. To allow you to navigate the screen either from side to side or up and down, many windows will open with scroll bars located usually along the right and bottom margins of the window. See Fig 2.10 – Two Scroll Bars, that shows both a horizontal and a vertical scroll bar.

Scroll Buttons

Scroll buttons are located at the top and bottom of the scroll bars. You can make the window scroll either by dragging the scroll bar slider with the mouse or by clicking directly on the top or bottom scroll buttons. See Fig 2.10 – Two Scroll Bars to view scroll buttons and sliders located on both the horizontal and vertical scroll bars.

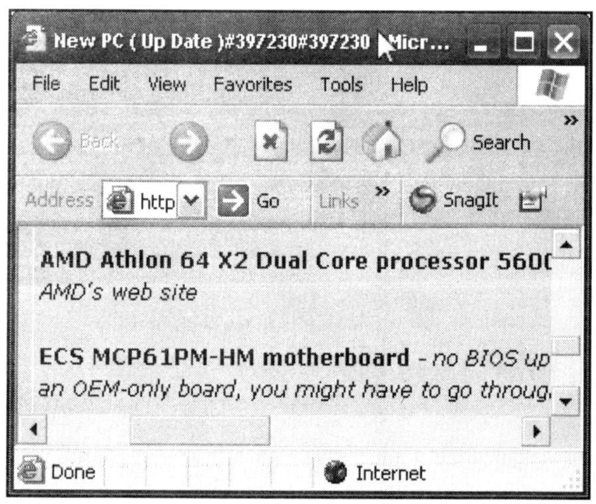

Fig 2.10 – Two Scroll Bars

Edit Boxes

The small white window often provided inside a dialogue box is called an Edit box or a Text box. You can enter a word or a command inside this box. If you make a mistake while typing, use the backspace or the insert key to edit the text. See Fig 2.08 – Help and Support.

List Boxes

Fig 2.11 – List Box shows a list of topics listed in the Windows Help and Support window. Use the arrow keys to select a topic and then click on the **Display** button for more information on the selected topic. You can open the Help and Support index by clicking **Start → Help and Support → Index** to display the list of topics arranged alphabetically.

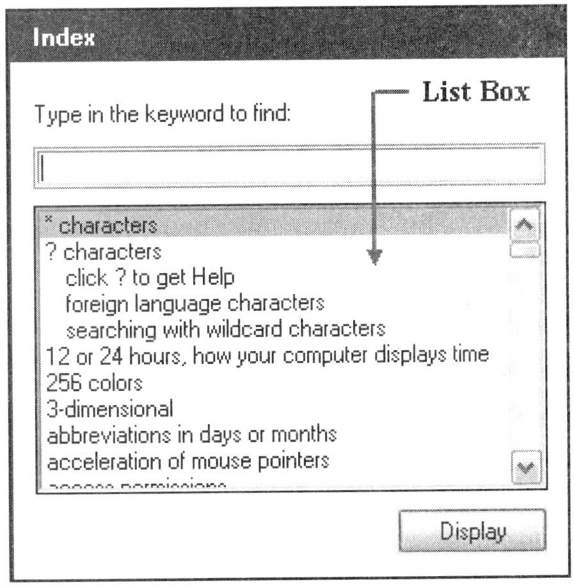

Fig 2.11 – Help and Support Index

Check Boxes

Somewhat like radio buttons, check boxes allow you to select options offered to you in a dialogue box. While radio buttons are used where you may select just one option out of two or more options, check boxes allow you to select several options at once. In Fig 2.12 – Taskbar and Start Menu properties dialogue box, you can see that 3 check boxes have been selected out of 5 under the group titled Taskbar appearance. You can open this dialogue box by right clicking on any vacant spot on the Windows Taskbar and then clicking on Properties, which is the last item in the pop-up menu that appears.

Fig 2.12 – Taskbar and Start Menu

Customising the Display

Minimising, Maximising and Moving Windows

Open the Control Panel of Windows by clicking on **Start → Settings → Control Panel.** The Control Panel window opens. You will observe three icons located at the top right hand corner of the window. They look like _, □ and ⊠. The first icon minimises the window into the taskbar, leaving the desktop free. The second icon opens the window to occupy the entire monitor screen while the third icon shuts the window down. If the window is fully open, then the second icon will change from □ to 🗗. Now clicking on the 🗗 icon will cause the window to change to a user selected size, smaller than the full screen size. See Fig 2.13 – Control Panel. We will discuss how to resize a window to any user selected size in the next section.

Fig 2.13 – Control Panel

To move a window on the desktop, click on the title bar of the window and with the left mouse button pressed down, drag the window to any desired position on the desktop. The window will stay anchored to the new position wherever you release the mouse button.

Resizing a Window

You can resize most windows by dragging its border with your mouse cursor. To do so, position the mouse cursor on the edge of the window so that it changes to a double headed arrow like this ⇔. Now, with the left mouse button pressed down, drag the border outwards to enlarge the window, or drag the border inwards to reduce the window size. You can change the window size both horizontally and vertically. See Fig 2.13 – Control Panel. You will observe a double headed arrow on the right vertical margin of the window indicating that the mouse is ready to drag that margin.

Active and Inactive Windows

If you have more than one window open on your desktop, only one window will be ready to receive your commands. This is the active window. Computer users sometimes use the phrase "the window has got focus". In other words, the window with focus is active. Only one window will be active at a time on your desktop. It is easy to switch the active window. Simply click on the title bar of the window that you wish to become active. You will observe that its title bar (of the selected window) will become brighter, while the title bars of other windows become lighter. See Fig 2.14 – Two Windows. You will notice that the "Run" window with the mouse cursor is the active window.

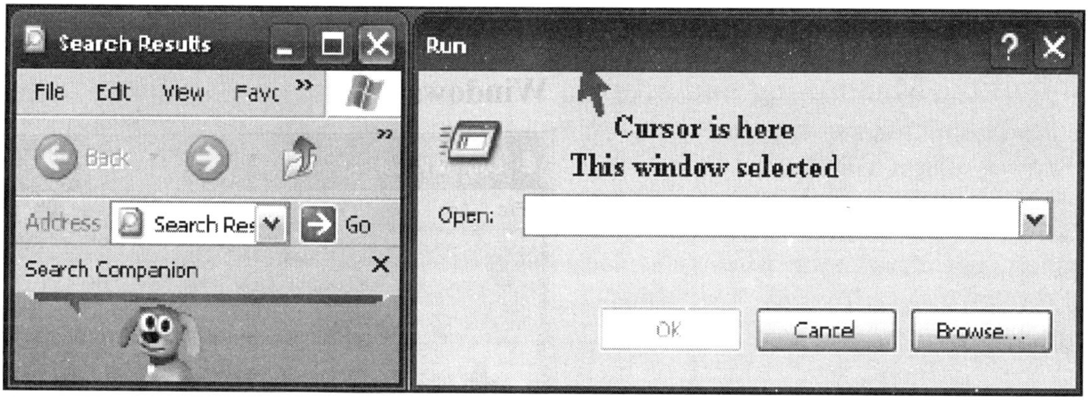

Fig 2.14 – Two Windows

The First Few Tasks

In order to become familiar with your computer and Windows XP, it is a good idea to practice some simple everyday tasks on your computer. We devote the rest of this chapter working on:

- Using the Windows Explorer
- Finding files on your computer
- Some simple file operations
- Emptying the Recycle Bin

The Windows Explorer

Programmes and data are stored in your computer's hard drive in folders and files. Folders are like the drawers in a filing cabinet while files are like individual files you store inside the drawer. Just as physical filing cabinets may have more than one drawer, a hard disk in your computer can have a number of folders, each folder containing several files.

To find and use programmes and data, you should know how to view, sort, copy, move and delete files and folders in your computer. The programme you will use is the Windows Explorer, which is a part of Windows. To launch Windows Explorer type **Start → Programs → Accessories → Windows Explorer** from your desktop. The Windows Explorer will open. See Fig 2.15 – Windows Explorer.

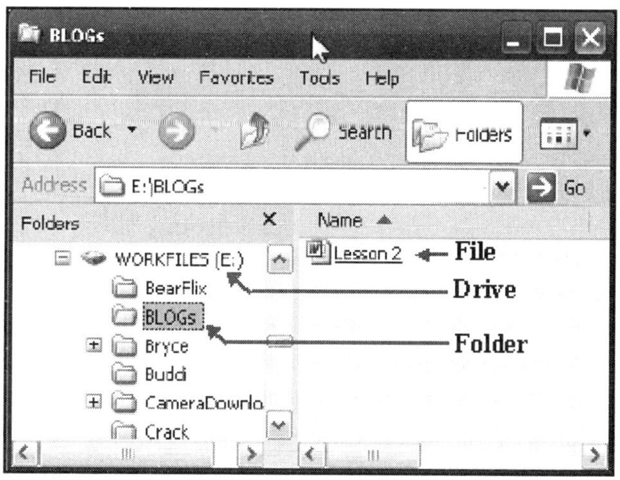

Fig 2.15 – Windows Explorer

The left pane of Windows Explorer (titled Folders) lists both drives and folders. You will notice that in the left pane, the drive E: (WORKFILES) has been expanded to display the folders in the drive. Also in the left pane, the folder BLOGs has been selected (grey coloured) to display the file Lesson 2 in the right pane (titled Name). By using both the panes, you can display all the drives, folders and files on the hard disk(s) of your computer.

The menu bar (just under the title bar) displays the menus of commands that Windows Explorer can perform for you. You will observe that the menu items are "File", "Edit", "View", "Favorites", "Tools", and "Help". Each menu item can be clicked to display its drop down menu.

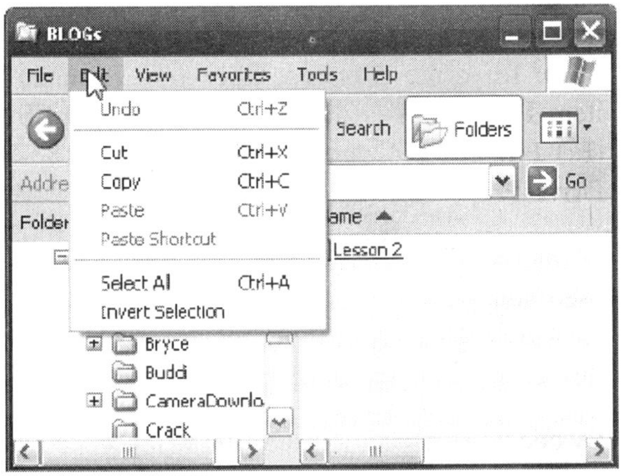

Fig 2.16 – Explorer Edit Menu

For instance, Fig 2.16 – Explorer Edit Menu displays the edit commands available.

These commands apply to the files displayed on the right pane. To work with folders and drives in the left pane, right click on the folder or drive to reveal its context sensitive menu that lists the commands you can give to the selected folder. For instance, in Fig 2.17 – Context Menu, you can see the commands available for the selected folder "Crack". For instance, you can rename the folder by left clicking on the menu item **Rename**. Some folders in the left pane will display a small + (plus) sign to the left of the folder's name.

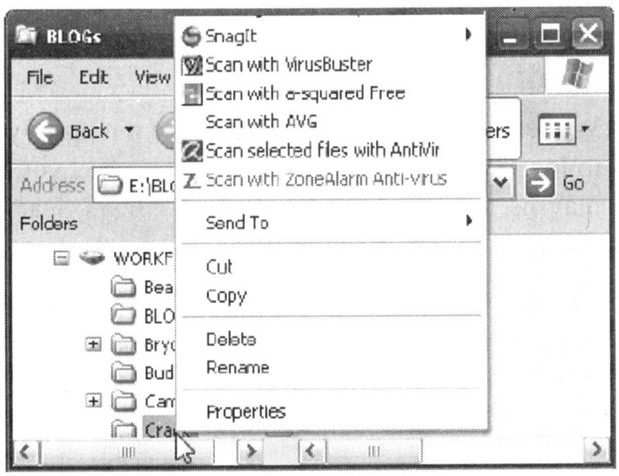

Fig 2.17 – Context Menu

In Fig 2.15 – Windows Explorer, for instance, there is a plus sign to the left of the folders named "Bryce" and "CameraDownloads". The + sign indicates that there are sub-folders within the main folder. You can display sub-folders by clicking on the + sign.

You can open more than one Windows Explorer window on your desktop at the same time. This is useful for comparing the contents of two folders that you may have on two different disk drives. You can also drag and drop files from one Explorer window to the other window.

Drive Properties

You can use the Windows Explorer to open the drive properties dialogue box to work with the disk drives on your computer. Open the Drive properties dialogue box by right clicking on the drive **WORKFILES (E:)** that we saw in Fig 2.15 – Windows Explorer. A context menu for drive E opens. Click on the menu item **Properties** to display the WORKFILES (E:) Properties dialogue box. See Fig 2.18 – Drive Properties Dialogue Box.

If the general tab is open, you will see the used and the free space available on the drive as well as the type of formatting (NTFS in this case).

By clicking on the Tools tab, you will get access to Error-checking, Defragmentation and Back-up tools that you can use on the drive.

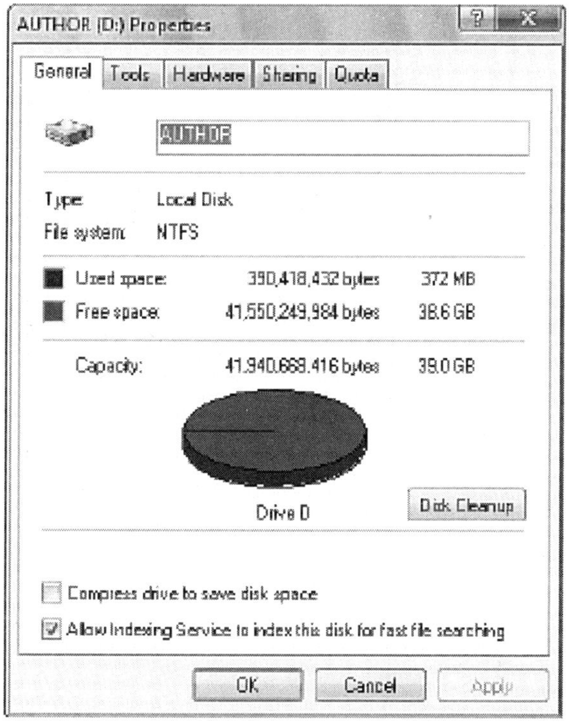

Fig 2.18 – Drive Properties Dialogue Box

Finding Files

While the Windows Explorer is like a map of your computer's drives, it is often faster and easier to locate a particular file (especially when you are not quite sure in which folder or drive the file may be located) by using the Windows Search utility.

Open this utility by clicking **Start ➔ Search ➔ All files and folders**. Now click the down arrow to the right of the Search Results box and select **My Computer** to display all the drives on your machine. Type the file name you are looking for (a part of the file name may also be sufficient) and click on the **Search** button to begin searching. See Fig 2. 19 – Search Dialogue Box.

In a short while, the Search Results dialogue box will open listing the files matching the name you have entered. The information on the right pane will also show the location of each file found. See Fig 2.20 – Search Results Dialogue Box.

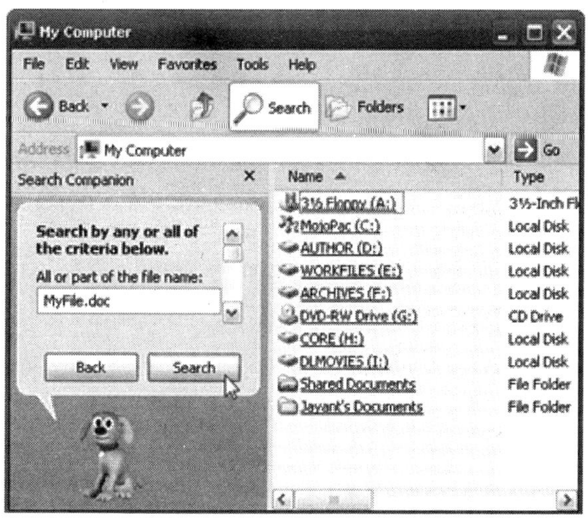

Fig 2.19 – Search Dialogue Box

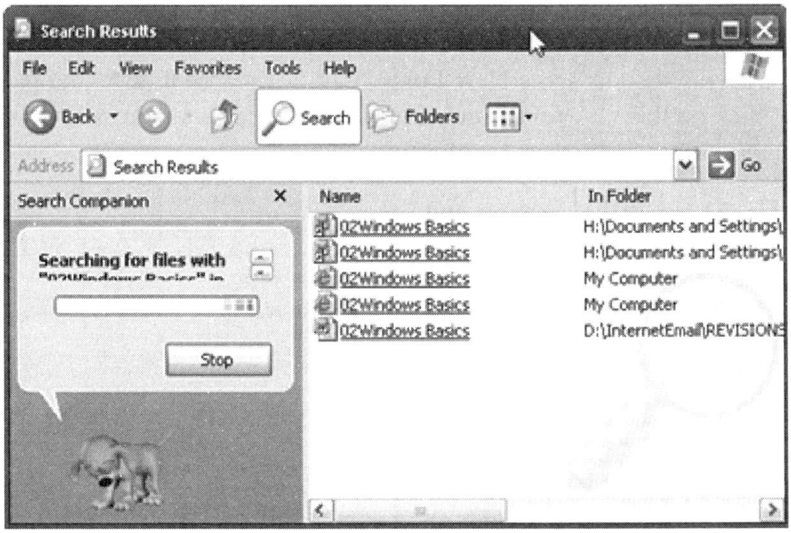

Fig 2.20 – Search Results Dialogue Box

File Operations

As we have already seen, programmes and data on your computer are arranged in a hierarchy of files, sub-folders, folders and drives. To arrange data and manipulate data efficiently, it is important to have a working knowledge of manipulation of files and folders. Generally speaking, drives contain folders. The folders in turn contain sub-folders or files and sub-folders also contain sub-sub-folders and files. See Fig 2.21 – Tree Structure. You will see a drive containing two folders. The first folder contains only one file while the second contains two sub-folders each containing a single file.

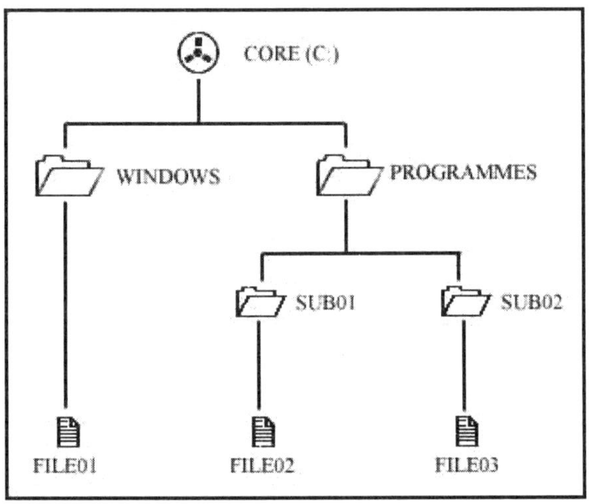

Fig 2.21 – Tree Structure

Creating Folders and Sub-Folders

Computer programmes that you may use save your work in the form of files. The files are automatically created when you save your work, either at a default location such as "My Documents", or in folders that you choose. You may be required, however, to create folders and sub-folders to organise your files.

Here is how you can create a new folder on a drive you select. Open Windows Explorer and select the drive you want in the left pane. Now click the **File menu** and click **New → Folder**. A blank folder with the default name New Folder will be created in the right pane of Windows Explorer. Right click on this new folder and select **Rename** from the drop down menu. Now you can type the name you have chosen for the folder.

The procedure is the same for creating and naming sub-folders. Begin by selecting a folder instead of a drive and follow the same procedure of clicking **File → New → Folder** to create a new sub-folder. Rename it as before.

Copying and Moving

The easiest way to copy a file from one location to another is to open two Windows Explorer windows side by side. Display the source file in one window and the destination folder in the other window. Now simply left click on the file and drag it with your mouse to the target folder. Release the mouse when you are done.

To move the file, open two Windows Explorer windows as before. Now right click on the target file and choose **Cut** in the drop down menu. Move to the second window and right click on the target folder. Click on **Paste** in the drop down menu. Your file will be transferred to the new location.

Deleting Files and Folders

You can delete any file or folder simply by right clicking on the file or folder and then clicking on the **Delete** option in the drop down menu that appears. The file or folder that you delete will be sent to the Recycle Bin. We will look at this special folder in the next section.

Recycle Bin

The Recycle Bin is a special folder on your computer's hard drive. You cannot delete this folder. Whenever you delete a file or folder from your hard drive, the contents are transferred to the Recycle Bin. By temporarily storing the deleted material in the Recycle Bin, you are given a chance to recover any accidentally deleted material before it is finally erased from your hard disk.

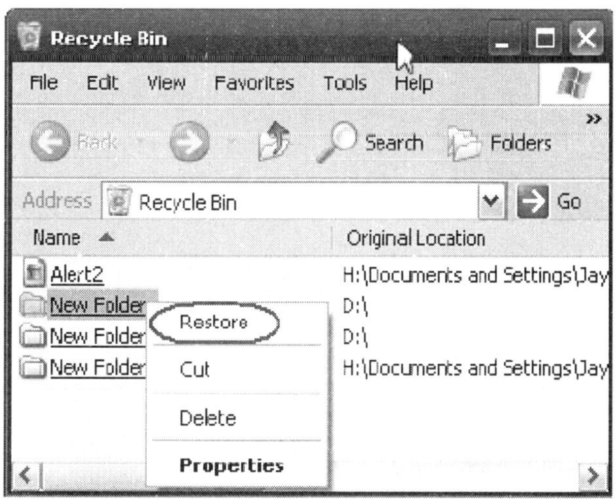

Fig 2.22 – Recycle Bin

To recover accidentally deleted material, open the Recycle Bin by right clicking on the Recycle Bin icon on your desktop and clicking on the **Restore** option on the drop down menu. The Recycle Bin window opens. See Fig 2.22 – Recycle Bin. In the left pane, you will see the current contents (files and folders) of the Recycle Bin. The right pane will indicate the original location of the deleted item. Right click on the item you want to restore and click on the Restore option in the drop down menu that appears. The selected item will be restored in its original location. Close the Recycle Bin when done.

ALERT

When you right click on the Recycle Bin icon, one option on the drop down menu lets you empty the Recycle Bin. Once you do so, the contents can no longer be recovered. If you delete a very large file or folder, there may not be enough space for the deleted item in the Recycle Bin. If so, the item will be permanently deleted without any chance of recovery!

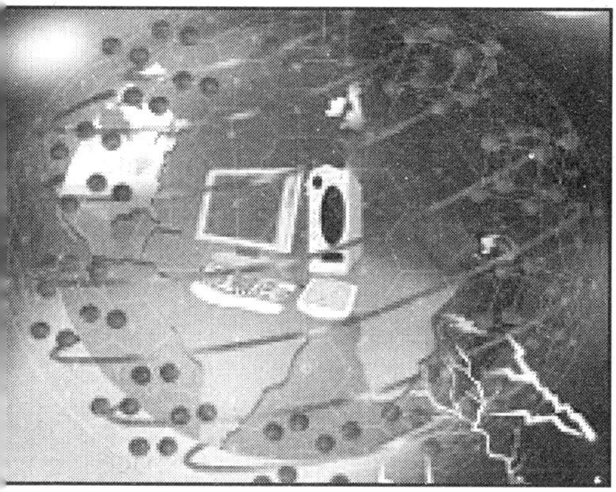

3. Connecting to the Internet

In this chapter:

- You are introduced to different types of Internet connections ranging from the slower dial-up connections to faster broadband connections using ISDN, DSL, cable modems and wireless modems.
- We discuss the hardware and software you will need to connect successfully to the Internet.
- We guide you through procedures for installing, connecting and testing your modem.
- We discuss the Internet connection wizard, a piece of software already included in your Windows operating system. We examine how to use this wizard to set up your Internet connection.
- We examine the two different procedures for setting up an Internet connection, the first using a slower dial-up connection and the second using a faster broadband ADSL connection.
- We look at the information you will need from your Internet Service Provider (ISP) while setting up your Internet connection.

Types of Connections

In order to use the Internet, you need to get connected to it. In recent years, just as the contents of the Internet have exploded in quantity and variety, so have the different means of connecting your computer to the Internet. India joined the Internet community only in 1980. By 1987, E-mail service had begun in a limited way. In 1995, the government's Videsh Sanchar Nigam Ltd. (VSNL) opened commercial access to the Internet.

However, after the VSNL monopoly was broken, many Internet Service Providers (ISPs) entered the field including Tata Indicom, AirTel, etc. Today there are a variety of services available to users in India, especially if you happen to live in a metropolitan city.

Before studying the two most common Internet connections in detail, let us take a look at various options that are available today.

Analogue (up to 56k)

Also called Dial-up access, it is economical but slow. Using a modem (modulating-demodulating unit) connected to your PC, you can connect to the Internet when your computer dials a phone number (which is provided by your ISP) and connects to the Internet. Dial-up is an analogue connection because data is sent over an analogue, public telephone network. The modem converts received analogue data to digital and vice versa. Because dial-up access uses normal telephone lines, the quality of the connection is not always good and data rates are limited. Typical Dial-up connection speeds range from 2400 bps to 56 Kbps. The term bps stands for bits per second and Kbps for kilobits per second.

ISDN

Integrated Services Digital Network (ISDN) is an international communications standard for sending voice, video, and data over digital telephone lines or normal telephone wires. Typical ISDN speeds range from 64 Kbps to 128 Kbps. ISDN is largely used by business enterprises.

DSL

DSL or Digital Subscriber Line is also called an "Always on" connection because it is always available without your having to dial-up your ISP. DSL uses existing 2-wire copper telephone line connected to your home, but transmits data in digital form. It is possible to receive analogue voice signals for your regular telephone and digital data for your computer at the same time over the same line. The two main categories of DSL for home subscribers are called ADSL and SDSL or Symmetrical DSL. ADSL is asynchronous DSL where the download speed is higher than the upload speed. SDSL or synchronous DSL has the same data transfer speed for both upload and download.

ADSL

ADSL is the most commonly deployed type of DSL in India. ADSL supports data rates from 1.5 to 9 Mbps (Megabits per second) when receiving data (known as the downstream rate) and from 16 to 640 Kbps when sending data (known as the upstream rate). ADSL requires a special ADSL modem to be connected to your computer.

Cable

Through the use of a cable modem you can have a broadband Internet connection that is designed to operate over cable TV lines. Cable Internet works by using TV channel space for data transmission, with certain channels used for downstream transmission, and other channels for upstream transmission. Because the coaxial cable used by cable TV provides much greater bandwidth than telephone lines, a cable modem can be used to achieve extremely fast upload and download speeds. However, in most cable modem installations, large number of users share the same bandwidth. This leads to a slow down of actual data transfer speeds.

Wireless Internet Connections

Wireless Internet or wireless broadband is one of the newest Internet connection types now available in India. Instead of using telephone or cable networks for your Internet connection, you use radio frequency bands transmitted wirelessly from your ISP to your home. Wireless Internet provides an always-on connection that can be accessed from anywhere — as long as you are geographically within a network coverage area. Wireless access is still relatively new, and it may be difficult to find a wireless service provider in some areas. It is typically more expensive and mainly available in metropolitan areas.

In this chapter, we will study analogue dial-up networking and ADSL Internet connections in detail since they are the two most common types in use in India. We shall also briefly cover wireless Internet since it is a strong, emerging trend.

Analogue Dial-up Networking

In this section, we will cover the essentials you need to know to purchase and set up a dial-up analogue network for connecting to the Internet. We will presume that you have selected analogue because that is what your ISP can supply, or you do not wish to spend the extra amount for a faster ADSL network.

Modem

The most important additional hardware you will need to buy is an analogue dial-up modem. You may choose a standard modem or one that has additional fax capability. You may prefer a slightly more expensive external modem, or a cheaper internal modem. The internal modem will require you to open the casing of the computer so that you can install the modem card in one of the free expansion slots of your computer's motherboard.

If you are reluctant to open the cover of your computer, you can choose a 56 Kbps modem conforming to the latest V91 protocol. The modem comes with its own cables and Direct Current (DC) power unit that you must plug in to a standard 220 volt socket. The power unit will supply 6 or 9 volts DC to the modem.

An external modem has the added advantage that it has indicating lamps to show power and data status. This is of great help if you are having problems accessing the Internet and wish to run diagnostics on your modem or network software. A typical set-up is shown in Fig 3.01 – Dial-up Modem Set-up.

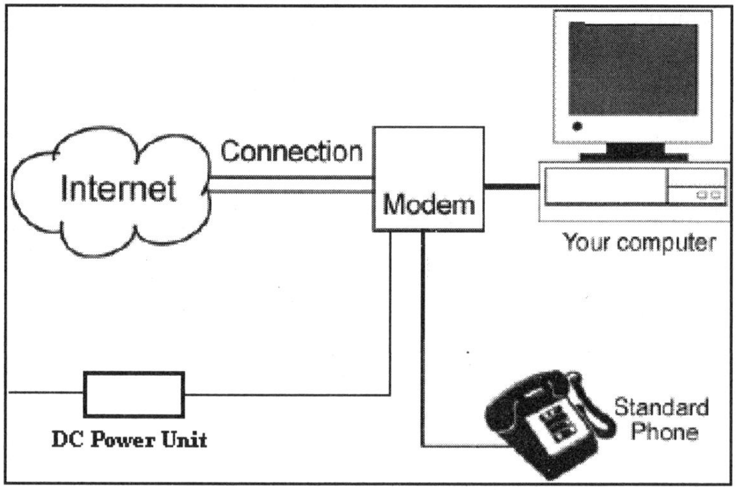

Fig 3.01 – Dial-up Modem Set-up

Your ISP

Your ISP will determine quite a few parameters of your Internet set-up. For instance, the ISP may have a list of approved makes of modems. They will usually supply the dial-up networking software and also their access telephone number you have to dial. Once you have subscribed to their Internet scheme, you will also be assigned a username and a password that you must enter to gain access to the ISP's network.

TIP

Choose from different schemes with care. If your work is mostly Web surfing and e-mailing, you may find a cheaper scheme quite adequate even though it limits the amount of data you can download every month. However, if your work involves large downloads such as music, graphics, programmes, etc, you may want to subscribe to a more expensive scheme with greater download limit.

Installing and Testing Your Modem

Set up your modem and provide the connections required. You will have to connect the telephone line to the appropriate RJ 11 socket at the back of the modem. Another RJ 11 socket allows you to connect your telephone to the telephone line through the modem. Plug in the DC power supplier to a 220 volt wall plug and connect the power jack to the back of the modem. Finally, connect the modem's communication port to the communication port at the back of your computer. See Fig 3.01 – Dial-up Modem Set-up.

Switch on power to the modem. Now switch your computer on. All modern modems are of the plug and play variety. Therefore, Windows will detect your modem.

If not, open the Control panel (**Start → Control panel**) and then click on the **Add hardware** icon. The Found New Hardware Wizard will be launched. See Fig 3.02 – Found New Hardware Wizard. Follow instructions on screen to install your new modem.

Fig 3.02 – Found New Hardware Wizard

NOTE

Windows may ask you to insert the CD-ROM containing software supplied by the modem manufacturer. Follow instructions on the screen to install software required to initialise your modem and install its device driver. A device driver or software driver is a computer programme allowing higher-level computer programme to interact with computer hardware devices such as your modem.

Once your modem has been installed, you may test its function. To do so, proceed as follows:

- Open the control panel (**Start → Control Panel**) and click on the **Phone** and **Modem** Options icon. The Phone and Modem Options dialogue box will open.
- Click on the **Modems** tab and then click on the **Properties** button at the bottom. The Modem Properties dialogue box opens.
- Open the **General** tab if it is not already open. Under Device status you should see the message "This device is working properly".

Your modem is ready for use. See Fig 3.03 – Modem Properties

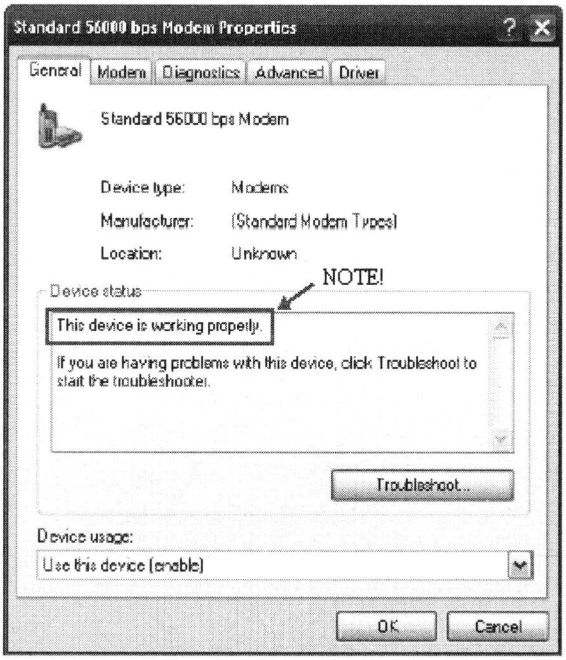

Fig 3.03 – Modem Properties

Connecting to the Internet

Make sure that you have the following information handy:

1. Your ISP's special phone number to be dialled for Internet connection
2. Your username and password supplied by your ISP
3. Any Dial-up networking software supplied by your ISP on a CD-ROM
4. Your Windows XP installation CD-ROM

To make a new network connection, launch the New Connection Wizard as follows:

Click **Start** ➔ **Control Panel** ➔ **Network Connections** ➔ **Create a new connection**. You should see the Network Connection Wizard. See Fig 3.04 – Network Connection Wizard, which shows the network connections page of the Control Panel with the network Tasks listed on the left.

Now follow these steps after opening the Network Connection Wizard:

1. Click **Connect to the Internet**, and then click **Next**.
2. Choose one of the following:
   - If you already have an account with an Internet Service Provider (ISP), click **Set-up my connection manually**, and then click **Next**.
   - If you have a CD from an ISP, click **Use the CD I got from an ISP** and then click **Next**.

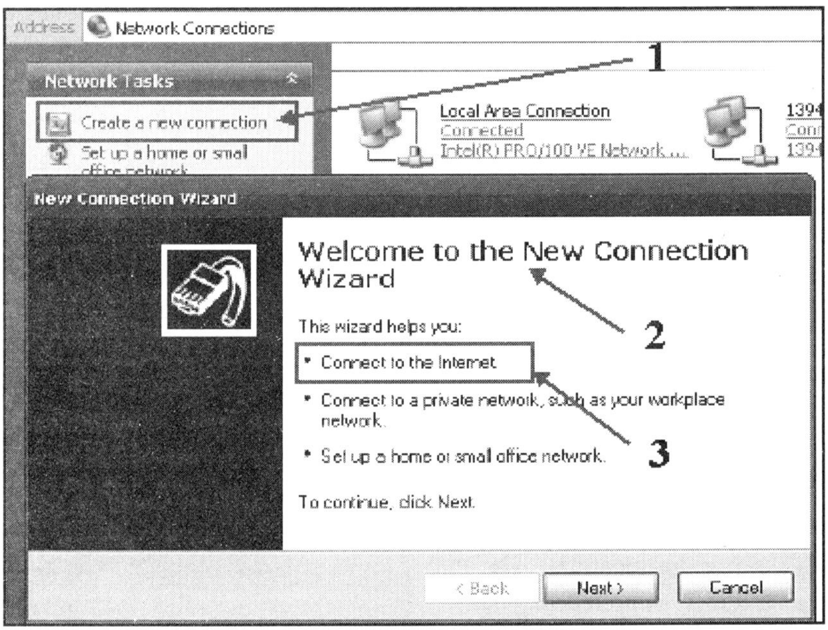

Fig 3.04 – Network Connection Wizard

- If you do not have an Internet account, click **Choose from a list of Internet service providers** (ISPs) and then click **Next**.

3. From your choice above, click one of the following:

   a. **Set-up my connection manually**.

   b. If you are connecting to your ISP using a standard 28.8 Kbps or 56 Kbps modem, click **Connect using a dial-up modem**, click **Next**, and follow the instructions in the wizard.

   c. **Use the CD I got from an ISP**. This is the preferred option since the software will configure the dial-up networking software and create an icon on your desktop. Click this icon to connect to the Internet through your ISP.

4. Click **Next**, and then click **Finish**. Insert the CD provided by your ISP and follow the instructions.

NOTE

In the past, if you were using Windows 98, you would be required to configure the connection properties including the TCP/IP Internet protocol. However, in Windows XP, Windows itself will do this configuring for you. If you have selected option 3.c, all you will need to do is to click on the Internet icon to connect to the Internet.

ADSL Always On Networking

If you have an ISP in your area offering ADSL network and you are ready to pay more for a much faster and more reliable Internet connection, then the "always on" Internet connection is the better choice over analogue dial-up networks. In addition to more reliable connection and higher data transfer speeds, you will be able to hold a telephone conversation while surfing the Internet or downloading information since the same telephone line will simultaneously carry both voice and data streams.

TIP

It is very likely that your ISP will provide you with a modem and also help to set up your Internet connection. If possible, request your ISP to supply a USB modem. It can be connected to your computer via one of the USB ports on your computer. If you already have a network card installed, you can use a standard ADSL network modem that will connect to your computer through its network card.

Your ISP will upgrade the telephone connection to your residence or office so that it is capable of ADSL transmission.

A typical ADSL network modem set-up is shown in Fig 3.05 – ADSL Set-up

You may note that the telephone line from your ISP is connected to a splitter. At the splitter, the voice and data streams are separated. The analogue voice connection goes to a standard telephone while the data stream is supplied to your computer through the ADSL modem.

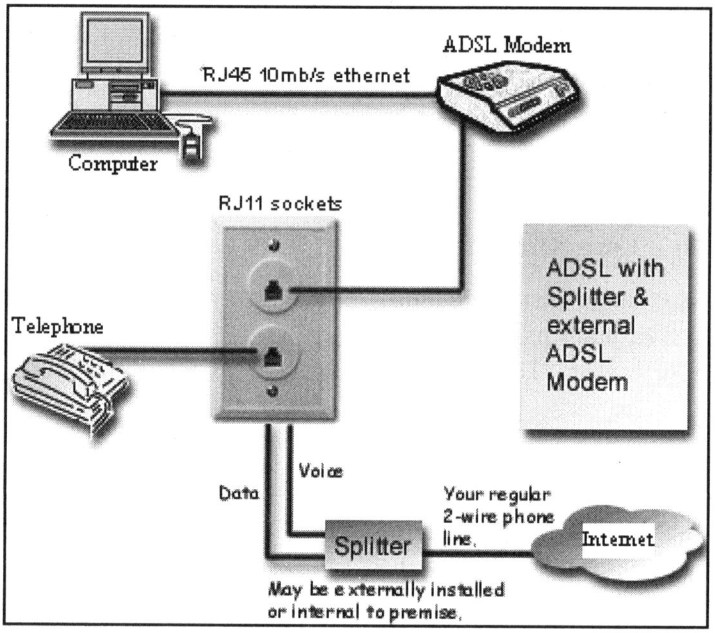

Fig 3.05 – ADSL Set-up

NOTE

If your ISP supplies you with a USB modem, it will be connected to one of the USB ports of your computer and the configuration protocol will be somewhat different. However, all the installation and configuration is normally undertaken by the ISP's engineers.

ALERT

Since the ADSL connection is always on, you need not dial your ISP to get connected. However, being always connected to the Internet, you will be more vulnerable to attack by virus or other malicious software, collectively called "Malware". It is essential therefore, that your computer is adequately protected against such attacks. We will discuss virus protection later in this book, in *Chapter 11 – Virus, Spam and Other Perils.*

Testing Your ADSL Connection

If you have difficulty in connecting through your "always on" connection, you may wish to check the status of the connection by opening the Website of your ISP. The procedures will differ depending on the protocol used by your ISP. We show you a typical procedure applicable to a well known ISP supplying high speed broadband connection for several years.

Follow these steps:

- Open your Web browser and type **http://192.168.1.1** in the address bar. Click on the **Go** button.
- The login window opens. See Fig 3.06 – Login Dialogue Box.
- Now enter username (usually admin) and password (usually password) and click the **OK** button. The Network Status window opens.

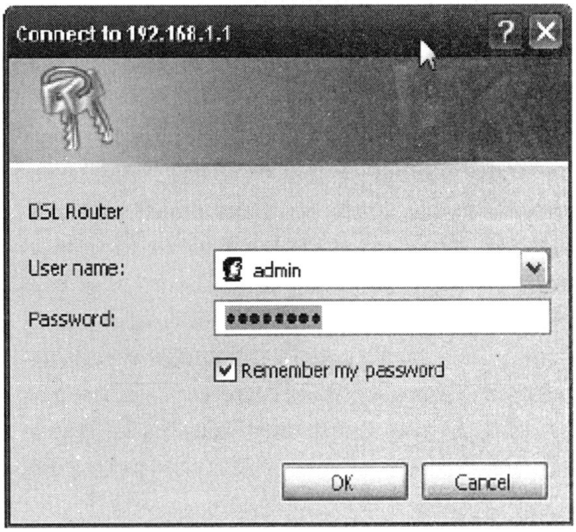

Fig 3.06 – Login Dialogue Box

The network status will be displayed in the marked area as shown in Fig 3.07 – Network Status. Note that the PPPoE protocol status reads "Enabled". It will read "Down" if the network is not working.

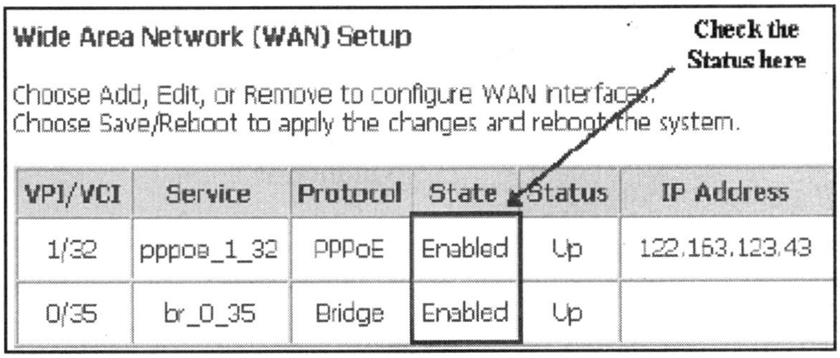

Fig 3.07 – Network Status

Wireless Internet Connection

Since wireless Internet connections do not require the installation of telephone lines, it is now gaining popularity in India, especially in metros and other large cities. You can get wireless broadband connection if your house or office is located sufficiently close to a wireless transmitting station owned by the ISP. In many parts of India, government owned MTNL and BSNL and private players such as Tata Indicom can provide wireless Internet services to you.

Wireless Modem

We have discussed computer hardware and software needs for other types of Internet connections. They remain basically the same for wireless broadband also except that the ADSL modem must be of the wireless variety. In most cases, the ISP will either supply the modem free or lease the modem to you depending on the tariff plan you choose.

For example, for a monthly tariff of Rs. 2000/- you may have to lease the modem while for Rs. 4000/- per month, the modem will be supplied free. The higher tariff plans generally provide you with faster connection speeds as well. Therefore, these plans suit users who use the Internet for business or for really large volumes of data transmission. See Fig 3.08 – Wireless Modem for a view of the rear panel of a typical modem capable of receiving wireless Internet connection. This model connects to your computer through a USB port and can act as a router (or hub) for other devices as well.

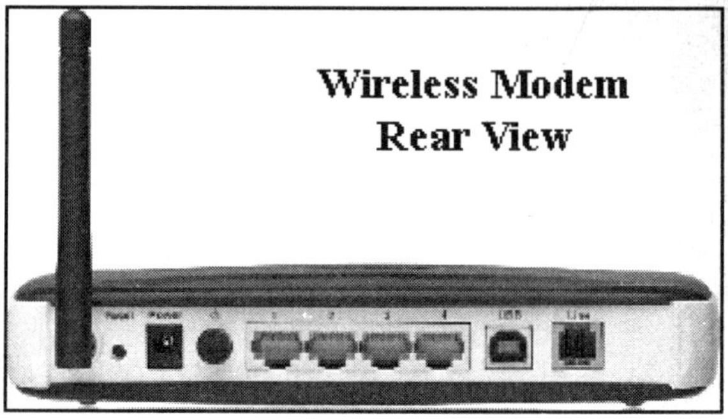

Fig 3.08 – Wireless Modem

NOTE

Note that while wireless modems will connect the modem to the Internet without telephone lines, you have to use cables to connect the modem to your computer. If you are looking for true wireless connectivity where your modem connects to your computer or computers without wires, you will need a wireless router. If you have more than one computer, including a laptop that you may wish to use around the house, then you will have to set up a local wireless network and use a wireless router as the Internet hub in your home.

4. Web Surfing

In this chapter:

- We discuss why people surf the Internet.
- You are introduced to the main tool for exploring the Internet, the Web browser.
- We take a closer look at the most popular Web browser, the Internet Explorer and study its layout, tools and command buttons.
- Since staying connected is expensive, we look at many ways to speed up things while you are connected to the Internet. Specifically, you learn how to use the AutoComplete feature, speed up Web page downloads and to find your favourite Web pages quickly.
- You get to know the Search Assistant, a useful feature on your Web browser.
- You learn to save Web pages on your hard disk so that you may browse through at your leisure, after you have gone offline.

Why Do We Surf?

Why is the Internet so addictive? To answer that question, we begin by looking at the main reasons for surfing the Internet. A moment's thought will convince us that our purpose is usually one of the following:

- To gather information
- To be entertained
- To do business on the Web (e-business)

The last item is recent, but its influence is growing. Until a couple of years ago, e-Bay was a foreign Website. Today, thousands of Web surfers in India buy and sell their products on the Indian avatar of e-Bay!

As you will soon discover, the Internet is all things to all people. Whether you want to communicate with business associates or friends quickly and cheaply, or you are looking for entertainment, or your need is information of any kind at all, it is out there on the Internet!

Surfing Software

As we have seen in *Chapter 1 – Introduction*, virtually all the Internet content is in HTML (or its successor XML) format. To read the text and graphics on a HTML page, the computer uses specialised software called a Web browser. Most of you have probably used the Web browser included in your Windows operating system. It is the familiar Internet Explorer (IE).

NOTE

While there are other Web browsers such as the Mozilla Firefox and Opera, for Windows users the Internet Explorer is the *de facto* industry standard. Since it is bundled with Windows, its code is very well integrated with the operating system. In fact, the programme code of the Internet Explorer is also used to run the Windows Explorer, the device you use to view the contents of your computer.

If you want to use other Web browsers such as Firefox or Opera, you will have to install them separately. Since the majority of Windows users will run IE on their machines, this chapter is based on the Internet Explorer. If you have Firefox or Opera, you will find that what we discuss here applies equally to them as well, with only minor variations. In particular, these two browsers have tabbed browsing capability. Only the latest version of Internet Explorer, IE 7.0 has tabbed browsing. IE 7.0 is available with the latest Windows operation system, Windows Vista.

NOTE

Tabbed browsing permits you to open several Websites in individual tabs on the same browser page, allowing you to switch from one Web page to another very easily, simply by clicking on the tab in which the page has been opened. We shall discuss tabbed browsing later in this chapter when we take a closer look at Firefox.

Components of Internet Explorer

Navigation Tools and Home Page

While Windows is being installed in your computer, it is programmed to select Microsoft Network as the default home page for your computer. However, you can change the default to any other Web page, or no Web page at all as your default home page. For the purpose of our discussion, let us assume that MSN is indeed your current default home page.

Connect to the Internet and you will see the MSN.com home page. The page is too long to fit inside the screen of your Web browser. You will have to scroll down the page to see all of it. See Fig 4.01 – MSN Home Page for a partial view of the page.

Let us open another Web page and focus on the navigation tools.

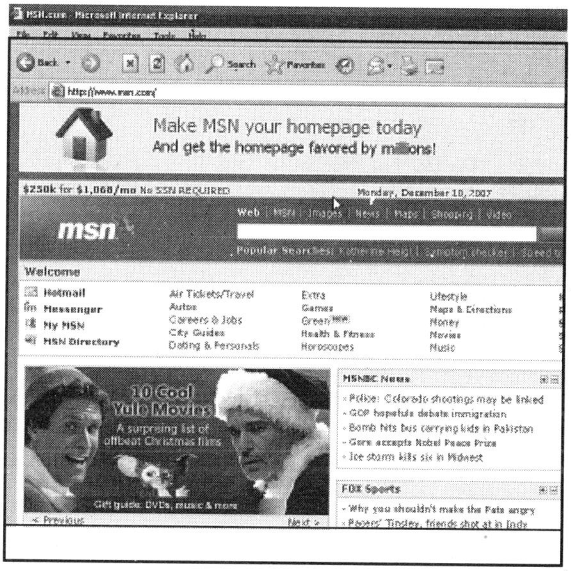

Fig 4.01 – MSN Home Page

You will notice four separate areas in the form of bands starting with the Title bar (In this case, AXN-India), then the Menu bar containing the menu items File, Edit, View, Favourites, Tools and Help. Below the menu bar is the Tool bar that contains forward and reverse navigation buttons, delete button, refresh button, home page button, search button, favourites button, etc. The last band is the address bar. You have to enter the URL (or Uniform Resource Locator) of the Web page you want to see in this space and then press the Go button to the right of the address bar. We will now examine each bar in detail. See Fig 4.02 – Navigation Tools and Menus.

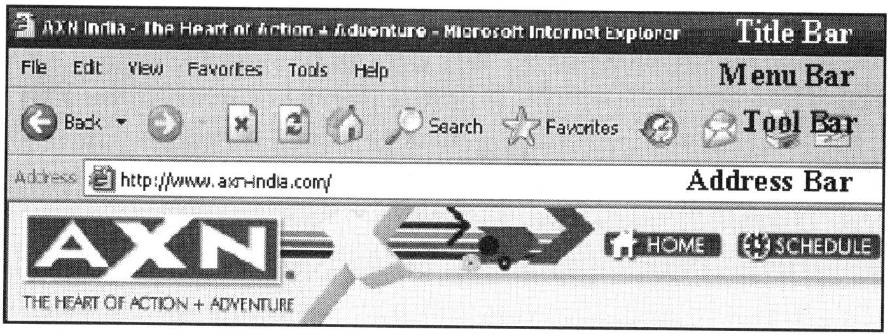

Fig 4.02 – Navigation Tools and Menus

Title Bar

The title bar contains the name of the Web page that is open in your browser. In the two examples we have just seen, the titles were MSN.com and AXN-India respectively.

Menu Bar

The menu bar contains menu items we have already mentioned. Clicking on any menu item will open its associated drop down list. For instance, the Edit menu has the following sub-menu items: Cut, Copy, Paste, Select All and Find. Of special interest to Web surfers is the Favorites menu item.

TIP

Clicking on this menu item will open a drop down list containing all the favourite Web pages that have been specially saved as Favorite or as Bookmark. You can also open the Favorites panel to the left of the Browser screen by clicking on the Favorites icon on the tool bar. To add a Web page to the favourites list, open the page you want and then click on Add to Favorites in the Favorites sub-menu. The browser remembers the URL of each favourite so that you can click on any favourite item and the requested page will open without your having to type the URL. See Fig 4.03 – Favorites Sub-menu.

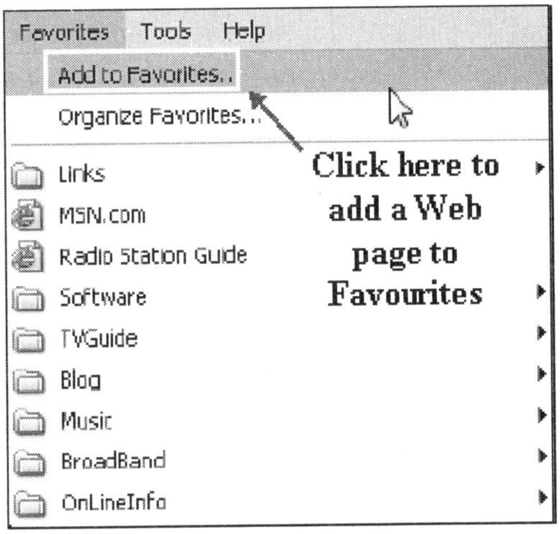

Fig 4.03 – Favorites Sub-menu

Tool Bar

The Tool bar, also called the Icon bar, contains important tools for navigating Web pages. At the extreme left are two arrow buttons that allow you to navigate back or forward in a set of Web pages. The next button will stop a Web page or picture download. The Refresh button refreshes the Web page, that is, the page is loaded afresh. The Home button will take you to the default home page, the Search button opens the Search assistant, and the Favourites button opens the list of favourites that you have already saved. The last button is the History button that lists the Web pages that you have already browsed. We will discuss the Search button and the History button in detail later in this chapter.

Address Bar

The address bar is where you have to enter the URL of the Web page that you wish to see. The data you enter in this space (also called an edit box) can be edited to correct errors while typing. Once a Web page has been saved as Favorite, it is not necessary to type its URL. It is enough to locate it in the Favorites drop down sub-menu and click on the item.

NOTE

Depending on your Web browser and its version, the details we have just discussed will vary. However, for all popular browsers, the tools are laid out in basically the same way. See Fig 4.04 – Tabbed Browser for a view of the Firefox browser showing three tabs. You can navigate from one tab to the next by simply clicking on the tab.

Home Page

We have seen earlier that Windows installs the MSN.com Web page as your home page by default. However, you can easily set your home page to any other Web page or simply a blank page.

Fig 4.04 – Tabbed Browser

Follow these simple steps:

- Connect to the Internet and launch your Web browser
- Go to the Web page you wish to set as your home page
- Click **Tools → Internet Options** on the tool bar of your browser. The Internet Options dialogue box opens.
- In the General Tab, under Home Page, click the **Use Current** button.
- Click **OK** to close the dialogue box.

Your home page will be reset. See Fig 4.05 – Internet Options Dialogue Box.

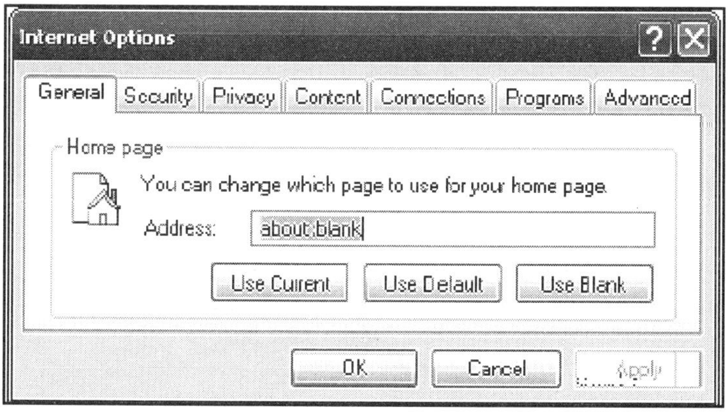

Fig 4.05 – Internet Options Dialogue Box

Using AutoComplete

The AutoComplete feature saves previous entries that you have made for Web addresses, forms, and passwords. Then, when you type information in one of these fields, AutoComplete suggests possible matches.

These matches can include folder and programme names you type into the Address bar, and search queries, stock quotes, or information for just about any other field you fill in on a Web page.

To use AutoComplete, start typing the Web address in the Address bar. If you've typed a similar entry before, AutoComplete lists possible matches as you type. If a suggestion in the list matches what you want to enter in that field, click the suggestion.

If no suggestion matches what you are typing, continue typing.

History

You can browse through Web pages that you have recently visited by opening the History panel on your browser by clicking on the History button on the tool bar. See Fig 4.06 – History Panel.

Surf Faster

In addition to the AutoComplete feature we saw just now, here are a few additional tips to speed up Web surfing so that you get what you need, fast.

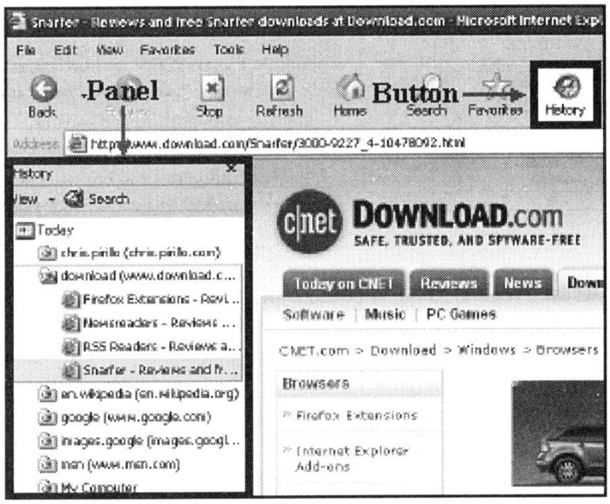

Fig 4.06 – History Panel

Speed Up Downloads

Internet Explorer is configured to strike a balance between downloading speed and pleasing graphics. Unless you have a very fast broadband Internet connection, you may wish to sacrifice some of the nice graphic effects in order to download Web pages faster. Do not worry, whatever changes you make can be easily restored if you do not like the results.

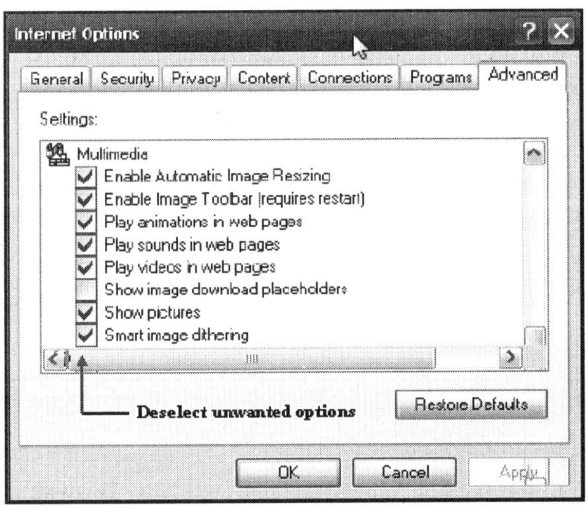

Fig 4.07 – Advanced Internet Options

Turn Off Unwanted Multimedia Options

- Open Internet Explorer and click **Tools → Internet Options**. Now click on the **Advanced** tab.
- Scroll down the list till you reach the heading "Multimedia". Deselect the check boxes (by clicking on any that has a tick mark) of those effects that you do not need.
- Click **OK** to close the dialogue box.

Should you wish to restore default settings in the future, open the same dialogue box and click the **Restore Defaults** button and then click **OK**. Your default settings will be restored.

Use the Search Feature

Click on the Search icon on Internet Explorer to open the Search panel to the left of the browser's page. Under the heading Search the Web, enter what you wish to search. Click the **Search** button to begin searching the Internet. In Fig 4.08 – Search Feature, you will notice that the user is searching for Antivirus software. The Search Results panel on the right lists part of the search results. Click on any item on the list for more information.

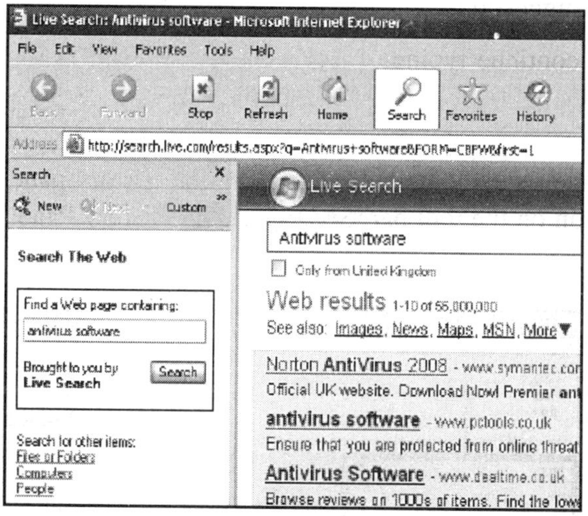

Fig 4.08 – Search Feature

Observe the bottom part of the Search panel on the left. You will observe that in addition to searching the Internet (or World Wide Web), the search feature can also search your own computer for files and folders by clicking File or Folders, search other computers that may be connected to your computer over a Local Area Network (LAN) by clicking Computers, or even search for the e-mail addresses of people by clicking People.

Browse Offline

By making a Web page available offline, you can open the page even when you are not connected to the Internet. If you wish to download a large quantity of Web pages quickly with the intention of going offline to browse through them at leisure, you should add the page to your favourites list and then make the page available offline.

After adding the target Web page to your Favourites list, it will appear in the left pane as you can see in Fig 4.09 – Offline Browsing. Now, follow the serial numbers 1 to 4 while reading the steps below:

1. Click the **Favorites** icon. The Favourites left panel opens.
2. Select the page you wish to browse offline.

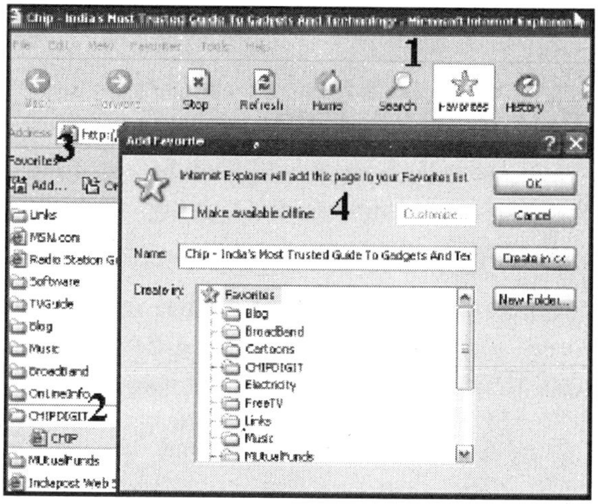

Fig 4.09 – Offline Browsing

3. Click the **Add** button, the Add Favorite dialogue box opens. See Fig 4.09 – Offline Browsing.
4. Check the box captioned Make Available Offline.
5. Click the **Customise** button to open the Offline Favorite Wizard. See Fig 4.10 – Offline Favorite Wizard.
6. Set the contents to be downloaded, the links to be saved and the schedule your computer should follow to update the page. You do so by selecting the options you want in the Wizard, advancing to the next option by clicking on the Next button.
7. Click the **Finish** button when you have finished with the Wizard.

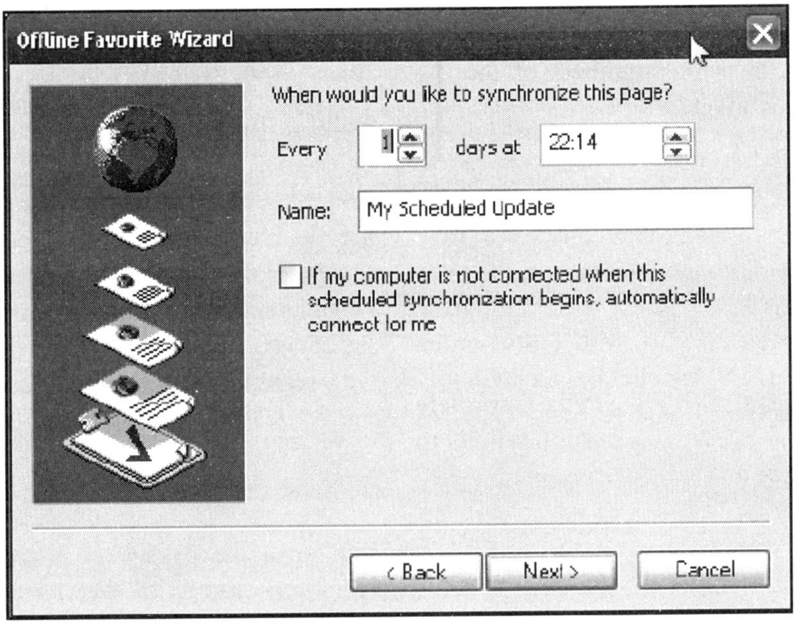

Fig 4.10 – Offline Favorite Wizard

Save a Web Page

While many Web pages will change over time and you will need to synchronise (or update) the Web page from time to time as explained in the previous section, there are many Web page content such as pictures, graphics, articles and reports that do not change over time.

You may wish to download and save such content on your hard disk for maintaining a permanent record without adding the Web page to your list of favourites. To do so open the Web page you wish to save on your hard disk using Internet Explorer and then proceed as follows:

1. Click on the **File** menu and select the **Save As...** option from the drop down sub-menu. The Save Web Page dialogue box will open.

2. Enter the destination folder where you want to save the Web page and either enter a file name for the Web page or accept the default filename. Click the **Save** button.

3. The file will be saved. You can observe the progress in the Save Web Page progress box. The box will automatically close when downloading is complete.

See Fig 4.11 – Save Web Page. The numbers 1, 2 and 3 on the graphic correspond to the serial numbers of the steps 1, 2 and 3 given above.

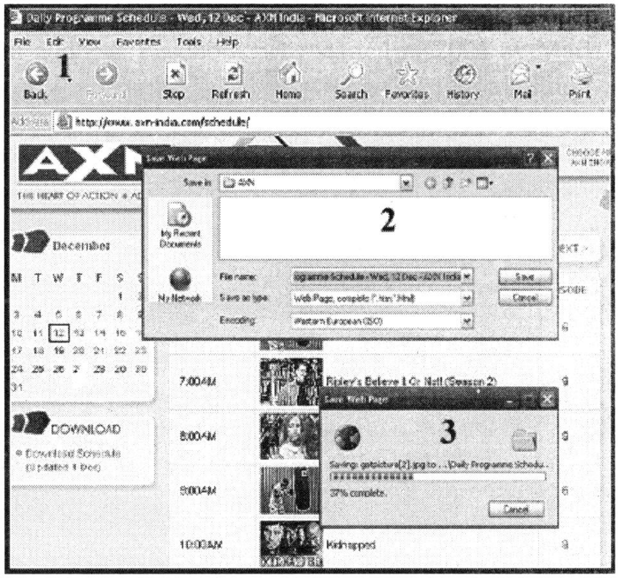

Fig 4.11 – Save Web Page

Saving Options

To save space on your hard disk, you may select different options while saving the Web page. If the data you wish to save is only the text, you can choose the **Text File Only** option.

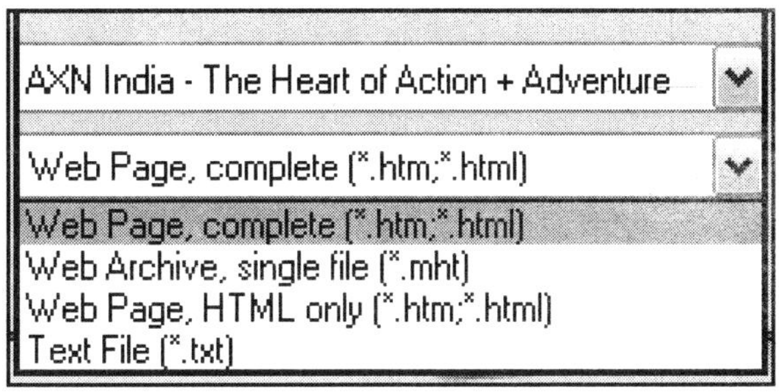

Fig 4.12 – Saving Options

On the other hand, the **Web Page Complete** option will save everything including links to other Web pages, but will occupy more space on your hard disk.

Your choice therefore, is a balance between what you wish to save and the amount of hard disk space that you can spare.

5. Web Searching

In this chapter:

- You are introduced to the art of effective Web searches for precisely the information you need from a sea of millions of Web pages.
- We discuss the two basic sources of information — Subject Directories and Search Engines. We discuss when to use directories and when to switch to search engines.
- Techniques for using Subject directories such as Yahoo!, Looksmart, etc. are discussed.
- We review two of the most popular Search engines — Google and AltaVista.
- You are introduced to Meta-search or multiple search engines such as Meta-crawler and Dogpile.
- We introduce you to two very powerful Web search software, both in the public domain (free to download and use) — the Crazy Browser and Copernic Agent Basic.
- Specific techniques to get the best out of these programmes are discussed in detail.

Searching the Web

The Internet is the single largest storehouse of information available to mankind. But since the Web is not indexed in any standard manner, finding information can appear quite intimidating even to an expert. Search engines are popular tools for locating Web pages, but they will usually display thousands of results. Search engines "crawl" through the Web and log the words from the Web pages they find in their databases. Because some search engines have logged the words from over one billion documents, results can be overwhelming. Without a clear search strategy, using a search engine is like wandering aimlessly in the stacks of a library trying to find a particular book.

In addition to search engines (such as AltaVista) there are also subject directories (such as Yahoo!) on the Internet. Certain types of information are best searched using a search engine. Other types of information will be found more easily if you access a subject directory. In both cases, you have to use a well thought out search strategy to get relevant information quickly.

NOTE

Successful searching involves two key steps. First, you begin by identifying the important key words in your topic. Second, you should have some idea about how to use the various search tools available on the Internet. Search strategies for search engines are very different from strategies for subject directories. Even amongst search engines, there are many differences in size, accuracy, features, and flexibility. Let us now look at subject directories and search engines in more detail.

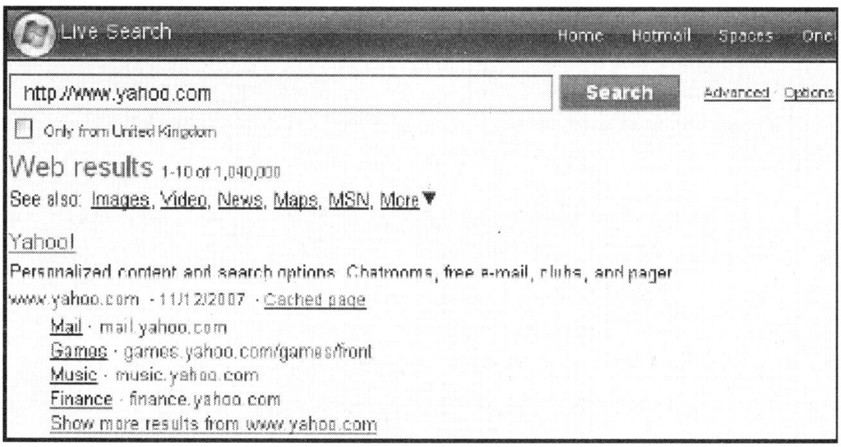

Fig 5.01 – Yahoo! Search Pages

Subject Directories

A subject directory is a catalogue of sites collected and organised by humans. Subject directories are often called subject "trees" because they start with a few main categories and then branch out into sub-categories, topics, and sub-topics. To find information on the Australian Open in golf, you have to click on **Sports** → **Golf** → **Australian Open** → **Read the Story**.

Because humans organise the Websites in subject directories, it is a good starting point if the directory includes the topic you are searching. If you do not have a precise idea of the information you need, you can use the directory's keyword search option instead of going through layers of categories and sub-categories.

Yahoo! is the largest subject directory on the Internet and is an excellent site for most general topics. For locating popular Websites, Looksmart (**http://www.furl.net**) is another good subject directory. For more scholarly topics, you can try the Open Directory (**http://www.dmoz.org/**)

Two other useful directories for scholarly research are the Internet Public Library (**http://www.ipl.org/**), and the WWW Virtual Library (**http://vlib.org/**)

TIP

However, directories cover only a small fraction of the pages available on the Web. Therefore, they are most effective for finding general information on popular or scholarly subjects. If you are looking for something specific, it is better to use a search engine. We will discuss various search engines in the following section.

Search Engines

Search engines are very different from subject directories. While humans organise and catalogue subject directories, search engines rely on computer programmes called spiders or robots to crawl the Web and log the words on each page. With a search engine, keywords related to a topic are typed into a search "box". The search engine then scans its database and displays a file (or files) with links to Websites containing the word or words specified.

Because these Internet databases are very large, search engines often return thousands of results. Without search strategies or techniques, finding what you need can be like looking for a needle in a haystack.

Besides the best known "Google", there are six major search engines—Yahoo!, AltaVista, Excite, Infoseek, Lycos, and HotBot. Each search engine has its own strengths and weaknesses. All these search engines ultimately depend on the size of their databases for their width of coverage. That is to say, the bigger the database they can access, the greater is their chance to get you the information you seek. From the point of view of the sheer volume of data registered with Google, it is certainly ahead of all other search engines.

Fig 5.02 – The Google Search Page

Since each database is indexed in a somewhat unique manner, it is useful to know exactly how to frame the query to get the best response from a search engine. All search engines use Boolean logic but with small differences. It is important to remember therefore, how to use Boolean operators such as “And”, “Or” “Not”, etc. to construct the appropriate query terms, which can dramatically improve its search performance.

It is also important to choose right key words in your query. For instance, to search for government’s legislation on Primary education, you may experiment with the key words: “Government”, “Education policy”, “Primary Education”. Some trial with different combinations of the key words will greatly improve your chances of getting the information you seek. Let us look at two popular search engines, Google and AltaVista, a little more closely.

Google

Google has the largest database at 1.5 billion pages and is very good at finding relevant results quickly. Google ranks a Web page based on the number of “important” pages that are linked to it. After a search, Google lists the most popular sites (i.e. sites with the most links) at the top of the displayed list.

Google supports OR (in all caps), but does not support full Boolean AND NOT. However, it does allow the implied Boolean minus sign (-). When multiple keywords are entered, all keywords are treated as “AND” queries. The plus sign (+) and the operator AND are not necessary when framing a query in Google.

NOTE

Google supports link searching and title, domain, and host searching when its Advanced Search page is used. Using the Image Search database, News Search database, or Discussion Group Search database, you can search for pictures/graphics, news articles, and newsgroup postings. Unlike other search engines, Google maintains a cached copy of each result in its own database. Thus, you can access the cached copy even if the original Website is temporarily down or the Web page is no longer available.

AltaVista

AltaVista currently claims to have one of the largest search engine databases containing over 550 million Websites. AltaVista offers both a Simplc Scarch and an Advanccd Search page. Simple Search requires the use of implied Boolean logic (plus and minus), while Advanced Search requires full Boolean logic (and, or, and not). The Advanced Search page also requires that the most important keyword appear in the “Sort by” search box so that the most relevant results are displayed at the top of the list. Both the Simple and Advanced search pages allow searching for phrases, titles of articles, links and domain names.

Near Searching

AltaVista has a number of powerful search features not found in other search engines. One such feature is the Advanced Search page is the NEAR search. A NEAR search will limit results displayed to pages where keywords appear within 10 words of each other. This is very useful in situations where an AND search produces too many results and a phrase search produces too few results. A phrase search is one in which a phrase (within quotes) is used to search the database.

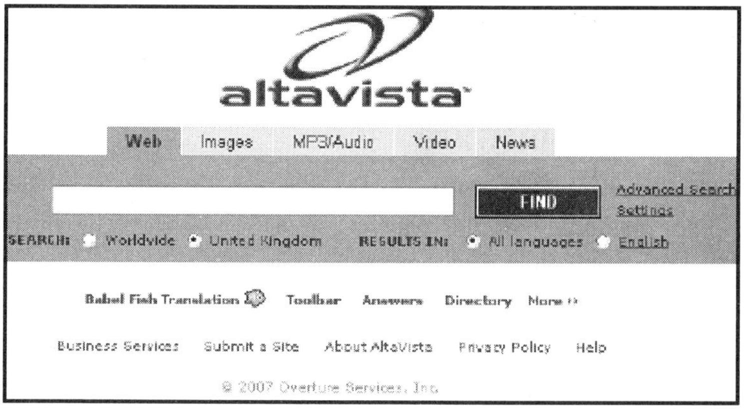

Fig 5.03 – The AltaVista Search Page

Meta-search Engines

Meta-search engines (also known as multi-threaded engines) search several major engines at once. Meta-search engines do not crawl through the Web or maintain a database of Web pages. Instead, they act as a middle agent, passing on the query to the major engines and then displaying the results. Because the major search engines often produce very different results, meta-search engines provide a quick way to determine which engines are retrieving the best match for the information you need.

Dogpile searches eight search engines and subject directories as well as newsgroups, business news, and newswires. Dogpile supports full Boolean logic and phrase searching.

Vivisimo clusters results from eight search engines and subject directories into convenient topic categories. It uses implied Boolean logic (+/-) and phrase searching.

MetaCrawler, uses seven search engines and subject directories. It uses implied Boolean logic (+/-) and phrase searching.

Fig 5.04 – Dogpile Search Page

ALERT

Meta-search engines are very convenient since you have to enter the search query only once and the software automatically employs multiple search engines at once. However, because the search engines used by Meta-searches vary considerably in their ability to interpret complex searches, it is best to use very simple search phrases.

Two Special Search Software

You can search the Web very efficiently using either subject directories or search engines with some practice and understanding of the way these devices work. However, there are some excellent free software that will do a very competent job of Web searching for you without your having to use Boolean logic or anything other than plain English questions.

TIP

We will now study two specialised Web search software in the rest of this chapter. Both are highly efficient and both are available as free downloads from their Websites. Therefore, you can use both of them legally. You can also update them when new versions become available. As you will see, one is good for a quick search while the other is meant for in-depth information gathering from the Internet.

The first of the two is called "Crazy Browser". This search software is built around the Internet Explorer. It will let you search any one of nine search engines to find answers to your query. It is quite fast and capable of finding general information, images, downloads, information from newsgroups, weather data, etc.

The downloaded data is volatile, that is, it will be lost once you close the browser unless the data is saved by you first on your hard disk.

The second software is called "Copernic Agent Basic". It is a much more elaborate programme that simultaneously searches the Internet using several search engines. The data is presented to you sorted in order of relevance and the summary of its finding is automatically saved for you to browse offline at leisure. However, the search takes longer, since it is more elaborate.

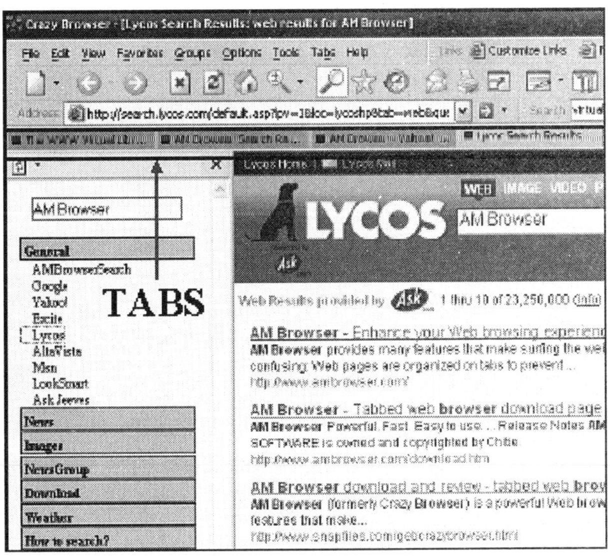

Fig 5.05 – Crazy Browser Tabs

Crazy Browser

Crazy Browser looks like a Web browser. It is built around Microsoft's Internet Explorer, providing many additional useful features missing in Internet Explorer such as tabbed browsing. It was originally known as AM Browser. Currently it is available as version 3.02 Beta. Since it is really an add-on, its size is very small, under 1 MB. It installs very easily and can be launched independently of Internet Explorer. See Fig 5.05 – Crazy Browser Tabs, which shows the main page with some tabs opened.

NOTE The colour scheme of Crazy Browser depends on the Windows theme that you have already chosen. There are seven main elements of the interface that can be removed or kept in sight as you want, starting with the six toolbar items and ending with the status bar. Let us find out more about these toolbars now.

The Standard Buttons toolbar contains mostly items that you can find inside Internet Explorer, like Go Back/Forward, Favorites, History and others. The extra functions available here allow you to open new tabs, edit current page or add external tools.

The left panel lists categories for Web search. For instance, there are separate categories for "General", "News", "Images", "Newsgroups", etc. By clicking the General category, you can expose the search engines that Crazy Browser can employ for a Web search. Depending on the version, you may have nine to fourteen search engines available.

A Simple Search

A simple search procedure will be like this. Let us assume that you wish to read reviews about the Canon PowerShot 710 Is digital camera. Proceed as follows:

1. Type the text of your search string ("Canon PowerShot 710 Is") in the text box of Crazy browser.
2. Click Google in the search engine list under the General heading.
3. You will see search results returned by Google in the right pane. Click on any of the headings for further information.
4. Click on any other search engine (such as AltaVista) for additional Websites.
5. AltaVista returns its own search results under a new tab. Click on the tab to see the new set of results which will replace the Google search results in the right pane.

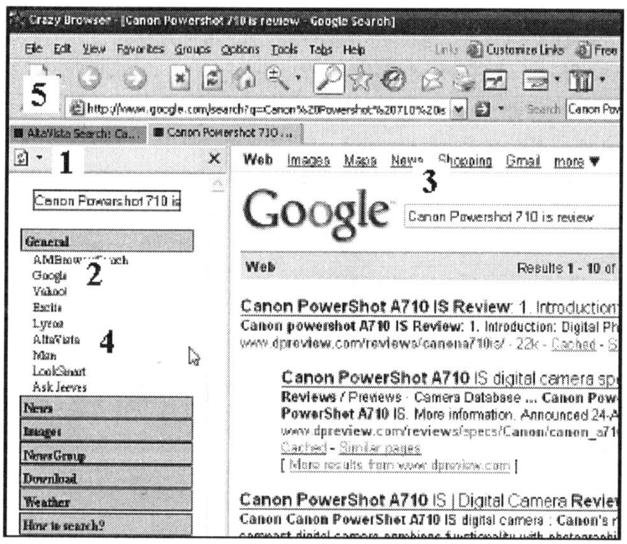

Fig 5.06 – Simple Search

See Fig 5.06 – Simple Search. The serial numbers in the above procedure matches the numbers in Fig 5.06.

NOTE

Crazy Browser has a smart popup blocker and an Advertisement blocker that do their jobs pretty well. In order to change their settings and much more, you have to choose the Advanced Options item from the Options menu. Once you are there, you will get an idea about how to set up Crazy Browser to your liking.

In summary, Crazy Browser is a fast, reliable and highly customisable browser. It does not use too much of your system's resources and has a lot of features that you will not find in Internet Explorer. It is amongst one of the best Internet Explorer based browsers. However, while it is fast, it is not as detailed as the next software we are going to discuss.

Copernic Agent Basic

Introduction

Copernic Agent Basic is a free new product replacing the former search tool known as Copernic 2000/2001. The new software comes with a completely new architecture and interface. By simultaneously using several search engines and information sources on the Web, it can find exactly what you are looking for.

Copernic Agent supports categories (such as The Web, Books, Movies, Music, etc.) to target appropriate search engines. It eliminates duplicate results, verifies and removes broken links, highlights keywords in result lists and Web pages, saves pages for offline browsing and finds keywords in results or Web pages with Boolean queries. Among other things, a quick search bar and the integrated Favourites menu will save you a substantial amount of search time.

Copernic Agent keeps a detailed search history with custom folders and sub-folders so that you may view and manage results at your convenience and update searches later to find new results quite easily. There are ways to customise menus, toolbars, search lists, search operations and options.

TIP

You can easily download the software by visiting the Copernic Website (**http://www.copernic.com**), and update it periodically by opening Copernic and clicking Tools ➔ **Check for Software Updates** while connected to the Internet. The free Copernic Agent Basic features nine predefined search categories, providing access to some eighty major information sources.

How Copernic Agent Operates

After finding information for you: Copernic also stores the results on your disk, organises them in a clear manner and removes duplicates automatically. You save the result pages on your computer's hard disk for offline browsing and consultation any time. Every time you connect Copernic to the Internet, it automatically updates its list of search engines.

Copernic is simple and easy to use. You need to enter your search string (the text you wish to use for searching) just once and Copernic will utilise nine different search engines to bring the results to you.

You may consult the results any time you like, and you can request an update on an existing search. Because Copernic is fast and stores the results on your disk, you will save on connection time.

Quick Search

See Fig 5.07 – Copernic Main Page. Follow these steps for a quick search:

1. Launch Copernic.
2. On the Quick Search pane at the left, enter the search string (in this case "conversational English") and click on the magnifying glass icon.
3. A list of Websites, also called headers or search results, appear in the right pane.
4. Click on any of the selected Website for more information.
5. An Internet Explorer window opens displaying the selected Website.

Fig 5.07 – Copernic Main Page

To open more related Web pages select another Website in the right pane and click on the Website. You can keep several Websites open if you have tabbed browsing capability as available with Internet Explorer 7. You can also save any of the Websites on your hard disk for future reference. The headers in the right pane are automatically saved by Copernic so that you can refresh and view the connected Websites later.

NOTE

New Search

A New or normal search (unlike Quick Search) can be launched from the main page of Copernic by clicking on the **New** icon on the toolbar. Alternatively, click on the **Search** item on the menu bar and then click **New**.

1. The New search window opens. See Fig 5.08 – New Search Window.
2. Enter the search string (in this case, "creative thinking puzzles").
3. Select the search option you want such as "All words", "Any words" or "Exact phrase".
4. Select the search category from the drop down list (in this case "The Web").

5. Modify the search engine settings if desired. Here fourteen search engines are enabled, returning ten results per page.
6. Select the display criteria under Analysis. Here the minimal criteria have been selected in which duplicate links are discarded.
7. Finally, click on **Search** button at the bottom of the window to start the search.

Sorting Searches

Search results are displayed on the right pane of the Main window. You can sort searches by Keywords, Update Date, Creation Date, Matches, Note, Category or Schedule according to your preference.

To customise the search sorting mode, click the Sort by header of the search list and select another sorting field from the drop down list. Another possible way is to select the Sort Searches command from the View menu, then select the desired sorting field.

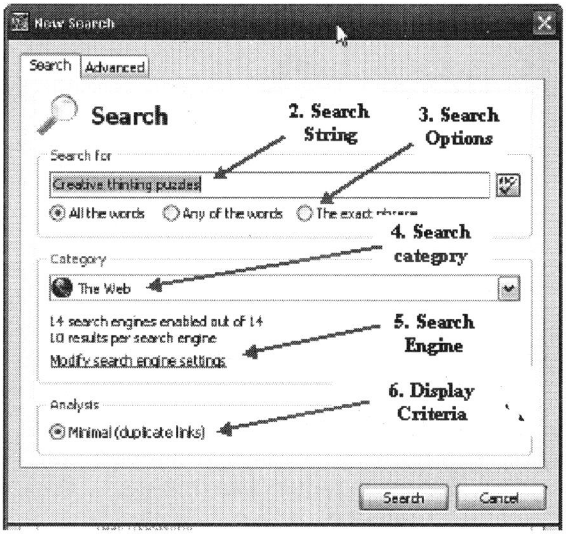

Fig 5.08 – New Search Window

Saving Pages

To save pages on your computer, select a search and click the **Save Pages** button on the Standard Toolbar. You may also select the Save Pages command from the Results menu. This will open the corresponding window. Before saving the pages, you may wish to select only the important pages. Do so by clicking only on the ones you want using the left mouse button while holding down the Ctrl key.

To decide how much of the Web page you wish to save, set the options on the Save Pages window by selecting the check boxes you want. The check boxes are:

- Save images embedded in pages: Also keeps images contained in Web pages. However, you should remember that downloading time may be greatly increased if your search contains many pages or some pages with numerous images.
- Save pages for selected results only: Downloads and saves only those pages corresponding to pre-selected results.

You can use a Save Page as command in the File menu to save the page as a file on your computer, a Web page or document related to a selected result.

6. E-mails

In this chapter:

- You are introduced to the history of e-mails, how it all began.
- We give you understanding of how e-mail appears to work and how it really works.
- We discuss e-mail front ends. These are software that the user will see and interact with.
- You are introduced to Web mail. We discuss and compare the top three — Gmail, Yahoo! and Hotmail.
- From Web mail, we move on to special software for e-mail management such as Outlook Express, Eudora and Mozilla Thunderbird.
- We take a close look at the most widely used software, Outlook Express.
- You are introduced to e-mail etiquette.
- We review the basics of protection against e-mail Virus.

How It All Began

E-mail is short for electronic mail. It is a method of transmitting data, text files, digital photos, and audio and video files from one computer to another over the Internet.

E-mails did not become popular until 1990. However, today it is perhaps the most important means for business and personal communications, and it is growing rapidly.

E-mail users create and send messages from individual computers using commercial programmes or mail-user agents (MUAs). An e-mail programme will enable the user to compose a message and send it via the Internet. To send the message, the user has to specify the address of the recipient(s) of the e-mails. If the user sends a message to more than one recipient, it is called broadcasting.

There are many different ways to write an e-mail address, depending on the e-mail destination. For instance, an inter-office message distributed over an Intranet, or an internal computer network, may have a simple scheme such as the person's name as the address. For e-mails meant to reach further destination over the Internet, the recipient's name is followed by the symbol @, followed by the domain name and then the organisation's name. In some cases, a country name may also be added. For instance, to send an e-mail to Mr. Roger Penrose working at a company in Australia, the address may read: rogerpenrose@worldwidetravels.com.au

E-mails generally contain headers and footers above and below the message. The information provided in these will include the sender's name, e-mail address, and the date the e-mail was sent. A user can store, delete, reply, or forward the message to others.

Most e-mail programmes allow you to attach files and photos to e-mails. These attachments permit users to append large text- or graphics-based files to e-mail messages. These files may include audio and video files and digital photographs.

NOTE

Ray Tomlinson invented Internet based e-mail in late 1971. Tomlinson worked as a computer engineer for Bolt Beranek and Newman (BBN) in the US. His company was hired in 1968 by the United States Defence Department to build the first Internet called ARPANET.

Tomlinson developed a file transfer protocol so that it could be used to send electronic messages to any computer on the ARPANET network. He chose the "@" symbol to tell which user was working at what computer. The "@" symbol is placed between the user's login name and the name of his/her host computer.

NOTE

The first e-mail was sent between two computers that were actually sitting besides each other. However, the ARPANET network was used as the connection between the two. The first e-mail message was "QWERTYUIOP". Look at the keyboard and you will see that this is just the letters on the first row of your keyboard.

How E-mail Really Works

In Fig 6.01 – How E-mail Works, the top part of the illustration shows the way that e-mail appears to work, moving straight from the sender's computer to the recipient's computer via the Internet. In actual practice, matters are a little more complicated. To give you an understanding of the basic mechanism of how e-mails are actually sent and received, the bottom part of the illustration shows you the six basic steps (A to F), involved. Follow the letters A to F as you read through the description of each step.

Step A: Sender creates and sends an e-mail

The originating sender creates an e-mail in his or her Mail User Agent or MUA and clicks 'Send'. The MUA is the software application the sender uses to compose and read e-mail. Popular MUAs include Outlook Express, Eudora, Outlook, etc.

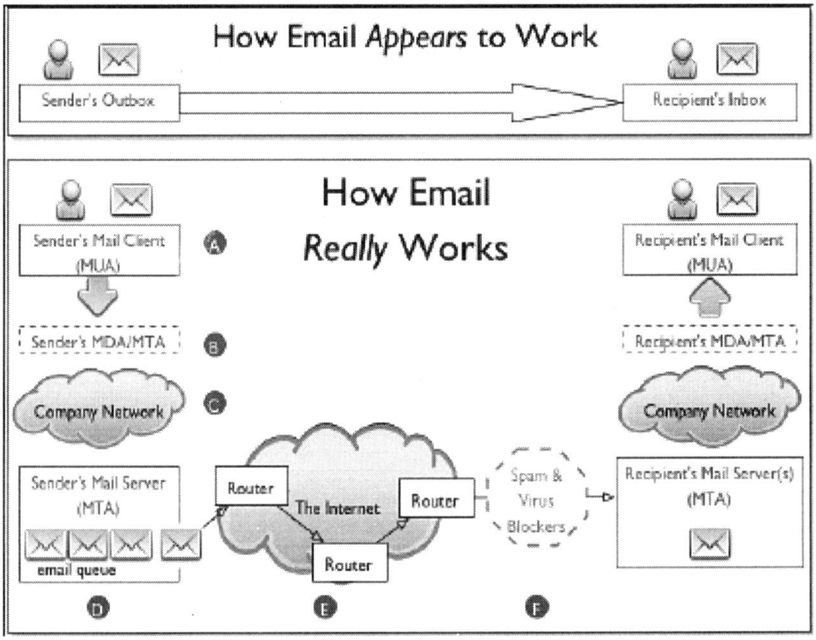

Fig 6.01 – How E-mail Works

Step B: Sender's Mail Delivery Agent (MDA) routes the e-mail

The sender's MUA transfers the e-mail to an MDA. The MDA accepts the e-mail, then routes it to local mailboxes or forwards it to a Mail Transfer Agent (MTA) if it is addressed to a far off recipient. In the diagram, an MDA forwards the e-mail to an MTA and it enters the first of a series of network clouds, labelled as a "Company Network" cloud. A network cloud is the name given to a collection of mail servers, DNS servers, routers, etc. These are Internet enabled devices that can send and receive data, providing links along a digital pathway for the e-mail to travel from sender to the recipient.

NOTE

Step C: Network cloud

The MTA will send the e-mail into a network cloud within a large company or Internet Service Provider (ISP) or into the largest network cloud in existence, the Internet. The links in the Internet are usually protected by firewalls, spam filters and mal-ware (here, mal-ware stands for any type of virus or other harmful software) detection software that may bounce or even delete an e-mail. A firewall is software that inspects network traffic such as e-mails passing through it, and denies or permits passage of the message based on a set of rules. When an e-mail is deleted by this kind of software, it may fail silently, so the sender is given no information about where or when the delivery failure occurred.

E-mail service providers and other companies that process a large volume of e-mail often have their own, private network clouds. These organisations commonly have multiple mail servers, and route all e-mail through a central gateway server also called a mail hub, that redistributes mail to whichever MTA is available. E-mail on these secondary MTAs must usually wait for the primary MTA to become available. When that happens, the secondary mail server transfers its messages to the primary MTA.

Step D: E-mail queue

The e-mail in the diagram is addressed to someone at another company, so it enters an e-mail queue with other outgoing e-mail messages. If there is a high volume of mail in the queue, the message will be delayed in the queue until the MTA finishes processing the messages ahead of it.

Step E: MTA to MTA transfer

When transferring an e-mail, the sending MTA handles all aspects of mail delivery until the message has been either accepted or rejected by the receiving MTA.

As the e-mail clears the queue, it enters the Internet network cloud, where it is routed along a host-to-host chain of servers. Each MTA in the Internet network cloud needs to "stop and ask directions" from the Domain Name System (DNS) in order to identify the next MTA in the delivery chain.

To find the recipient's IP address and mailbox, the MTA must drill down through the Domain Name System (DNS), which consists of a set of servers distributed across the Internet, until it reaches the local domain of the recipient. Then, the sending MTA asks if the host will accept messages for the recipient's username. If accepted, the MTA transfers the message.

Step F: Firewalls, spam and virus filters

The transfer process described in the last step is somewhat simplified. An e-mail may be transferred to more than one MTA within a network cloud and is likely to be passed to at least one firewall before it reaches its destination.

An e-mail encountering a firewall may be tested by spam and virus filters before it is allowed to pass inside the firewall. These filters test to see if the message qualifies as undesirable e-mail or spam or other forms of mal-ware. If the message contains mal-ware, the file is usually quarantined and the sender is notified. If the message is identified as spam, it will probably be deleted without notifying the sender.

We will discuss anti-virus and anti-spam measures in *Chapter 11 – Virus, Spam and Other Perils* later in this book.

E-mail Front Ends

So far, we have been studying the way e-mails are moved across the Internet. As you have seen, several Internet devices must work together to ensure that the e-mail you send reaches the correct destination. As a user however, you are required only to deal with an interactive front end that lets you compose and send e-mails or receive and read e-mails.

Front ends can be divided into two basic classes. The simplest ones are called Web mail front ends. These are Websites of the e-mail service provider that you can open in any Web browser connected to the Internet. The major drawback here is that all activity like reading or composing e-mails can only be done as long as you are online.

While this may not be a major drawback for personal e-mails, for business purposes however, this is inadequate. In business, you will receive and send perhaps hundreds of e-mails.

Some e-mails will need your immediate attention, whereas others will have to be retained in easily located folders on your computer. Above all, you will want to read and reply to e-mails while offline in order to conserve Internet expenses. For such situations, you will require specialised software that will allow you to use e-mails effectively in your business.

In the following sections, we will look at both of these types of e-mail front ends.

Web Mail

For personal use there are free Web-based e-mail programmes called Web mails. If you have a Web mail account, you can login to your account from any computer using the computer's Web browser and Internet connection. Therefore, it is not necessary to configure separate e-mail client software such as Outlook Express with your ISP's access number, your username and password; you have only to open the Web mail's Website and login with your username and password.

Some major examples of e-mail services that provide a Web mail interface include Hotmail, Gmail and Yahoo!. The main drawback of Web mail is that you can read or reply to e-mails only while you are online. In contrast, if you are using software such as Outlook Express, you can download all your mail online, then read and reply offline. You will, of course, have to go back online to send your replies.

In general, since all activity on Web mail has to be done online, it is most convenient if you have a fast broadband connection. You can configure Outlook Express on your computer to download your e-mail from Gmail or Hotmail while online and then read and reply to your e-mail while you are offline.

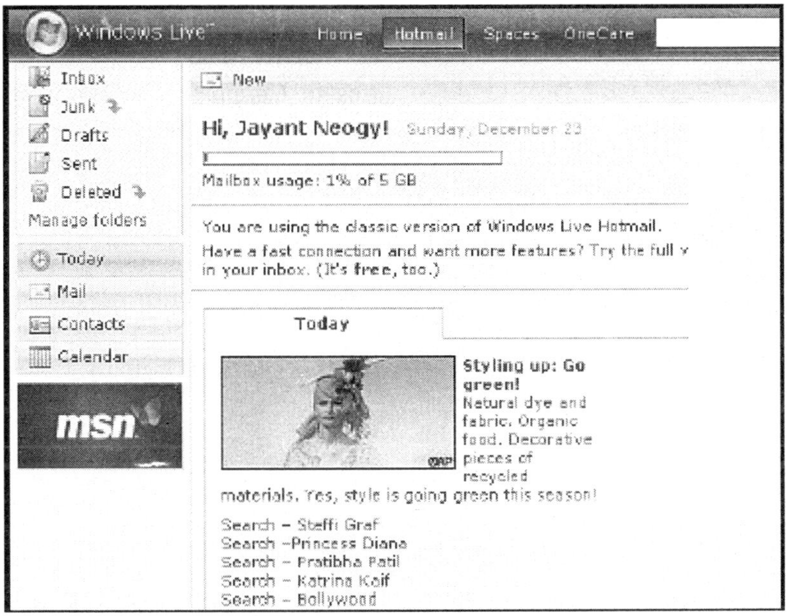

Fig 6.02 – Hotmail Sign In

However, if you are away from your own computer, you can still access your Gmail or Hotmail account from any other Internet-connected computer, using just its browser, to read your mail online. See Fig 6.02 – Hotmail Sign In.

In this case, the Website has been opened in the Firefox Web browser. However, it could be opened using any other browser such as Internet Explorer or Opera.

All the three Web mails mentioned here, Gmail, Hotmail and Yahoo! are leaders world-wide in terms of number of users. All of them (in the basic form) are free. It is a matter of personal choice as to which Web mail you may wish to use. Here is a brief comparison of the three to help you to pick one. See Fig 6.03 – Comparison of Web Mails.

Service	**Gmail**	**Yahoo! Mail**	**Hotmail**
Storage capacity	2 Gigabyte	1 Gigabyte	250 Megabyte
Spam Filtering	A	A	B
Search Efficiency	A-	B-	C
User Experience	A+	A-	B

Fig 6.03 – Comparison of Web Mails

You may notice that Gmail has scored the highest as far as user experience goes. It is not surprising therefore, that its user base has been growing steadily over the years. See Fig 6.04 – E-mail Users in the US.

Gmail appears to score over all other Web mail applications because its performance (speed) is consistently fast and it is easy to sort e-mails received and archived. Gmail also offers more storage. However, Yahoo! and Live Hotmail offer more Microsoft Outlook-like user interfaces.

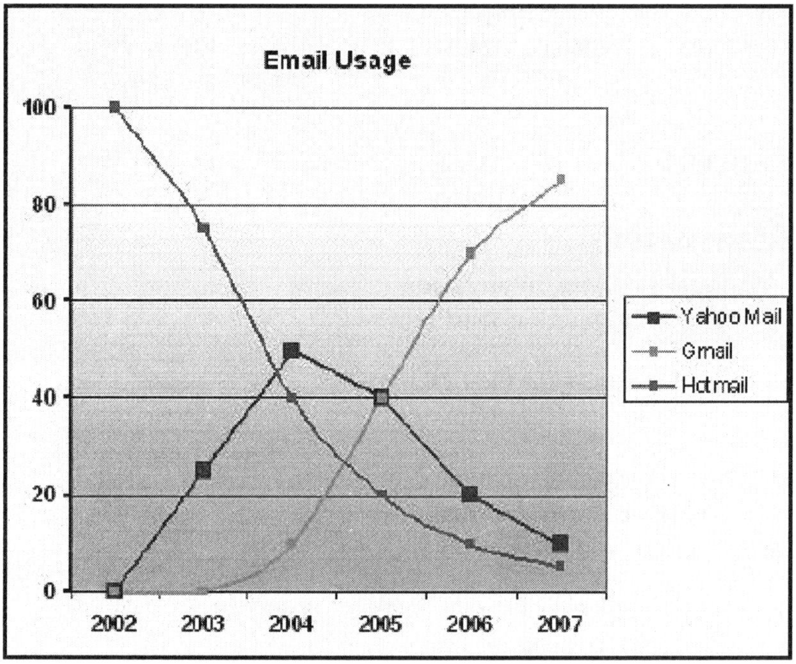

Fig 6.04 – E-mail Users in the US

So, if you are looking for speed and quick search capabilities, Gmail is for you. If you are looking for greater similarity with Microsoft Outlook online, pick Yahoo! Mail. If however, you have business usages in mind, you may look beyond Web mails, at specialised e-mail software that will allow you to work offline, store e-mails in separate folders, and provide you with capability to protect yourself against unwanted e-mails (called Spam) and against invasion by computer viruses.

Special Front Ends

As we have discussed, for business use or even for personal use, we may wish for greater capability in the front end software. In particular, we will want the software to automatically download all our incoming mail into our software's inbox and upload all outgoing mail that we may have composed and placed already into our software's outbox. In addition, we would like to filter out unwanted or dangerous e-mails.

To accomplish these tasks, we will require software that use the Post Office Protocol 3 (POP3) for downloading and Simple Mail Transfer Protocol (SMTP) for uploading e-mail. Many software programmes are capable of this including Windows Outlook Express, Microsoft Office Outlook, Eudora, IncrediMail, Pegasus Mail and a host of others.

While each of these has their own strengths and weaknesses, they function largely in the same way. The most popular software amongst these is Outlook Express, which comes bundled with Windows and therefore, is available free on all computers running Windows. If you have Windows XP with Service Pack 2 installed, you will have Outlook Express 6.0 already installed in your machine.

Outlook Express

Outlook Express Set-up

Basically, Outlook Express set-up involves configuring e-mail accounts. You cannot use Outlook Express until you have configured at least one e-mail account.

When you open Outlook Express for the first time, a wizard guides you through the account set-up process. However, new e-mail accounts can be set up at any time.

Outlook express allows you to set up multiple e-mail accounts. Each e-mail account will correspond to a mailbox on an e-mail server (normally your ISP or Internet Service Provider). Before proceeding with the set-up, you need to obtain your account details from your e-mail provider, which includes.

- SMTP server - This is used to send e-mail.
- POP3 server -This is used to receive e-mail.
- Account name - This is your login name to receive e-mail.
- Account password - This is your login password to receive e-mail.

To set up an e-mail account, proceed as follows:

1. Select **Tools** → **Accounts** → **Mail** and click **Add** and select **Mail**.
2. The Internet connection wizard page will appear. See Fig 6.05 – Internet Connection Wizard. Enter your display name in the box. The display name can be anything you want and will appear in the form filled on your outgoing messages. It is normally your name.

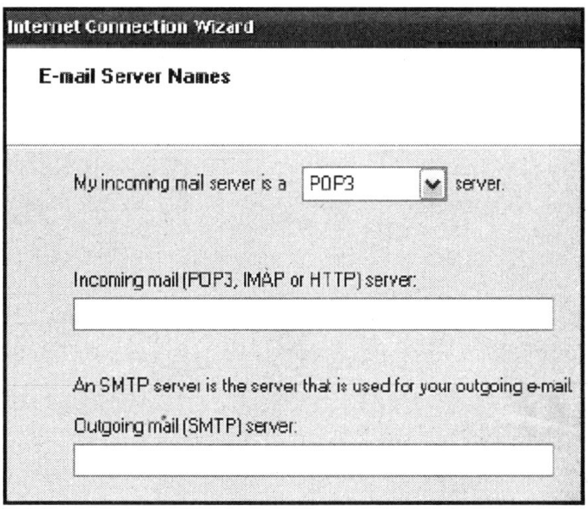

Fig 6.05 – Internet Connection Wizard

3. Click **Next**. A page will appear prompting for your e-mail address. This is the reply address for all e-mails that you send. Enter the e-mail address given to you by your e-mail provider.

4. Click **Next**. A page will appear prompting for your e-mail server names. The first box is a drop down box where you select the connection protocol such as POP3. Enter the server names given by your e-mail provider.

5. Click **Next**. A page appears prompting for your account name and password. Enter these details and ensure the Remember Password box is ticked so that you will not have to type it manually each time you try to receive e-mails.

6. Click **Next** and then click **Finish** to complete the e-mail account set-up.

The new account is created and appears in the list along with any other pre-configured accounts. See Fig 6.06 - Internet Accounts.

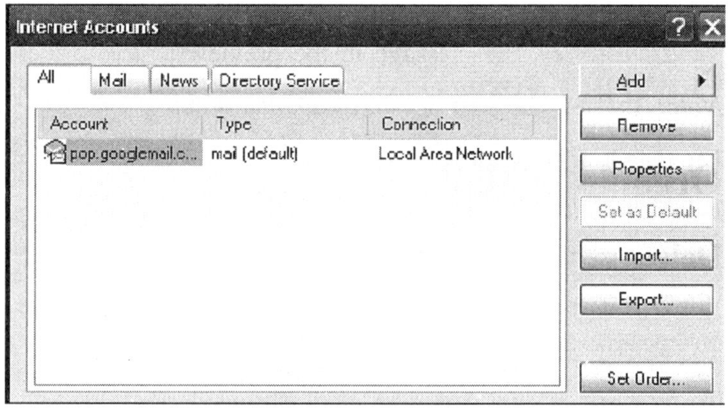

Fig 6.06 – Internet Accounts

Since Hotmail is a free e-mail account offered to you when you configure Outlook Express, you may wish to subscribe to Hotmail. Thereby, at no extra cost, you can set up your first e-mail account on your computer.

Proceed as follows to set up your msn Hotmail account in Microsoft Outlook Express:

1. In Outlook Express, click **Accounts** on the Tools menu.

2. In the Internet Accounts dialogue box, click **Add**, and then click **Mail**.

3. Use the following information to complete the Internet Connection Wizard. See Fig 6.05 – Internet Connection Wizard

On the Internet E-mail Address page, click the option **I already have an e-mail address that I'd like to use.** Enter your Hotmail address.

On the E-mail Server Name page, click **HTTP** in the **My incoming mail server is ...** box.

In the box **My HTTP service provider is...,"** click **Hotmail**. No other information needs be entered on this page.

4. Follow the remaining instructions to finish the wizard.

Getting Started

After you have set up your e-mail account or accounts, it is time to connect to the Internet and receive and send e-mails to your friends, relatives or business associates. We begin with receiving and organising mail.

To read your messages

After Outlook Express downloads your messages, or after you click the Send/Recv button on the toolbar, you can read messages either in a separate window or in the preview pane.

1. Click the **Inbox** icon on either the Outlook bar or the Folders list.
2. To view the message in the preview pane, click the message in the message list.

Note: To view the message in a separate window, double-click the message in the message list.

Organising Mail

Delete unwanted mail

1. In the message list, select the message.
2. On the toolbar, click **Delete**.

To restore a deleted message, open the Deleted Items folder, and then drag the message back to the Inbox or other folder.

To find e-mail messages

1. On the Edit menu, point to Find, and then click **Message**.
2. Enter criteria in the search fields.

Outlook Express searches the currently selected folder by default. To search in another folders, click Browse, and then select the folder you want to search.

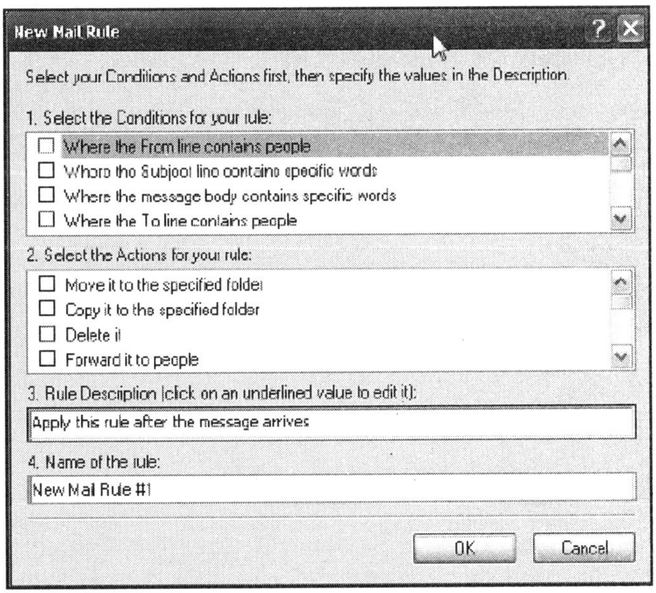

Fig 6.07 – New Message Rules

Managing e-mail messages with rules

When you have large volumes of incoming e-mail, Outlook Express can help you process it more efficiently by using rules to automatically sort incoming messages, highlight certain messages in colour, automatically reply to or forward certain messages, and do much more.

To create a rule for e-mail messages:

1. On the Tools menu, point to Message Rules, and then click **Mail**. See Fig 6.07 – New Message Rules. Note however that message rules cannot be created for IMAP or HTTP e-mail accounts.
2. If this is the first rule you are creating, proceed to step 3. Otherwise, on the Mail Rules tab, click **New** and proceed to step 4.
3. Select the conditions for your rule by selecting the desired check boxes in the Conditions section. (You must select at least one condition.)

TIP

You can specify multiple conditions for a single rule by selecting more than one check box. Click the underlined hyperlink in the Rule Description section to specify whether all of the rule conditions must be met before the specified action occurs (and), or whether at least one must be met.

Specify the actions for your rule by selecting the desired check boxes in the Actions section. (You must select at least one condition.)

1. Click the underlined hyperlinks in the Rule Description section to specify the conditions or actions for your rule.

TIP

You can click "contains people" or "contains specific words" in the Rule Description section to specify the people or words you'd like Outlook Express to look for in messages. If you enter multiple people or multiple words per condition, use the Options button in the Select People or Type Specific Words dialogue boxes to further customise the condition.

2. In the Name of the rule text box, select the default name or type a new name for your rule, and then click OK.

You can create a new rule by selecting an existing one on the Message Rules tab and clicking Copy. This is helpful when the new rule you want to create is similar to an existing one.

Increasing your disk space

There are several things you can do to reduce the amount of space that e-mail and newsgroup messages take up on your hard disk. The most convenient one is to compress the folder or folders that contain mail already downloaded. To do so, proceed as follows:

3. Select an e-mail folder.
4. On the File menu, point to Folder, and then click Compact.

Back up Mail

To back up any folder that contains important e-mails you wish to preserve, find the folder file, and then copy it to a back up folder, floppy disk, or network drive. Outlook Express e-mail folders have a .dbx extension (for example, "Sent Items.dbx").

Sending E-mail

Creating an e-mail

In the opening page of Outlook Express, click on Create a New Mail Message. The New Mail dialogue box will open. You will notice that the From line has already been filled by Outlook Express showing your default e-mail address. Fill in the e-mail address of the Recipient (To:), addresses of those who will receive copies (Cc:) and the subject matter (Subject:). See Fig 6.08 – New Message Dialogue Box.

Click inside the message area to start typing the message. Before starting, you can click on the Format tab located on the top menu bar and choose either Plain Text or Rich Text as your format option. While rich text will permit you additional text format options and will allow you to embed pictures and other graphics, you may wish to choose the plain text format if:

- You wish to reduce the size of the e-mail and do not need to embed pictures or graphics
- You know that the recipient does not have the capability to read rich text in his or her computer.

Special Formatting

When you want to add special emphasis or structure to message text such as bold text, colour, or bulleted lists, you can use Hypertext Mark-up Language (HTML), the standard for formatting text for the Internet. HTML formatting also enables you to include graphics and links to Websites in your messages. As explained earlier, HTML formatting is turned by selecting Rich Text in the Format menu.

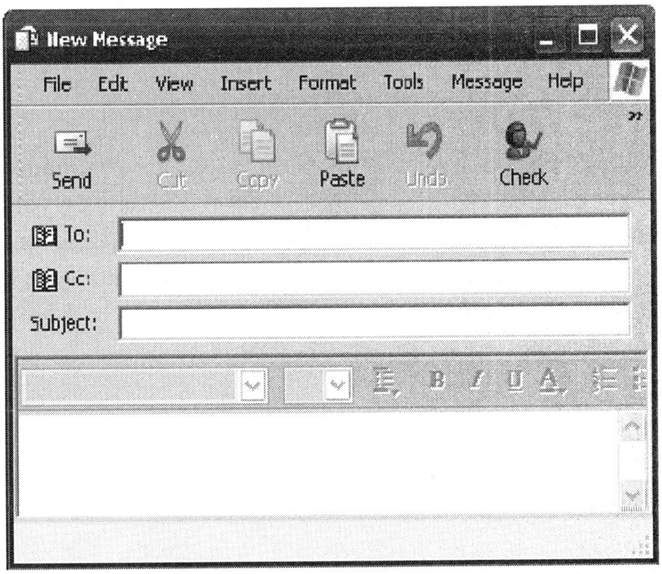

Fig 6.08 – New Message Dialogue Box

Rich Text Format

After selecting Rich Text format option, you can change the way the text looks for all your messages or you can make changes to selected text within a message.

To change the text style for all messages, do the following:

1. On the **Tools** menu, click Options.
2. On the Compose tab, click **Font Settings**.

To format text within individual messages, do the following:

1. Select the text you want to format.
2. To change the font for an entire message, on the Edit menu, click **Select All**.
3. On the formatting toolbar, click the buttons for the options you want.

Special Stationery

With Outlook Express stationery, you can create attractive messages for both e-mail and newsgroups. Stationery is a template that can include a background image, unique text font colours, and custom margins.

To apply stationery to all your outgoing messages, do the following:

1. On the Tools menu, click **Options**, and then click the **Compose** tab.
2. Under Stationery, select the Mail or News check box (or both), and then click **Select**.

TIP

To apply stationery to an individual message on the Message menu, point to New Message Using, and then select a stationery style. To apply or change stationery after you start a message on the Format menu, point to Apply Stationery, and then select a stationery style.

Insert Picture

In addition to rich formatting, you can add to your e-mail's impact by embedding pictures and graphics in the body of the e-mail. Such embellishments are often needed in business e-mails such as newsletters, promotional literature, etc. To insert a graphic or picture, proceed as follows:

1. Click the place in the message where you want the image to appear.
2. On the Insert menu, click **Picture**, and then click **Browse** to find the image file.
3. Enter Layout and Spacing information for the image file as needed.

Attachments

NOTE

You must make sure that you have selected the Rich Text option before you try to embed a picture, a graphic or some Web address (URL) in your e-mail. In case you do not wish to send the main message in rich text format, you can attach the photograph or graphic to your plain text e-mail.

To do so proceed as follows:

1. Open a new mail message dialogue box by clicking on the **New Mail** message option on the opening page of Outlook Express as described earlier.

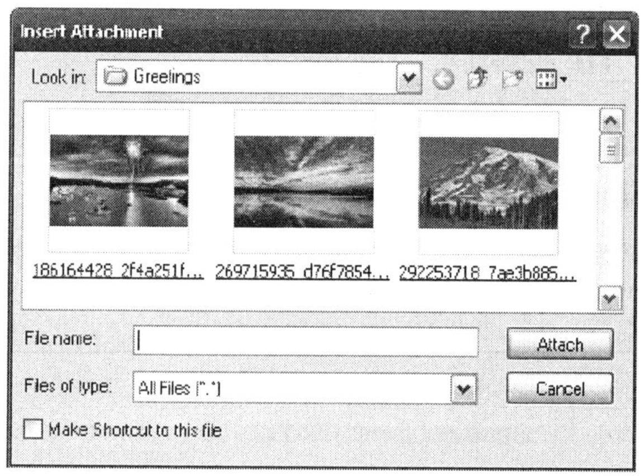

Fig 6.09 – Insert Attachment Dialogue Box

2. Select Plain Text under the Format tab of the New Message dialogue box.
3. Click on the **Insert** tab and then click on the **File Attachment** option. (This is the only available option if you have selected Plain Text earlier). The Insert Attachment dialogue box opens. See Fig 6.09 – Insert Attachment Dialogue Box.
4. Navigate to the folder and file you wish to attach and select the file. The New Message dialogue box will now show an added line Attach: which will be followed by the file name you have selected.

Send the mail as usual after clicking on the **Send** icon on the New Message dialogue box. Your e-mail will be sent along with its attached file.

Working Offline

You may recall our discussion about the ability of Outlook Express to let you read and compose replies to your e-mail while you are offline. We examine this capability that sets Outlook Express apart from browser based Web mails.

You can set up Outlook Express to automatically disconnect after downloading e-mail messages into your Inbox and uploading your replies waiting in the Outbox. After you are offline, you can read the downloaded e-mails and compose replies. When you click the Send icon of the New Message dialogue box, the replies are temporarily stored in the Outbox of Outlook Express. By doing so, you reduce the cost of being connected longer online.

To set up Outlook Express to reduce online time, proceed as follows:

1. On the Tools menu, click Options.
2. On the Connection tab, select the Hang up after sending and receiving check box.

TIP

To reconnect to send or receive messages, on the Tools menu, point to Send and Receive, and then select the option you want.

If you select an IMAP folder when you are offline, and you have not checked Work Offline from the File menu, Outlook Exprcss will rcconncct, and will not hang up when you click Send/Recv.

Tips and Tricks

As you continue with Outlook Express, you will want to use some time and effort saving tricks and tips like these.

Add Contacts to your Address Book

When you receive e-mail, you can add the sender's name and e-mail address to your Address Book from within Outlook Express. To do so, proceed as follows:

1. Open the message.
2. On the Tools menu, point to Add to Address Book, and then select the user you want to add.

You can also set up Outlook Express so that people whose messages you reply to are automatically added to your Address Book.

1. In Outlook Express, on the Tools menu, click **Options**.
2. On the Send tab, select the automatically put people I reply to in my Address Book check box.

Open Internet Explorer from Outlook Express

You may wish to explore the Internet without having to exit Outlook Express and then launch your Internet Explorer Web browser. To do so, proceed as follows:

On the Help menu, point to Microsoft on the Web, and then click the Web option you want. For example, click Search the Web to look for a Website, a person, a company, or an organisation. Or, click Best of the Web to open the MSN Web page that lists some of the best sites on the Web. See Fig 6.10 – Microsoft on the Web.

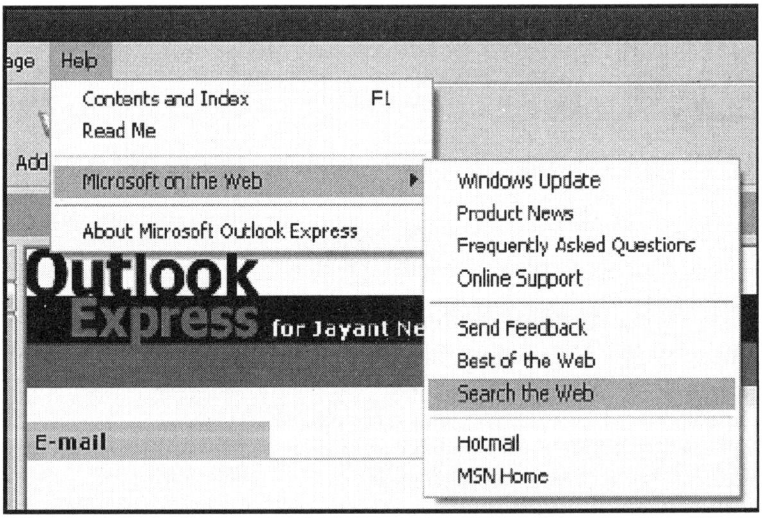

Fig 6.10 – Microsoft on the Web

Open Outlook Express from your Web browser

You can set Outlook Express to be your default e-mail programme, so that whenever you click an e-mail link on a Web page or choose the e-mail command in your Web browser, Outlook Express opens automatically. To do so, proceed as follows:

1. On the Tools menu, click **Options**, and then click the **General** tab.
2. In the Default Messaging Programs area, click **Make Default** for news or e-mail. See Fig 6.11 – Options Dialogue Box

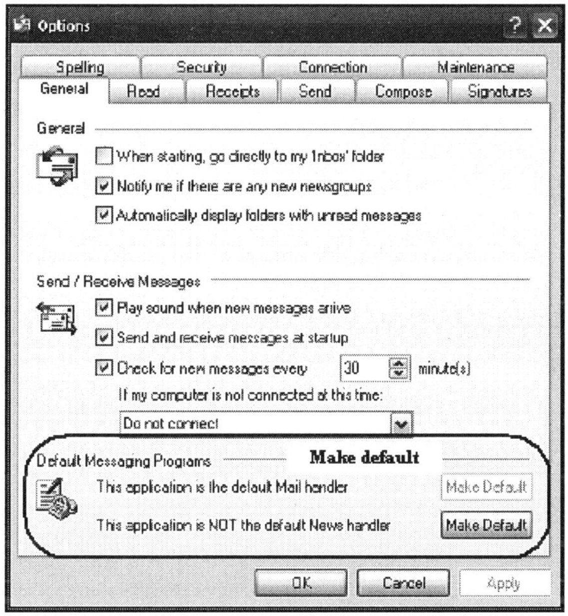

Fig 6.11 – Options Dialogue Box

E-mail Tips

To ensure that your e-mails create the right impression, be it in personal relationships or in business, there are two important areas that you should pay attention. Firstly, there are some rules or e-mail etiquette that you may wish to observe in all your correspondence. While less important in personal e-mail to friends, etiquette is vital in all business correspondence.

You must also ensure that you do not send annoying, unwanted or potentially harmful e-mails. You may unwittingly do so if your own computer is infected. On the other hand, some simple precautions will protect your own computer from virus attack.

We use the rest of this chapter discussing etiquette and virus protection.

E-mail Etiquette

Here are some useful tips for e-mail etiquette, particularly for business e-mails:

1. E-mail is frequently written quickly and often poorly. The tips that follow should help you to write e-mail that will create a good impression, so important in business
2. Pay attention to punctuation, spelling, grammar and capitals. Many e-mail messages contain poor spelling and grammar, incorrect use of capital letters and/or poor punctuation. Such messages look amateurish and inevitably produce a poor impression of the sender.
3. Your subject line should be descriptive. Many people get dozens (or even hundreds) of e-mail messages per day, and with so much of it is spam (i.e. unsolicited sales messages). Therefore, your message may be deleted unread if the subject line makes it look unimportant or appears to be a sales message. Another reason to make your subject clear is to help the recipient find your e-mail easily at a later date.
4. Use short paragraphs and leave lines between them. On-screen text is harder to read than printed text due to its lower resolution. You can make things easier for your readers by using short, clearly separated paragraphs.

5. Do not send unsolicited attachments. Large files will cause delays in downloading, especially if the recipient does not have a fast broadband connection. Be polite and ask first.
6. Ensure that your PC is protected against viruses. Unless you take suitable precautions (like regularly downloading the latest definition file for your antivirus software), you run the risk of your machine becoming virus infected. Far worse, you run the risk of unknowingly sending virus-infected e-mail messages to everyone in your address book. This is not a way to win friends.
7. Do not type in ALL CAPITALS. There are two reasons for this. First, text in all capitals is harder to read. Second, typing in all capitals is considered a faux pas by most Internet users, and doing so may see your message ignored.

Virus Protection

We discuss virus protection in detail in *Chapter 11 – Virus, Spam and Other Perils*. In this section, we mention only the very basic precautions that you can take to protect your own computer and that of your recipients.

Incoming Mail

We begin with your own computer's defences and look at some basic precautions to avoid picking up harmful virus.

TIP

A very important precaution is never to open an e-mail attachment unless you know and trust the sender. E-mail attachments may be in the form of HTML documents, Microsoft Word or Excel documents. Such attachments may contain active content such as macros. Viruses may hide inside the active content and be released within your computer when you open the attachment.

Since plain text does not contain any active content and hence cannot hide viruses, you can force Outlook Express to read all e-mails in plain text. Do the following:

1. Start Outlook Express and click **Tools** ➔ **Options**.
2. In the Options dialogue box, click the **Read** tab.
3. Select the check box against Read all messages in plain text.
4. Click **OK** and exit Outlook Express.

ALERT

While this will stop all active content, some e-mails may not read correctly in the plain text format. If the source of the e-mail is a known and trusted one, deselect the check box to read mail that may be in HTML format. You may restore the safer option after you have read the HTML e-mail.

Outgoing Mail

The most important precaution you can take to avoid infecting the computers of your recipients is to make sure that your own computer is not infected by a virus. Use at least two good anti-virus programmes, update their virus signature files regularly and periodically scan your computer with your anti-virus programmes.

If you install certain anti-virus software such as AVG, the programme will scan both incoming and outgoing e-mails for virus infection and will alert you if any infection is detected. See Fig 6.12 – AVG E-mail Scanner.

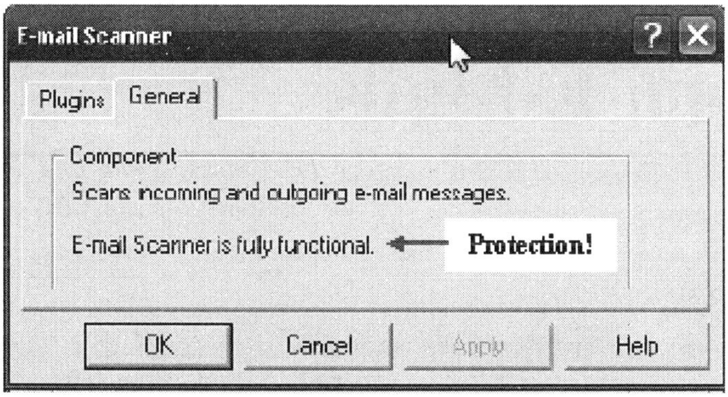

Fig 6.12 – AVG E-mail Scanner

7. Beyond E-Mails

In this chapter:

- We examine Internet communication applications that go beyond e-mails. We take a close look at Blogs and Blogging, the new form of diaries and journals on the Internet.
- We look at the rapid growth of Instant Messaging through Internet applications such as America Online's Instant Messenger, Microsoft's Windows Messenger, Google Talk, etc.
- We examine the techniques and benefits of Internet chat programmes such as ICQ, mIRC, etc. as well as recently launched applications in India such as Indiatimes chat.
- We examine the Voice over Internet Protocol, look at applications such as Skype and examine its future and growth potential in India.
- You are introduced to the fundamentals of the most rapidly growing phenomena on the Internet, that of Blogging. We tell you how you can get started with your very own Blog.

Introduction

E-mail is the very first application used for communication on the Internet. Even today, e-mails continue to be very widely used for both personal as well as business communications. However, a whole new generation of new, fast and convenient applications are finding place in the armoury of the Internet user.

NOTE

Some of these applications are blurring the lines between the Internet and the conventional telephone networks. Others are being used for video-conferencing and transfer of large data files. Yet other applications are being used to exchange information over the Internet between individuals or between groups in collaborative ways that were not considered possible only a decade or so ago.

The forces driving rapid advancement in the field of Internet communications are:

- Rapid proliferation of the personal computer
- Spread of the use of high speed broadband Internet
- Aggressive marketing of new technologies by Internet Service Providers

We begin this chapter with a look at some of the most promising technologies in this fast developing field, starting with Instant Messaging or IM.

Instant Messaging

Overview

Instant messaging (IM) lets you to have real-time communication with other users on the Internet. IM allows easy collaboration amongst a group of users. It is closer to genuine conversation than e-mail's "letter" format. In contrast to e-mail, each user knows whether the other users are available online. This is because IM systems allow the user to display an online status or away message for other users (called peers) to see.

People are not forced to reply immediately to incoming messages. So, IM is actually less intrusive than a telephone call. Some systems do allow the sending of messages to people not currently logged on (offline messages), thus removing much of the difference between IM and e-mail.

In certain cases, IM includes additional features, such as video conferencing, by using Web-cams. Other IM systems include Voice over Internet Protocol (VoIP) that allows peers to talk directly for free over the Internet.

TIP

It is possible to save a conversation for later reference. Instant messages are recorded (logged in) in local message history files, thus providing permanent records for future reference much like e-mails. IM allows quick exchange of information like URLs or brief excerpts from documents that is difficult to communicate via telephone.

NOTE

With the exception of e-mail, few applications in computing history have become as popular as quickly as Instant Messaging (IM). Building on a base of IM use on home computers, IM now represents a revolution in corporate communications. In the US, it has been observed that more than 50% of all business to client communications is in the form of IM.

IM is popular partly because, as its name suggests, the communication is instant. IM also fits in with the no nonsense "just the facts" style of business communication that we seem to like today, even in personal communications.

The Beginnings of IM

NOTE

The beginnings of IM can be traced back to 1996 when a handful of companies started producing client software that allowed you to chat in real-time with other people who had the same software. The pioneer of IM was Mirabilis in the US with its ICQ (short for "I Seek You") client. Soon major Internet players such as AOL, MSN (Microsoft), and Yahoo! followed suit with their own client software.

Today, AOL is regarded as the leader in IM. As the world's largest ISP, it provides AOL's Instant Messenger (AIM) to its subscribers. Other vendors like MSN and Yahoo! have sought to catch up with AOL but have so far been unable to do so. Though not as big as AOL yet, the fastest growing IM network is Microsoft's MSN Messenger which is bundled with Windows XP and therefore, available to most personal computer users.

IM Standards

Although IM's acceptance has been rapid and widespread, even now there are no standards that define how the different IM products communicate with each other. This means that IM users can interact only with others who are also on the same network. For IM providers like AOL or MSN, this lack of inter-operability is not really a major issue since their products are to be found on virtually each PC in use today.

TIP

To combat the problem of no inter-operability, some companies are producing IM clients that act as a front end to the different networks. One such product is Trillian Pro, from Cerulean Studios, which allows you to connect to ICQ, AIM, MSN Messenger, Yahoo! Messenger and IRC networks through a single interface.

It is hoped that in the near future, two protocols called SIP (Session Initiation Protocol) and SIMPLE (SIP for Instant Messaging and Presence Leveraging Extensions) will allow IM users true inter-operability. While this is not a real issue for individual users, it will make business to business and business to client communications much smoother.

ALERT

Like any form of technology, instant messaging (IM) can have good and bad uses. With the right parameters it can be a tool to develop friendships among people from every corner of the earth. However, the anonymity that this medium provides can lead to misuse as well.

Some Rules

Here are some rules one should observe for good IM:

- Use good spelling and grammar. It is common to allow sloppy, improper spelling and grammar to creep into online communication. Spawned by text messaging on cell phones, "text- speak" can appear in instant messaging as well. By typing full sentences that are grammatically correct, you will become a more effective writer and communicator.
- Select names and profile with care. IM programmes give you some freedom of expression, allowing you to select the name that is to be displayed and the picture that goes into your profile. But be sure to use judgement and select appropriate pictures. Be equally careful of what you include in your profile and avoid displaying any information that may be damaging.
- Online privacy is extremely important—and in some cases, it is a matter of safety. Never give out other people's screen names or e-mail addresses, unless you have been given permission. This would be akin to giving a phone number or address without permission.

Using Instant Messenger

America Online (AOL) provides an instant messenger that is perhaps the most widely used IM system in the world. To understand exactly how an IM system works, let us take a look at the steps below:

1. Go to the AOL's download page (use Google Search if required) and get a copy of the free software client for your computer.
2. Install the software and open the client.
3. The client tries to connect to the server. It uses a proprietary protocol for communication.
4. Once the client is connected to the server, you can enter your name and password to log in to the server. If this is your first time on, you can sign up for an account and immediately begin using it. When the server verifies your name and password, you are logged in.
5. The client sends the server the connection information (IP address and number of the port assigned to the client) of the computer you are using. It also provides the user with the names of everyone in your contacts list.
6. The server creates a temporary file that has the connection information for you and the list of your contacts. It then checks to see if any of the users in your contact list are currently logged in.

7. If the server finds any of your contacts logged in, it sends a message back to the client on your computer with the connection information for that user. The server also sends your connection information to the people in your contact list that are signed on.
8. When your client gets the connection information for a person in your contact list, it changes the status of that person to "online." You click on the name of a person in your contact list showing who is online, and a window opens that you can enter text into. You enter a message and click "send" or hit return to communicate with that person.
9. Because your client has the IP address and port number for the computer of the person that you sent the message to, your message is sent directly to the client on that person's computer. In other words, the server is not involved at this point. All communication is directly between the two clients.
10. The other person gets your instant message and responds. The window that each of you sees on your respective computers expands to include a scrolling dialogue of the conversation. Each person's instant messages appear in this window on both computers.

When the conversation is complete, you close the message window. Eventually, you go offline and exit. When this happens, your client sends a message to the server to terminate the session. The server sends a message to the client of each person on your contact list who is currently online to indicate that you have logged off. Finally, the server deletes the temporary file that contained the connection information for your client. In the clients of your contacts that are online, your name moves to the offline status section.

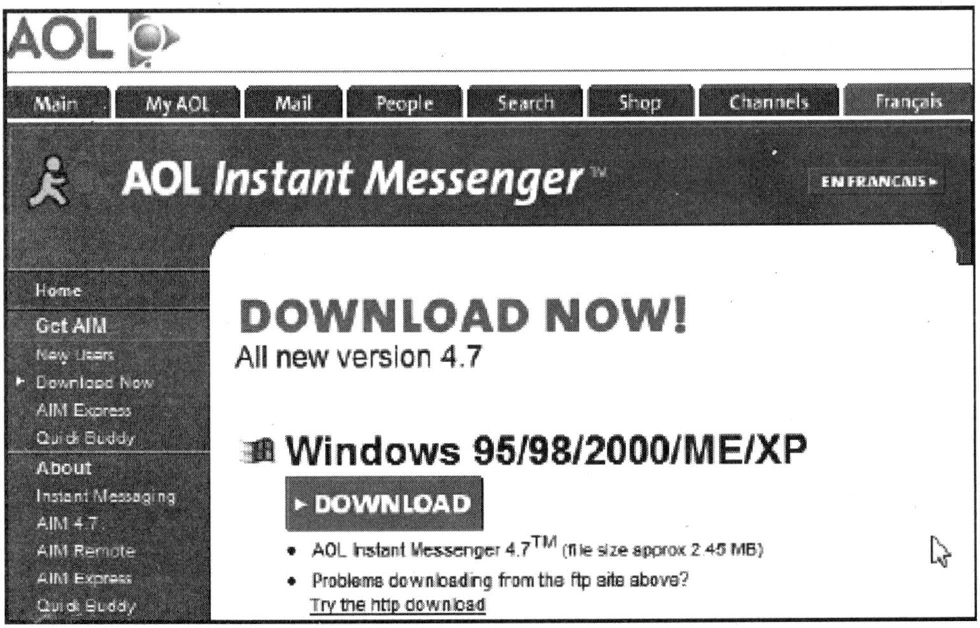

Fig 7.01 – AOL Instant Messenger

Internet Chat

Introduction

To give the application its full name, Internet Relay Chat, or IRC, is a means of chatting online in real-time through a client application like mIRC, through which data is sent via connected servers to various computers which are in turn connected to those servers all across the world.

Internet Relay Chat has been in use since 1988 when it was invented by an individual called Jarkko Oikarinen, and in the years since has provided a means for users to meet people of a like-minded nature to communicate in much the same way as the users of a Citizen's Band or Ham radio.

Using mIRC

To use IRC you will have to download and install a "client" programme that allows you to connect to the chat network. The IRC client works just like a browser that allows you to surf the Internet and look at Web pages. Instead of surfing, the IRC client allows you to send and receive messages to other users.

NOTE

One of the simplest and most comprehensive clients is mIRC, which is available for free download from **www.mirc.co.uk**. Once you download and install this programme, it will ask you to put in your name, nickname and e-mail address so that you can be identified by other users of the Internet chat rooms.

When you have provided the details, click on the file menu and then click on Connect. You will be connected to the chat room. The programme will pop up with a window listing all the channels that are currently open. Each channel specifies the subject matter being discussed.

To join a channel, simply double click on it and a new window will pop up. On the right hand side of this window you will see a list of names of people currently active in the channel. On the left hand side, you will see what they are saying. To contribute to the discussion, type in whatever you wish to say and press Enter. If you want to talk with a particular person one-on-one over the Internet, just double click on their name on the right hand side of the screen and a new window will pop up, in which you can write a private message that will be visible to only that person.

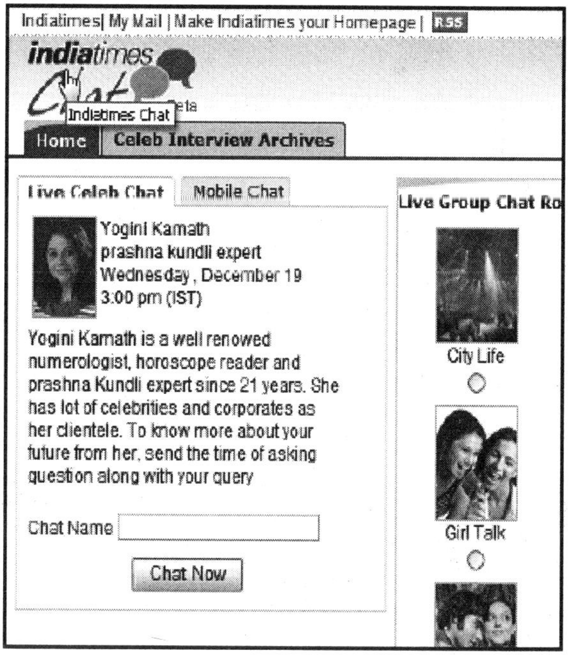

Fig 7.02 – Indiatimes Chat

For more information on IRC, you can go to the mIRC Website (**www.mirc.co.uk**) and look up the frequently asked questions (FAQ) section. Another good source of information is at www.irchelp.org.

TIP

On the Internet, there are a number of chat clients available, designed especially for the Indian audience such as Rediff Bol and Indiatimes Chat. You can download the Indiatimes Chat software from the Times of India Website at **http://www.Indiatimes.com**. See Fig 7.02. for a view of the Indiatimes Chat software.

Comparison with IM

Since we have already discussed instant messaging (IM) in this chapter, it is interesting to compare IM and IRC as methods of interconnecting with other users on the Internet. Here is a brief comparison of the two.

Online Chat is a way of linking with many people at once in real-time. You can enter some chat rooms simply through the Internet such as Yahoo! Chat. Some others require a separate software programme. Online chat rooms allow multiple users to join in a conversation and see what the other online users are typing. Typically chat rooms deal with certain themes, such as Teen Chat, Macintosh Chat, or Religious Chat. Using online chat, you can meet new people in an anonymous environment. You will need to choose a "screen name" to join a chat room, but the screen name can be whatever you would like it to be.

On the other hand, Instant Messaging, or IM is a way of communicating online with a select group of people, usually as individuals. To instant message someone, you need to know his or her screen name. You can save your friends' screen names in a list called a "Buddy List." In the instant messaging world, your screen name is likely to be more permanent than with online chat. Unlike online chat, you will have to use an instant messaging programme, such as AOL Instant Messenger or MSN Messenger. While online, you can open IM windows with many of your friends at once and type messages back and forth.

Voice over Internet Protocol

So far what we have discussed is the exchange of text messages, similar to e-mails. However, using the Internet and a broadband connection, it is possible for a PC or laptop user to dial other computers or even normal analogue telephones. The technology that makes this possible is called Voice over Internet Protocol or VoIP.

Basic Technology

Voice over Internet Protocol is actually a family of technologies that enable voice communications using Internet Protocol (IP) networks like the Internet. Developers and entrepreneurs have created an industry around VoIP technology in its many forms. They include desktop applications, telephone services, and corporate phone systems.

NOTE

VoIP is the core technology behind a range of applications from something as simple as voice-chat software loaded on a desktop PC to full-scale IP-based telecommunications networks used by large corporations. To the enterprise network engineer, VoIP is a way to simplify the corporate network and improve its telephone performance. To the home user, it is a convenient and money saving way to make phone calls from the home computer or laptop.

Background

The VoIP concept is not new. It was initially introduced in the 1990s. However, until broadband Internet became available to provide the bandwidth required, VoIP was no substitute for the conventional telephone network already in place. That is why Internet phone applications launched at that time had a rather short life. Once the novelty wore off, applications such as "Phonewala" (launched in India) did not have many users.

Due to bad sound quality, the first generation applications such as Microsoft's NetMeeting did not survive beyond 2003.

Things changed dramatically however by late 2005 when a freeware programme called Skype was launched using VoIP technology on broadband Internet connected computers.

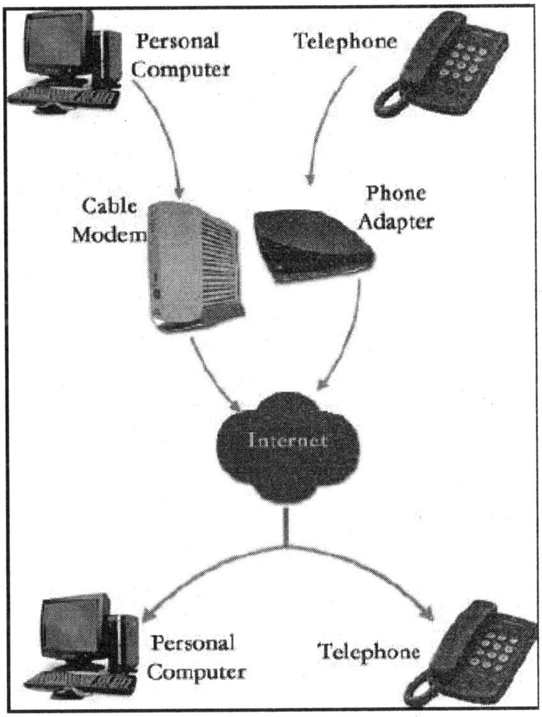

Fig 7.03 – How VoIP Works

Skype in Action

Skype is an instant messaging programme that uses a peer-to-peer global voice network, modelled on the Kazaa media desktop software. Kazaa is a peer-to-peer file sharing network application that can be downloaded for free. Skype is also a free peer-to-peer voice network application that you can download from the Internet and install on your computer. You can use Skype to call other people on your list of "buddies" who are also using Skype. All you need is broadband Internet connection, a microphone, and a pair speakers or headphones.

While several instant messaging services such as AIM or Windows Messenger also has voice calling facility, what sets Skype apart is its voice quality and versatility. Skype works in almost any broadband-connected network environment. Even networks with firewalls can be navigated by Skype while many other applications are unable to do so. Skype's variable-bit rate sound codec ensures much better sound quality than its predecessors.

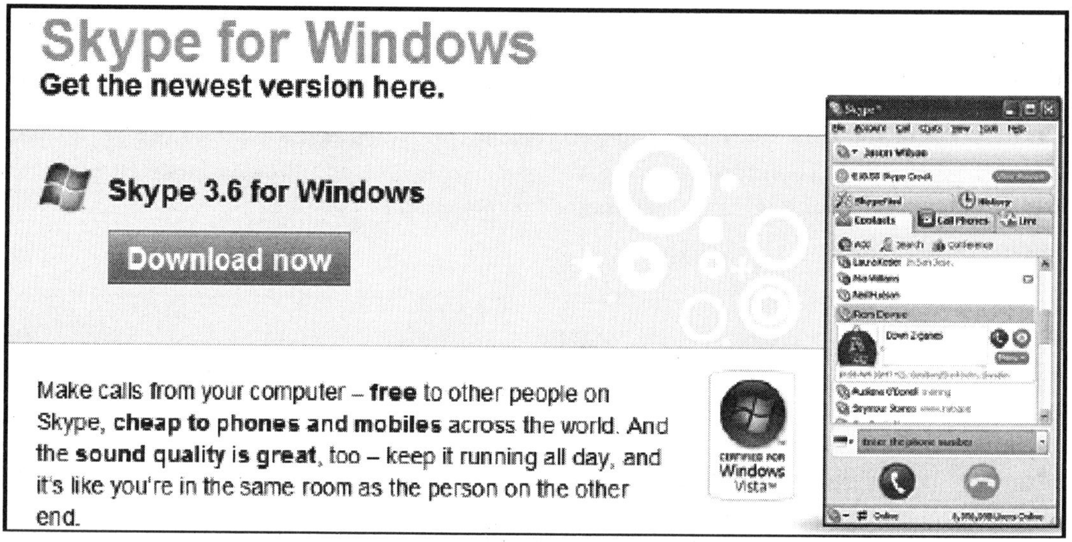

Fig 7.04 – Skype for Windows

NOTE

Today, Skype has over 150 million users. Skype now allows its users to call regular phone numbers from their PCs, a feature known as SkypeOut. Skype also offers a voicemail service and can route incoming calls to a certain phone number right to a user's desktop PC. Some of the recent add-on features of Skype include Video conferencing, integration with Microsoft Outlook and personal answering machine capability.

IP Telephony

Skype is not alone in exploiting the capabilities of VoIP and broadband Internet. A number of telephone service providers (especially in the US) have developed a number of services using IP telephony. As a result, not just individual PC users but corporate customers too are upgrading their IP networks to support voice applications. The trend, therefore, is for digital data networks and VoIP to converge into a single entity that carries both voice and data, leading to significant cost saving for business users.

VoIP for Cell Phones

NOTE

A host of brand new VoIP-enabled cell phones will soon be ready for action. Soon it will be possible for a corporate user to receive a call on the cell phone while driving and then continuing that call on the corporate Wi-Fi network as the user walks into the front office, all without any interruption to the call-in-progress. The cell network will just "hand over" the call to the corporate Wi-Fi network at the right time and without any intervention by the user.

Functionality

VoIP has many advantages over the traditional public telephone networks. Some are listed below:

- VoIP can transmit more than one telephone call down the same broadband-connected telephone line. Therefore, with VoIP, you can add another telephone line in your home or office without having to lay another physical telephone cable.
- VoIP gives you extra features such as 3-way calling, call forwarding, automatic redial, and caller identification at no extra cost.
- Since the VoIP transmission is digital in nature, it is only necessary to encrypt and authenticate the existing data stream to give you a secure and tamper proof telephone connection.
- Only an Internet connection is needed to get a connection to a VoIP provider. For instance, call centre agents using VoIP phones can work from anywhere with a sufficiently fast and stable Internet connection.
- VoIP can be easily integrated with other services available over the Internet such as video conversation, message or data file exchange in parallel with the conversation, audio conferencing, managing address books, and passing information about whether others such as friends or colleagues are available online or not.

Reliability

While the quality of speech is as good as what you can get on an analogue telephone, the reliability is affected by power failures. If power fails at a user's household, while the analogue telephone will continue to work, the VoIP link will be lost unless you have an uninterrupted source of back-up power.

Integration

Integration of a VoIP network into the existing Plain Old Telephone System (POTS) is not easy since VoIP protocols do not conform to the E164 protocol used by POTS. Therefore, though hand-held telephone sets are now available that can be plugged into a VoIP network, computer support is required at the point of origin of the call.

NOTE

Since mobile telephones are penetrating very rapidly all over the world including India, VoIP has to wait for the introduction of "dual mode" mobile phones that will allow the user's mobile to switch automatically from a cellular network ordinarily used by mobile phones to a WiFi network required by VoIP.

VoIP in India

In India, VoIP telephony can be used for making phone calls from a PC to another PC. You can also call another PC or a regular telephone abroad. Since VoIP cannot be used to access traditional telephony devices within the country; it is curbing the growth of VoIP in India. Greater availability of personal computers and more widespread broadband availability will surely accelerate the growth of VoIP technology in India.

Blogs and Blogging

From Internet communications, we move on to a very different but very significant topic, the phenomena of Blogs on the Internet. At the time of writing, India has over 40,000 active Bloggers and over 400,000 registered Bloggers. Although small compared to the population worldwide, it is still a very significant number, one that is growing rapidly.

We devote the rest of this chapter to the study and understanding of this phenomenon. We also give you advice and help about starting your own Blog, should you be so inclined.

What is a Blog?

The most concise definition of a Blog is a Website in which a person may list entries or posts in chronological order. The subject matter may be personal musings, poetry, political comment, amusing thoughts or information in any particular field in which the Blog's author has something to say.

NOTE

For the purposes of this book, we define a Blog as an online diary. That is to say, it is a diary of your thoughts that you keep online instead of in a traditional book. It can be a place for you to express yourself and share your dreams, or it can be a forum for you to talk about events and views that are important to you.

People write Blogs on the Internet (or, just Blog on the Internet) because Blogs are an interesting way of interacting with other people online. Blogs have sometimes been described as a virtual campfire, where one can share one's thoughts on the Web and let other people comment on these thoughts.

Blogs are not Private

Historically, a diary is thought of as something that is private. You write your most intimate thoughts and dreams in your diary. Therefore, you really do not want anyone else to read what is in your private diary.

However, this is not true of Blogs. Blogs are online and out there for the entire world to see, and read. They can be read by anyone, including family, friends, your parents or your children as well as complete strangers.

ALERT

Privacy goes out the window when you are writing online. Some Blog hosting sites do offer privacy features that allow you limited control over who can read your Blog. However, most of us write Blogs because we want to reach a wider audience and therefore, privacy features appear to defeat the very purpose of writing Blogs

Most Blogs are not private. You can read them and other people can read yours. Most Blog hosting services also allow people to post comments to your Blog entries as we shall see a little later in this section.

You can meet a lot of interesting people online, and one of the best ways to do this is by creating your own Blog, letting other people post comments to the entries, and then posting back to them what *you* think about their comments.

Types of Blogs

There are multiple types or Blog genres. Here are the most common:

Personal diary – This is probably the most obvious use of a Blog. Write about what you do every day or about things you think about or dreams you have for the future. A few examples are given here.

Krissy.nu	(**http://www.krissy.nu**)
Life Unscripted	(**http://fivestrongs.Blogspot.com/**)
Ninetynine Problems	(**http://:ninetynine.org**)

Fig 7.05 – Life Unscripted

Activist Blogs – Do you believe something needs to be changed or fixed? Make others see your point of view. Blog about what you believe in and rally the masses. A good example of this is The Scientific Activist. (**http://scienceBlogs.com/scientificactivist**)

News – Keep a Blog of the latest big news events. Talk about what you think about what is going on in the world or any given niche. The World Newser is a high profile world news Blog (**http://Blogs.abcnews.com/theworldnewser**), while the Art News Blog (**http://www.artnewsworld.com**) covers the art world.

Politics – Left-wing, right-wing, libertarian or socialist, if you are passionate about politics, you can become a member of the chattering class by joining the Internet pundits. Crooks and Liars (**http://crooksandliars.com**) and Free Republic (**http://freerepublic.com**) are two examples.

Celebrities and Gossip – Let other fans know what's going on with your favourite celebrities and shows. Dish the dirt like they do on TMZ.com. (**http://tmz.com**)

NOTE

Hobby – If you have a favourite hobby, it is very likely that a lot of other people on the Internet are interested in the same thing. Write about it and invite others to join you. Cooking with Amy (**http://cookingwithamy.Blogspot.com**) is great for the culinary enthusiasts. Another example, In Your Face Remote Control Hobbies illustrate how (**http://remotecontrolhobbies.Blogspot.com**) just about every hobby has a Blog dedicated to it.

Technology Blogs – Because of the technological nature of the Internet, technology enthusiasts are very popular on the Internet. CNET even has its own Blog network that includes Crave, the gadget Blog (**http://crave.cnet.com**), and Green Tech, a Blog about keeping technology clean. (**http://Blogs.cnet.com/8300**)

Corporate Blogs – Corporations are finding Blogs as excellent opportunities to get their message out and communicate with customers. Dell's Direct2Dell is an active example. (**http://direct2dell.com/one2one/default.aspx**)

Industry Blogs – Industry Blogs provide great opportunities to network with your peers and find out what's going on with your profession. Commercial real estate agents might be interested in Jordan Crouch's Adventures in Mortgage Banking Blog, for example. (**http://jordancrouch.wordpress.com**)

Blog Hosting

Blog Hosting Platform

TIP

Creating your own Blog is actually pretty simple since there are many sites willing to display (host) your Blog on the Internet. There are many dedicated Blog hosting services that will manage running the Blog software. So you only need to concern yourself with the writing of the material or your Blog. Building a Blog using one of these Blog hosts is quite easy. All you have to do is to sign up for the service and create and fill up the content in the Blog host's software.

Your work is made easier since the host provides you with a wide choice of pre-designed templates that take care of layout, fonts and colour schemes.

Here are some of the Blog hosting services available today. Also, some social networking sites, such as MySpace and Facebook, allow you to set up Blogs. We will look at social networking sites later in this book. Some of the major Blog hosting sites include:

Blogger	**http://Blogger.com/home**
LiveJournal	**http://livejournal.com**
TypePad	**http://typepad.com**
MovableType	**http://movabletype.org**
WordPress	**http://wordpress.com**
Open Diary	**http://opendiary.com**
AOL	**http://peopleconnection.aol.com/Blogs**
Yahoo!	**http://360.yahoo.com/login.html**
MSN	**http://spaces.live.com**

Fig 7.06 – The Blogger Site

Hosting sites like Blogger make it easy to build and run a Blog. Blogger is a free site, so you have to pay nothing for hosting your Blog. If you already have a Website provider, check if they now offer to host Blogs. If not, you can use Blogger or some such host.

TIP

There are many reasons to use a Blog hosting service instead of doing all the work of administering Blog software on a server yourself. The main reason is of course, ease of use. Blog hosting services offer features that would require you to do a lot of Web designing and programming. It is usually beyond the scope of the average Blog writer.

If you go to the Blogger site (**http://Blogger.com/home**), you will see the opening page as shown in Fig 7.06 – The Blogger Site. Fig 7.07 shows the sign in page for WordPress.

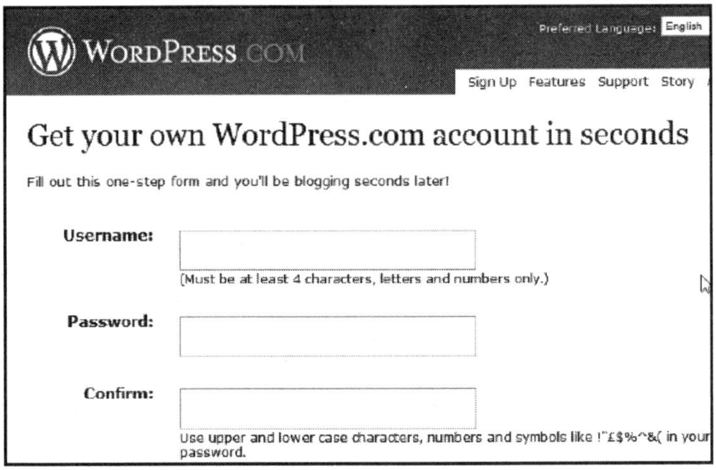

Fig 7.07 – WordPress Sign In

As you start using the facilities of the site, you will see many features such as:

Easy posting – Just click a button and start posting your Blog entry. No HTML or other coding knowledge necessary.

Profile page – You will fill up a profile page that provides your readers with information about yourself, who you are and what the reader may expect to find in your Blog.

Interaction – Browse the service to see what other Bloggers are writing about. Post comments on their Blog entries and let them post comments on yours.

Advertise – When you create a Blog with a Blog host, your Blog will be entered into the host's database. This will allow others to search for your Blog posts from the Blog host's pages.

Make money – Some of the Blog services offer you the ability to include advertisements in your Blog. Advertisements will generate income for you.

Multimedia – Blog hosting sites simplify adding music and video to you Blog. Many hosts offer convenient upload options for pictures, music clips and even videos.

Templates – Blog hosts have a variety of templates that you can use to design your Blog. By using a template you can make sure that your Blog has an attractive and relevant background and layout. See Fig 7.08 – Blog Templates.

Fig 7.08 – Blog Templates

Statistics – Find out how many people are visiting your Blog and what kinds of comments are being made.

Dedicated e-mail – With a dedicated e-mail address, you do not have to post your personal e-mail address on your Blog. Users can still contact you directly, but you maintain privacy.

Photos – Adding and uploading photos is simple too, often done with the click of a button.

For a small personal Blog, it probably makes most sense to start your Blog on a dedicated Blog hosting platform such as **Blogger.com**.

Your Own Design

If you have experience managing a Website and want more control, you will probably want to host your own version of Blog software through a server-side Blog hosting arrangement.

When searching for a Website host, look for one that will let you host your own domain name. You should consider buying a domain name for your site. Having your own domain name gives you more control and makes it easier for search engines, and people, to find your site.

TIP

The positive side of building your own Blog site, especially if you have your own domain name, is that you can put whatever you want on your Blog, you make the rules because you own the site. Also, you can layout the pages for your Website any way you want them. Add a photo album, add pages about different family members or add information on hobbies. In other words, do what you want with your Blog design.

You can build a Blog from scratch, but it requires technical knowledge. Also, you will have to find your own Blog templates, create your own HTML pages. You will also have to keep track of the visitor statistics. In this book, we will only cover dedicated Blog hosting platforms as we have already discussed.

Blog Entries (Posts)

Blog entries, or posts, make up the heart of your Blog. The quality of the content in a post will determine how many people visit your Blog. To have a good Blog you must write interesting Blog entries. If your Blog is boring, not one will read it.

You will be surprised what people will be willing to read about when it is in a Blog. Even if you have a boring life, it may seem interesting to someone on the outside looking in. When they read about your life, they find it interesting because it's different from their own.

ALERT

Everything you write is public. If you are employed, your employer may have specific guidelines about what you may reveal regarding work in your Blog. Therefore, even if you write your Blog at home and in private, make sure that no work related disclosures causes your employer to take offence.

Writing Meaningful Blog Entries

Here are five tried and tested pointers for writing meaningful entries.

1. Find a theme for your Blog. This does not mean that you should write your whole Blog about just one thing. On the contrary, your Blog should contain many things. Mix them up to keep people interested. But, if your Blog is going to be a personal Blog about you and your daily life, then that is what your focus and emphasis should be. If you run a News Blog, and one of your entries is about the new furniture you bought, your readers will be turned off.

   NOTE

2. Find a writing style that comes naturally to you. Choose the way you want to write your Blog. Do you want it to be serious and down to earth, or funny? Consider the tone you wish to use. Do you want to use proper grammar all the time, or throw some slang in there? Add your own sense of style and personality to your Blog.

   TIP

3. Be honest and sincere. People will not read a Blog that is written by an author who does not know what he or she is talking about. Blog readers are very intelligent; they can always spot a faker or a liar.

4. Proper spelling, grammar and punctuation are a must. You will instantly lose credibility with your readers if you incorrectly spell words. Frequency is also important. Blog posts are meant to be regularly updated. The more often you post, the better. As such, most successful Blogs have short, daily posts at a minimum.

5. Writing meaningful entries begins by writing a catchy and relevant title. Think of your daily newspaper. Generally, the titles are catchy, descriptive and yet, short.

Comments

Comments allow readers to add their thoughts to your posts. Comments make a Blog more interesting. They let your readers tell you what they think about your writing. It is an excellent way to get a feedback and be forewarned if readers find your entries boring or offensive.

NOTE

Sometimes advertisements or spam will pop up in your comments section. You should read every comment posted to your Blog and delete spam or advertisements of any sort. Spam and advertisements distract your readers from the real message. Eventually, they may get turned off. Some Blog hosts have spam filters to help you keep control on this problem.

ALERT

Be wary of offensive or incendiary posts containing coarse or insulting language. Readers often take advantage of the Web's anonymity by being rude and hurtful while writing comments. It is a good idea to enforce proper decorum to keep your Blog a welcoming place. Otherwise, you will not only lose readers, you may also be accused under new cyber-crime laws.

Graphics and Photos

Why Add Photos?

A picture is worth a thousand words. Wherever possible you should add pictures and graphics to your Blog to make it interesting. Graphics allow you to personalise your Blog and make it stand out. If you like, say flowers, decorate your site with flowers. If you like nature, decorate your Blog using a nature theme.

TIP Photos can also be added to create a feeling and add to a story that you're writing on your Blog. If you are writing about your baby's first tooth, add a photo of your baby smiling. It is a great way to connect with your readers. Your readers will be more likely to read your Blog if it has photos on it. People love to look at photos. Conversely, a plain page with just text is very boring and will drive readers away.

Finding Graphics

Graphics can be found free all over the Internet. Try going to your favourite search engine (such as Google) and typing in "free graphics" or "free clip art." You'll find free graphics of every kind. If you add a word to your search term, like "free graphics cats," you will find free graphics about cats.

ALERT Be careful that you do not use art that does not belong to you. If you see a picture on another Website or Blog that you think makes a good addition to your Blog, be sure to get permission from the site administrator before using it. Do not use a copyrighted image. If you upload a photo of someone, make sure they have no objection.

Adding Graphics and Photos

The Blog editor software used by most Blog hosts allows you to add graphics and photos to your Blog. Though the process may be slightly different for each Blog, here is the most common method that should work with most Blog editors.

When you enter your Blog posts, you will see a little icon in the editor that looks like a little, tiny photo, most often a tree. When you hold your mouse over it, the cursor tool tip will say "add image". When you click on the icon, a pop-up window will open that you can use to add your photo or graphic to your Blog entry. Follow these steps:

- If the graphic or photo that you want to add to your Blog entry is on your computer, click on the Browse button and locate and choose the photo or graphic from your computer.
- If the graphic or photo that you want to add to your Blog entry is on the Internet, copy and paste the URL of the photo in the photo URL box.
- Click on the button to upload your graphic or photo and add it to your Blog.

- Your photo should now be showing on your Blog entry. Finish writing your Blog entry and save.

Before you start writing a Blog entry, it is a good idea to keep all the graphics you want to use organised in a specific folder on your hard drive.

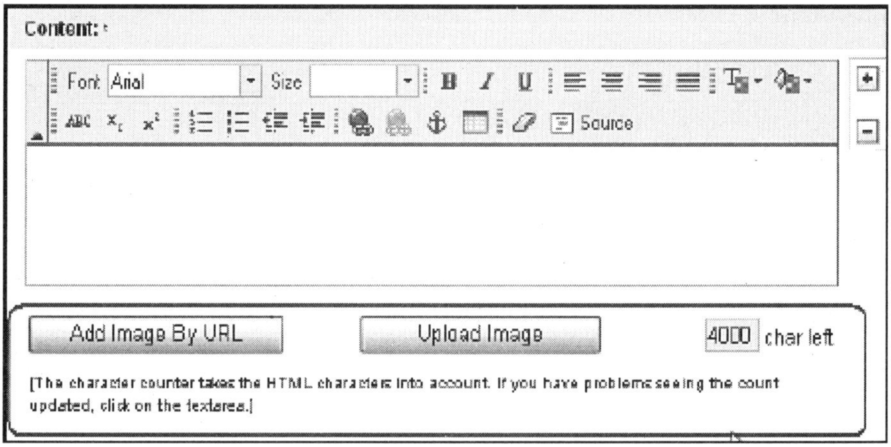

Fig 7.09 – Insert Graphics

Layouts & Applications

Templates make your Blog visually attractive. Applications are used to make your Blog more interactive for your readers. Templates are essentially HTML code that you enter into your Blog and then tweak the layout and design. There are many different kinds of templates and many of them come in different themes.

Applications are short programmes (often written in JavaScript) that will do special things when the reader clicks on the icon of the application. For instance, an application can display current news headlines, show weather report or even play a simple game.

Blog Templates

Templates for your Blog can be found, free, all over the Internet. Start by going to Google, or your favourite search engine and typing in "Blog template", or something similar. If you are using Blogger, or another well known Blog host, type in the name of the Blog host, such as "Blogger template". You will find a number of Websites that offer free Blog templates that you can use.

To add templates, do the following:

- Find the template that you want to use for your Blog and download it to your computer.
- Open the template with your computer's text programme (ie: Notepad) or HTML editor.
- Copy the entire code.
- Open the template page in the settings of your Blog host's editor.

- Save the code that is already in your Blog template settings to another text file, just in case you decide to change back to your original template later.
- Delete the code from the Blog host's editor.
- Paste the code of the template you have chosen for your new Blog design into the Blog host's editor.
- Save the template.
- Click "republishes" or "rebuild" on your Blog.

Your new template should be viewable on your Blog after the rebuild is finished.

Applications

Applications are tools or interesting things that you can add to your site so your readers can interact with the application. They come in many different varieties. Applications can be games that your readers will be able to play from your Blog, virtual pets, weather reports, the latest news updates, or any number of other things. These are great for spicing up your posts and keeping your readers engaged, and in turn, likely to spend more time on your site.

For applications, as for templates, go to Google, or your favourite search engine and type "Blog add-ons" or "Website add-ons". You will see lists of applications that you can add to make you Blog interactive and interesting.

Do the following to add applications:

- Search through the applications that are available to you online. There are applications for passwords, forums and chat boards. There are also applications for online "post it" notes, games and many other things.
- When you find the Web application you want to add to your Blog, find the code that goes with it.
- Copy the code on a text editor on your computer (you can use Notepad).
- Go to the page on your Blog that you want to add the Web application, or create a new page, and open up the HTML editor for your Blog.
- Paste the code into the page. Then save the page.

Getting Your Blog Noticed

Since you will want as many readers as possible to read your Blog, you will want to make your Blog noticeable. The best way to do so is to register your Blog with search engines that readers will use to locate Blogs that are of interest to them. It is also necessary to optimise your Blog for search engines so that your Blog is listed near the top of the list when a reader uses a search engine that you have used to register your Blog.

Fig 7.10 – A Community Blog

We discuss this topic in the following section.

Registering

There are many different search engines. It is really time-consuming to register your site with all of them. Therefore, just choose the top search engines such as Google, Yahoo!, and AOL (powered by Google).

ALERT

Add links to the search engines on your main Blog page. Carefully read the rules for adding links to each particular search engine. Sometimes you can only add a certain number in total, sometimes you can only add links every two months. If you add too many links, the search engines may consider your site to be a spam site and ignore your Blog. It is a good idea to start by just registering with Google.

Blogs are a work in progress. Your Blog too, will evolve over time. It will take some time and trials till you find your subject and an appreciative audience. Get started by writing a post a day and see what responses you get. Regularly read other Blogs of similar interest and leave comments to get to know others who will eventually link to your Blog and bring you more readers.

Optimisation

The most important part of Search Engine Optimisation (SEO) involves selecting appropriate keyword phrases. Choosing a keyword phrase for each page on your Blog is an essential part of SEO. Before you start writing a Blog entry, think about what you are going to be writing about. Then think about the key words you would type into a search engine describing what you are writing about. While you are writing your Blog entry, make sure to include the search phrase in your entry, several times at least. Use the same keyword phrase in the title of the page and at least twice in the first paragraph.

NOTE

Some Blog hosts will allow you to enter keywords into a keyword section. Use the keyword phrase that you have chosen to write about here. Also enter any other phrases from the article that you think people may use to search for your Blog entry. If there is a description box for you to enter a description of your Blog entry, make sure that your description also has the keyword phrase in it.

8. Entertainment on the Net

In this chapter:

- Your computer and the Internet can be a source of fun and games! We look at the streaming media technology that brings music and videos to your computer in rich colour and full motion.
- We look at the software you need to play music and videos as well as the Websites from where you can download contents of your choice.
- We look at Windows Media Player which is bundled with your Windows operating system and at some other media-playing software.
- When the fun ends, the games begin! From streaming media, we move to games on the Internet. We look at different types of games available on the Internet such as adventure games, arcade games and multi-player games.

Your Computer as an Entertainer

The Internet is seductive. Once you begin, surfing can easily become an addiction. The Internet has the power to be all things to all people! No matter what you may start with, such as e-mail or Web surfing, you will soon find yourself getting involved in the Internet's thousand and one delights! A great deal of the Internet's attraction lies in the entertainment it can bring to you through your computer screen and speakers. You can listen to music, play a music video or watch a movie with colour and sound. You can also play games, buy things, or even gamble! The new technology that makes all this available to you in rich colour, full motion and in stereophonic sound is called "streaming media". Streaming media allows you to view what you see on your computer screen as if you were watching a TV programme brought to you via cable. Streaming media technology brings prime time entertainment to your computer from the Internet.

Not so long ago, when the Internet was young and transfer speed was 2400 Kbps, all that you could download were pages of plain text. Because of speed limitations, there was much controversy whether still pictures could ever be sent over the Internet! Since then, on the one hand, data transmission speeds have increased significantly. On the other hand, software developers have found ways of compressing the data. As a result, it is now possible to fit in much more information in the digital data stream and send it to your computer much faster than before. In the past, you had to first download and save a media file. Now, the file (music or video) can start playing almost as soon as the download starts. This is streaming media!

Streaming Media

Streaming media works like this:

1. Music or video is formatted in an audio or video media file.
2. The media file is compressed, using special technology.
3. The compressed media file is converted into a special format that the media server computers on the Internet can understand.
4. When you log on to a media server on the Internet, the media is "streamed" to you. This means that the media begins to play music or video on your computer as it is being received. In the past, the entire file had to be downloaded and saved on your computer before the media would begin to play. In streaming media, therefore, there is a much shorter waiting period before you can see and hear the broadcast.
5. As soon as you are connected to the media server, your computer detects the format (or codec) of the programme being broadcast. It launches the appropriate software for playing the streaming media being received.

NOTE You must have the required software such as Windows Media Player, Apple's QuickTime or RealOne player installed on your computer. If not, you will see a message window telling you that the required software is available for download. If you wish, you can download the programme right away. After you have installed it, you can start watching your selected programme.

Streaming Media Sources

Several companies offer streaming media. They will usually also offer the software that you require for viewing the media. Many are free. In some cases, instead of a complete stand-alone programme, you can download a smaller "plug-in" that works with your Web browser that allows you to watch streaming media. This is a rapidly developing field and changes are fast and frequent. For example, Microsoft's "NetShow" has now been replaced by its latest version of Windows Media Player. We will now look at some current media sources and the associated software for streaming media.

Windows Media Player

Windows Media Player is built into your Windows software. With Windows Me, 2000 or XP, you will have version 7 installed. All these versions will allow you to connect to numerous video or music stations as well as to the Websites of major newspapers so that you can listen to music, watch video films (usually promotional trailers) and live news broadcasts on your computer.

Since the media player is already installed with Windows, all you have to do is launch the software and connect to the Internet. You can also play media files already downloaded earlier.

Fig 8.01 – Windows Media Player

When you click on the media player icon on your desktop or the quick launch taskbar, the media player main window opens. You must be connected to the Internet to visit Internet media servers and watch streaming media.

Select the Media Guide button to connect to Microsoft's own Website, **WindowsMedia.com** to download information about radio stations or video sources for listening to music, watching music video or a live news broadcast.

Windows Media Player does more than just connect you to Internet sources and play what you wish. It helps you to save what you download, organise the digital files on your hard disk and play the media later offline if you wish to hear or see what you had downloaded earlier. It allows you to organise your computer as a music and video entertainment centre.

MacroMedia ShockWave

MacroMedia's ShockWave (now acquired by Adobe) is a very popular streaming media technology. If you have their plug-in (software) installed, you can get access to a very rich variety of both video and audio presentations. ShockWave programmes are very popular for their high quality of graphics and excellent animation. You can download entertainment material or games from ShockWave's own Website or from a number of independent Websites using ShockWave's technology. You can download free versions of the ShockWave software from these Websites as well.

Fig 8.02 – ShockWave Player

Real Networks

Originally known as RealPlayer, the latest software, which is called RealOne is available free for download from the Internet. You must be patient while downloading though, since this version is over 8 MB in size!

Fig 8.03 – The Real Player

The companion music source is RealAudio. RealAudio was the Internet standard for streaming audio files until WinAmp and music in MP3 format became more popular.

Real networks have gone beyond streaming media and introduced live broadcasts on the Internet, now known as Webcasting.

At their Website, they offer music, a variety of games and video clips. You can either download the media for later playing, or stream the media for instant play.

WinAmp

WinAmp is the most popular source of music on the Internet. The very popular MP3 format is used exclusively at this site. You can download the latest WinAmp MP3 player (version 2.78) from this site. After installation, you can use the Win Amp player to locate, download and play **MP3 music** from the WinAmp Website and many other sites around the world.

In addition to the player itself, many "skins" and plug-ins are available that enhance the appearance and add to the functions of the WinAmp player. For instance, a plug-in will generate on-screen VU meters for each channel just as you have on a real music amplifier.

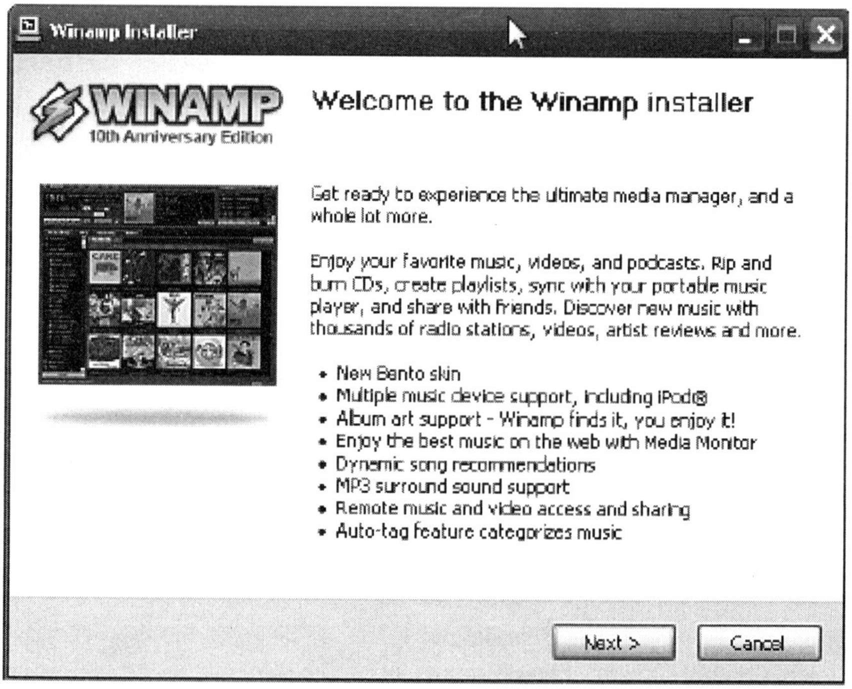

Fig 8.04 – Installing WinAmp

Games

The Internet started out as a vast computer network for sharing information. Then it became a means of communicating as well. Today, the Internet is growing into a full-fledged entertainment medium. A significant part of that entertainment is online games.

Online games began as text-based multi-user games that involved solving puzzles and fighting against many magical opponents. A favourite location for such games was inside the dungeon of some imaginary castle! From text, the games have progressed to detailed characterisation, intricate plots, sound and dazzling graphics. The first commercial online game was Doom II, based on the classic arcade game style of shoot first! Gradually many other categories of games were added such as flight simulators, war games, strategy games and board games.

Fig 8.05 – Multiplayer Website

More and more games are Internet enabled these days. It means that you can log on to an appropriate Website and play the game online with other online opponents. However, dial-up networking connections are generally not fast enough for you to get the most out of an Internet game. You will need a cable modem or an ISDN connection with data transfer speeds of 128 Kpbs or so to get the full flavour of gaming.

Where To Go

To join in on an online game, you must log on to an Internet game server computer. The most convenient way is to start an Internet-enabled game on your computer and then select the "network play" option. While online, enter the address (URL) of the game server, such as **http://www.avalon-rpg.com** and connect to the Website in the usual way.

When connection is established, the Internet games server takes on the role of a server and your computer becomes one of the clients connected to the games server just like any client-server network. The server programme sends game status information to each client player, which is displayed on each client's screen. Player inputs are uploaded to the server where they are processed and the resultant changes in the game status flows back to each player. Game servers are usually robotic, with no humans at the keyboard.

Some of the popular game sites are:

- **http://www.heat.net**
- **http://www.gamestorm.com**
- **http://www.10six.com**
- **http://www.playsite.com**
- **http://www.station.sony.com**

There are, of course, very many other game sites and more are joining in each day!

Computer games can be played against the computer itself, such as a game of chess. Some arcade type games are more fun if two human opponents play, using joysticks attached to the computer. However, there is more novelty if you can seek out an invisible opponent in some far off corner of the world, and play an online game with him or her! If you have a fast Internet connection, go for it!

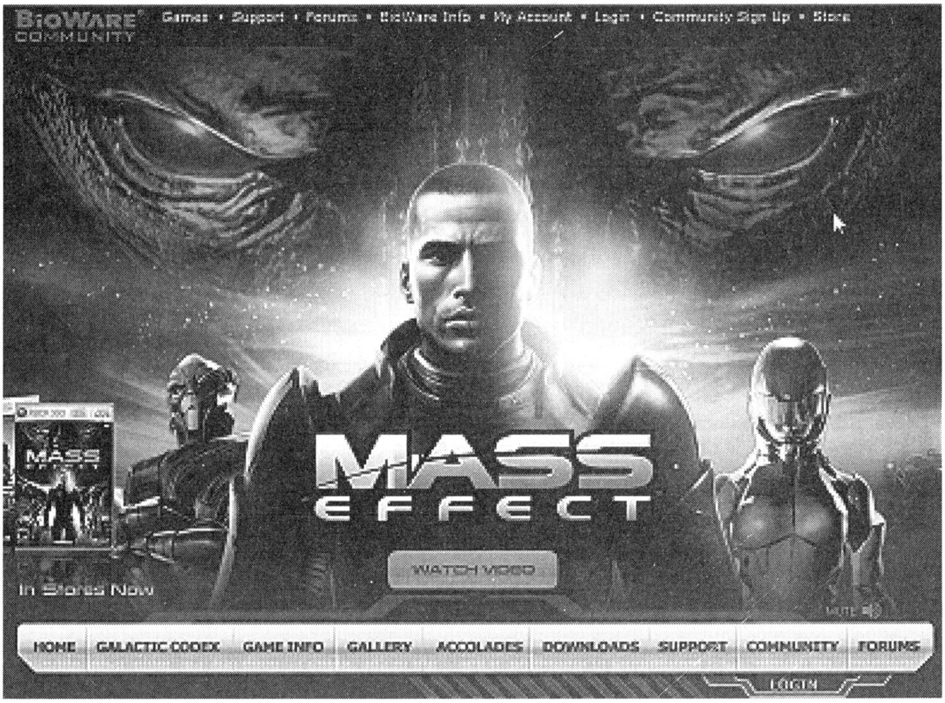

Fig 8.06 – MassEffect Website

Online gaming is a vast subject. Entire books have been written on it. The popularity of this entertainment in India will grow with faster Internet connections.

Fig 8.07 – Online Gambling Site

Eventually, all forms of gaming that include multi-player games, arcade games and even online gambling may become commonplace in India! So take a break from work and have fun!

9. Social Networking

In this chapter:

- We introduce you to one of the fastest growing phenomenon on the Internet – Social Networking.
- We examine the four basic types of social networks and examine some rules of network etiquette as well as some guidelines for maintaining network security.
- We take a look at some of the popular social networking sites such as MySpace, Orkut and Facebook. You are introduced to two Indian sites as well.
- Some media sharing sites are discussed next, where you can share videos, audio clips and photographs. We look at the Indian site, iShare.
- It is the turn of business networking sites next and the workings of Biznik, LinkedIn and Ryze are explained to you.
- To help you organise information and media content from the Internet, you can use Bookmarking sites. Their functions are explained to you along with details of three popular sites.

Social Networking

Introduction

The phenomenon of using the Internet to set up special interest groups for exchanging information is not new. To do so, the scientist community in the US had begun to use the Internet and e-mail as early as the 1970s. What is new, however, is the absolutely unprecedented rate at which social networking has grown recently all over the world as well as India.

Human beings have always needed the safety, the security and the warm feeling that comes to people when they belong to a group of like-minded individuals and are able to communicate with each other. You have only to look at the tremendous popularity of the cell phone in India to appreciate this desire for communication.

It is interesting to see that the personal computer (PC), which is supposed to be personal and for individual use, has now become the most powerful tool for forming groups on the Internet. These groups are not confined geographically, but stretch right across the whole world in the form of social networks.

NOTE

No contemporary book on the Internet like the one you are reading now can possibly ignore this development. Therefore, we have included this entire chapter to acquaint you with the trend, explaining how you can use your PC to join Internet-based social networking groups such as MySpace, Facebook and Orkut, and other networking sites. We tell you how to do so, what you can do at these Websites and how you should protect yourself from the many dangers that lurk out there.

Background

The origin of social networking can be traced back to 1988 when the first Internet Relay Chat (IRC) programme was written at the University of Oulu in Finland. The popularity of IRC as a platform for users to chat with each other significantly increased in the US during the Gulf War in 1991.

Then IRC developed the ability of file sharing between users. Thereafter channels or chat-rooms were established where users sharing a common interest could chat with each other and exchange photographs or text documents using file sharing software. IRC was followed by a host of "messenger" services as we have already seen in *Chapter 7 – Beyond E-Mails.*

The first truly social networking site was launched in 1995 called **Classmates.com**. It was used by people to look for old classmates on the Internet with whom they had lost contact. Social networking as we know it was launched in 2002 with the Website **Friendster.com**. Since then, social networking sites have been set up regularly, many in India. We will take a look at some of the most popular sites as we progress with this chapter.

Types of Networks

Since social networking is a means of exchanging information and to get to know new people, the types of networks you will come across on the Internet are as varied as humanity itself. Broadly speaking, all network users want to increase their circle of friends and to share information. However, there is much diversity in who we want to befriend and what information we seek.

Based on the interests of networking groups, we can broadly classify social networking into four broad categories. We look at each in turn.

Writing Based

Blogs fall in this category. Blogs are started by people who have something to say and wish to share their thoughts with others. Blogs are read by surfers who are looking for something interesting to read. Topics covered by Blogs may range from intimate personal details in an online diary to political, religious or philosophical musings. There are enough Blogs on the Internet to cater to almost any interest that a surfer may have. We have already dealt with Blogs in *Chapter 7 – Beyond E-mails.*

Finding Friends

NOTE

This is perhaps the most powerful motivation for using a social network. The friendship people seek may range from finding people with similar interests to finding dates, life partners or simply to flirt in a rather anonymous and therefore, seemingly safe environment.

ALERT

There are networking Websites of a sexual nature as well. They provide opportunity for sexual adventuring. This category includes very dangerous Websites that may lure children or unsuspecting young visitors into danger. You need to be constantly on guard against the predators that lurk in these places on the Internet. We will discuss more about defensive measures in *Chapter 10 – Sharks in the Ocean*, later in this book.

Business Networks

TIP

While one can use any networking Website for building up business contacts, it is much better to be focussed and go to specialised Websites that promote business partnerships. These Websites are frequently used by professionals to build up a circle of contacts that can be used to look for jobs, advertise about oneself and to keep track of job and business opportunities in India and abroad.

Although many official relationships are built up at the workplace, career conscious individuals use business networking sites to broaden contacts beyond their immediate work environments.

Specialised Information

While finding friends, dating and business networking attract literally millions of surfers, there are many more looking for specialised information rather than social or business interactions. Such people need focussed information on a variety of fields like vintage cars, outdoor cooking, solution to software problems and a host of other topics.

NOTE

Websites that allow members to share specialised information are called Forums. There are forums on virtually every subject that you can think of. In addition to rather general sources of information such as Wikipedia and Yahoo! Answers, there are specialised forums such as one on Windows Vista, Microsoft Office suit, etc.

No matter what your interest is, there will always be several networking sites that will suit your needs. Subscribe to a few sites that interest you and you will get to exchange information on your favourite topics.

Etiquette

Although the anonymity of the Internet may encourage us to be somewhat uninhibited in what we say to others at a networking site, it is important to remember that we are ultimately dealing with people. Therefore, certain rules of behaviour or etiquette apply to whatever we say, even on the Internet.

While there is no published guide book on the subject, even relatively informal sites such as MySpace or Orkut expect that the members of the site will observe a certain level of decorum. Here are some guidelines for you to consider:

- If you do not want to use your own name, choose an interesting or amusing nickname. Avoid something that sounds weird. It may attract the wrong kind of friends.
- Select sites with care. The topics being discussed should interest you. Choose topics about which you have some knowledge. Otherwise, you will not be able to contribute meaningfully to discussions.
- Add friends to your "buddy" list with care. Pick the ones who are really interested in the subjects discussed in the site.
- Take part in the discussions. After all, you have joined a group (or site) because you want to socialise. Give help to others by posting helpful information or hints if requested by others.
- Be careful of the language you use. Avoid being insulting or provocative. This leads to acrimony (often called "flame wars") and irritates others.

Security

In addition to being pleasant, dignified and polite, it is also necessary to be careful. There is always the chance that there are some site users with bad intentions. Here are some guidelines for your own safety:

- Avoid giving personal details such as your postal address or cell phone number in your personal profile when you sign into a social networking Website. Many surfers prefer using a nickname to preserve anonymity.
- Under no circumstance should you post your password or bank account in any networking site.
- Be extremely careful about agreeing to physical meetings with any "friend" you may make on a Website.
- Avoid parting with any sensitive information regarding your personal life or your professional life that may be used against you in the future.

With these guidelines, we believe that you will have safe, pleasant and satisfying social or business experience on the Internet. We devote the rest of this chapter examining specific Websites that can help you to:

- Find friends
- Share media files (photographs, audio and video files)
- Join special interest groups
- Set up business networks

Finding Friends

Finding friends to socialise with is the most common reason why people join social networks. The hectic schedules of our present working life leave us with very little time to socialise in the old and traditional ways such as by writing and posting long letters, telephoning friends or even physically visiting them. Instead, we relax and unwind at the end of a tiring day by going online to chat with our Internet friends. Finding online friends therefore, is a very important first step.

To help you do so, we examine three very popular international sites and two Indian sites in the pages that follow.

Myspace

Located at **http://www.myspace.com**, it is the most popular of all the networking sites. It was started in 2003 by Tom Anderson and Chris DeWolf and bought over by Rupert Murdoch's news corporation in 2005.

Myspace provides the user with all facilities that a social networking site can provide. After joining, you can add pictures to share with your friends, write Blogs, make new friends, share music and video files, etc.

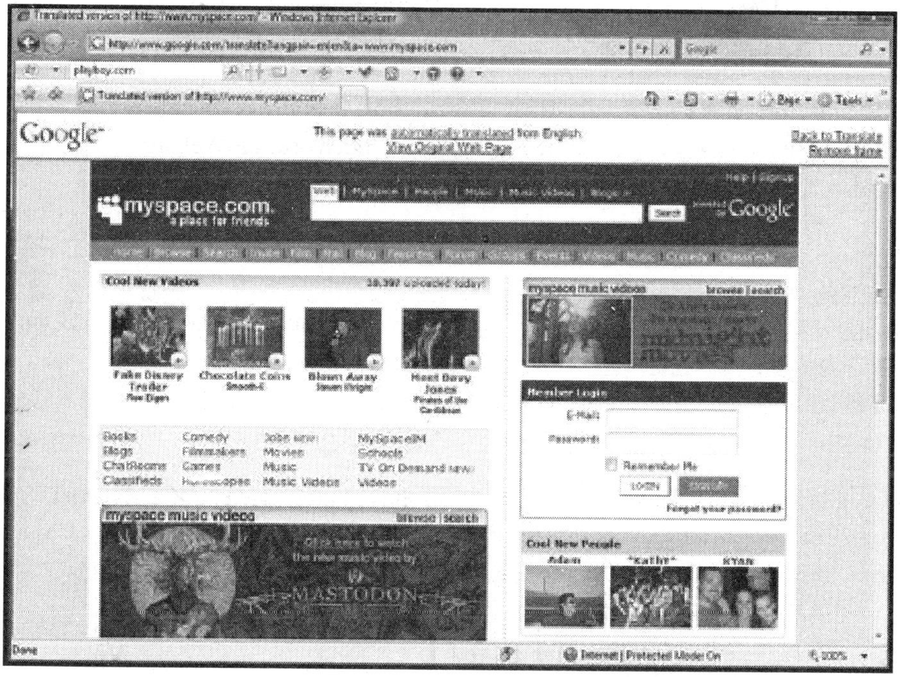

Fig 9.01 – MySpace Screen

Myspace allows you to customise your personal profile completely. You can choose colours and fonts, select whatever application you want to embed in your profile and adjust the look and feel of your profile exactly as you want.

After setting up your profile, you can start looking for people to add to your "Friend" list. To start off, you can browse through profiles listed in the main page and add anyone to your Friend list that appears to be interesting.

You can communicate with your friends by using the site's message board and using Instant Messenger. If you are looking for people with special interests, visit the "Groups" section. You can add music or video clips from the site's collection to your profile so that you can share them with your friends.

ALERT

A word of caution is necessary. Being the most popular social networking site on the Internet, Myspace attracts all kinds of users, including some who are sexual predators and a real threat to the underage users. It has been reported that the site has virus that you can pick up while browsing. There may be attempts at "phishing" which means that attempts may be made to trick you into disclosing your private financial information such as your credit card number or bank account number. So, be very careful!

Orkut

Orkut is undoubtedly the most popular site for the young people of India. It is also the most popular in other countries like Brazil. Started in 2004 by Orkut Buyukkokten, a Turkish engineer working for Google, the site first became popular in Brazil. It has now many devoted followers in India and Pakistan as well. Orkut can be reached at **http://www.orkut.com**.

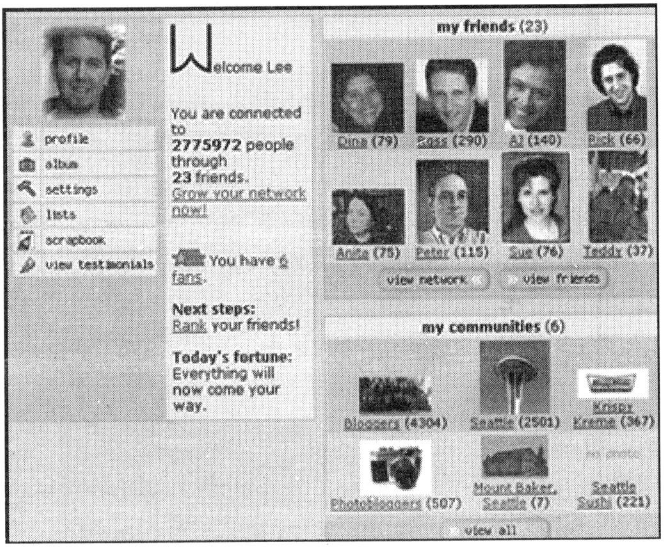

Fig 9.02 – Orkut Page

Orkut has a very user friendly and uncluttered Website. When you open the profiles of other members, you can add selected members to your friend list by simply clicking on the "Add as Friend" tab. To communicate with members, you use what is called a "Scrap". A scrap is somewhat like a simplified e-mail that you can send to one or more members.

Special interest groups are called Communities. Each community has an "owner" and may have an additional moderator who keeps track of the postings and communications. You can upload up to 12 photographs and add them to your profile. You can also add videos from YouTube (now acquired by Google) or from Google video.

If you use Google Talk for instant messaging, you can launch this application while still within Orkut and contact any of your friends who may be registered in your Google Talk list.

ALERT

Like all social networking sites, Orkut too has been blamed for different things. For instance, there are examples of political parties using Orkut to propagate hate against those they do not like. There have been cases of cyber-stalking on Orkut and some hate groups have used the site to broadcast anti-India propaganda.

The risks associated with virus infection, "phishing" and other malicious software apply to Orkut as to other Websites. Despite the risks, Orkut is easily the most popular Website in India, particularly for the youth.

Facebook

Located at **http://www.facebook.com**, this Website used to be the most popular till losing the crown to MySpace. It began as a cyber-meeting place exclusively for college students. At that time, you had to have a college identity card to join Facebook. Now however, Facebook is open for membership to anyone with a valid e-mail address. Facebook was started in 2004 by Mark Zukerberg of Harvard University. Within a year, the membership had swollen to over a million. Growth has been very rapid especially after membership was thrown open to non-college students as well.

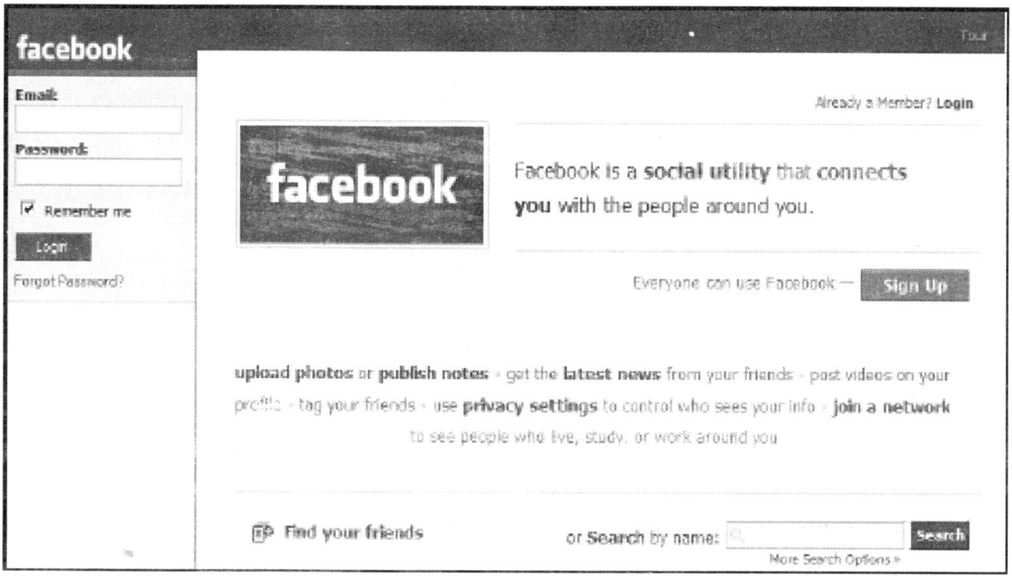

Fig 9.03 – Facebook Sign up Page

Facebook's profile pages are customisable, but not to the same extent as MySpace or Orkut. On the plus side, the pages load faster and the security features are quite good. For example, users can view the profiles of only their friends.

NOTE

Facebook has two similar areas called Network and Group. Networks are collection of affiliated colleges and institutions. In India, the IITs and the IIMs are all part of the Facebook network. Groups on the other hand are collections of individuals with similar interests, sometimes from the same geographic location. Groups in Facebook are much like communities in Orkut.

NOTE

Facebook has many add-on features (called applications) and more are being added by users. For instance, you can add an application that will list the books you have read. The Marketplace in Facebook is a feature that has been added recently. Here you can carry out business deals such as buying and selling things.

The site layout of Facebook is a little complex. However, by looking up the built-in help section, you should be able to get all the information you need about Facebook.

Indian Sites

In our highly social environment built amongst closely connected communities, it is not surprising that India has set up her own social networking sites.

Fropper

This is essentially a dating site. The user's profile is called Zone and the user can upload photos. An area called Relationships is used exclusively for dating. Users can enter this area only by using a separate login name. You will find the Fropper site at **http://www.fropper.com**.

BigAdda

This much advertised Indian networking site is accessible at **http://www.bigadda.com**. However, it appears to be still evolving. Many profiles are incomplete and the activity is still slow.

Fig 9.04 – Fropper Registration Page

Indian networking sites appear to be clones of foreign sites with very little added features. Therefore they fail to attract current networking users away from the hugely popular international sites such as Facebook or Orkut.

Sharing Media

Certain networking sites specialise in sharing video, music clips or photographs. While basically similar to the Websites we have discussed so far, their Web addresses may be of interest to those who wish to share media files on the Internet.

For videos, the following sites are very popular:

- YouTube **http://www.youtube.com**
- Flickr **http://www.flickr.com**
- Dailymotion **http://www.dailymotion.com**

For music clips, you may wish to visit some of these sites:

- Cylive **http://www.cylive.com**
- Twango **http://www.twango.com**
- iShare **http://ishare.rediff.com/**

NOTE

Special mention should be made here about iShare, India's only media sharing portal launched by Rediff.com. The site allows users to share video, music and photographs. The Website has a clean and streamlined look. There are separate tabs for navigating to five main areas named Video, Audio, Music, Home and My Home. My Home is the personal Web page where you can list your uploaded media files, store your favourites and open a scrapbook to jot down thoughts, reminders and comments.

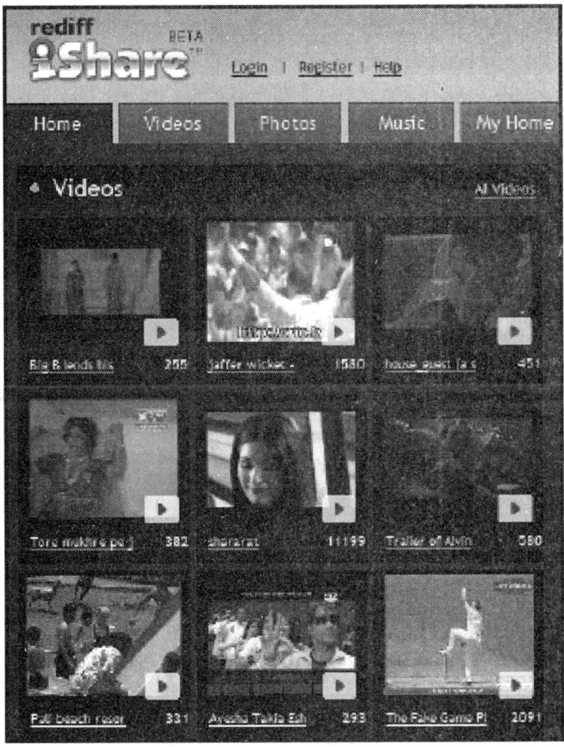

Fig 9.05 – Rediff's iShare Site

Business Networking

Introduction

Successful business professionals depend on a large and active network of business contacts to further their careers by getting to know the right people and identify business and job opportunities. They network with selected people and business networking sites put them in touch with people that matter.

Fig 9.06 – Biznik Main Page

We look at three popular business networking sites in this section.

Biznik

Located ate **http://www.biznik.com**, this site caters to independent professionals and small business owners. Biznik works on the principle that collaboration and cooperation is better for all concerned rather than cutthroat competition.

Biznik allows you to network with professionals or businessmen in your own field or in closely related fields. You can use this site to exchange business information or organise events where you can invite others with similar interests. Some of Biznik's services are free while others are charged.

LinkedIn

LinkedIn's strength lies in locating potential business associates or business contacts that you may use to look for a job, find a collaborator, a sales agency or a financier. LinkedIn has a numerically large network of members that assist you to find the kind of contact you are looking for. The site address is **http://www.linkedin.com**.

To use LinkedIn successfully, it is important that your profile is detailed and is updated regularly. A very useful feature of LinkedIn is that it will enter information on job opportunities based on your professional profile, automatically in your home page. With 11 million members, LinkedIn is an excellent site for serious business professionals.

Ryze

Ryze is one of the oldest business networking sites located at **http://www.ryze.com**. It has the flavour of an old boy's network like many old schools and institutions. The procedure for creating a profile is the same as other business networks. In Ryze, it is important to include your photograph to ensure that more people read your profile.

To increase your list of contacts, you can opt for the paid "Gold" account. In addition to contacts, you can visit the Events page to find out about upcoming business events or enter information about some event being sponsored by you or your company.

Similarly, visit the classified page of Ryze to read about other's products and services. You can also advertise your own products or services here.

Bookmarking

Introduction

To get good responses and be "popular" on a social network, it is very important that you contribute regularly to the discussions in your group, upload music, video and photographs and otherwise participate in the community in which you are a member. This is much like any social gathering where your popularity depends on what you can bring into your group.

NOTE

To contribute, you need content such as media files or up-to-date information in your areas of interest. While the Internet certainly has much more information than what you may ever need, it is very difficult to remember later where to find something interesting that you have seen while browsing. It is simply not enough to mark a site as your favourite (or bookmark it) in your Web browser. Instead, you can use special Bookmarking sites.

After registering at one of these sites, you can store all your bookmarks, organise them in the way you want and even categorise them by adding "Tags" to your bookmarks. Tags are single word labels that you can attach to your bookmarks. Let us say that you visit several Websites displayed by car manufacturers. Instead of listing the sites by name, you can tag them as "Cars" so that all of them will be conveniently displayed in a single group.

NOTE

You can have both private and public bookmarks. Private bookmarks are visible only to yourself, to be used as a convenient reference for your research. Public bookmarks on the other hand, may be viewed by any visitor to the bookmark site. However, no one else except the author can alter, edit or delete either private or public bookmarks.

We take a look at some of the more popular bookmark sites in the remainder of this chapter.

Del.icio.us

Located at **http://del.icio.us**, this site was started by Joshua Schachter in 2003. After Yahoo! acquired it in 2005, it has become the most popular site for bookmarks. Since the procedures at these sites are basically the same, we describe what you have to do to use this site in some detail. Register at this site by filling in the personal details required.

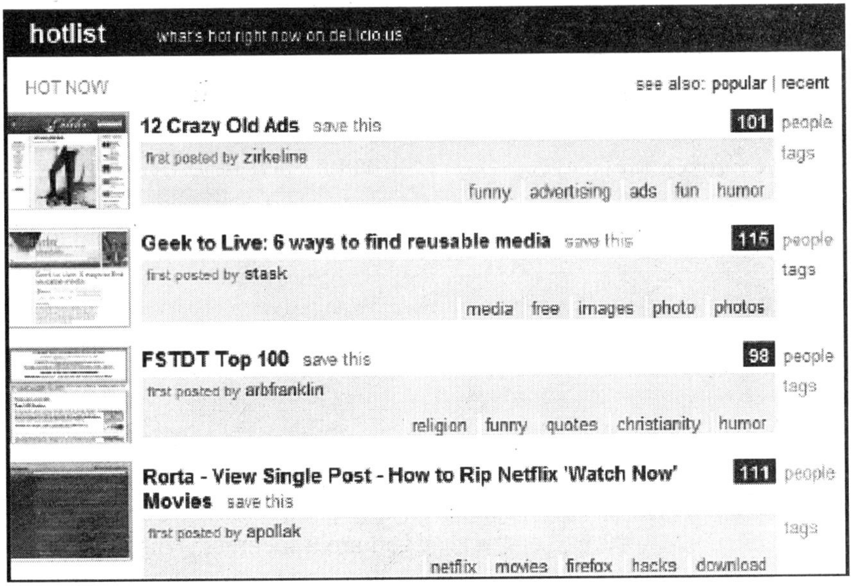

Fig 9.07 – Del.icio.us Hotlist

- Install buttons (button icons) on your favourite browser.
- Import and upload your browser bookmarks to the site.

Your browser should now show two buttons marked "Del.icio.us" and "Tag" respectively. Click on the Del.icio.us button to go to the bookmark sites Web page. You should see your uploaded bookmarks listed there.

Click on the Tag button to add a tag to a bookmark as we have already discussed. Ordinarily, all the bookmarks you upload will be available for viewing by the public. To hide them from view to all but you, select the "Private Saving" option from the "Settings" menu.

StumbleUpon

Available at **http://www.stumbleupon.com**, this bookmarking Website is currently owned by eBay. The site has a very innovative toolbar which adds to its popularity. After registering, and recording the subjects you are interested in, you can download and add the StumbleUpon toolbar to your favourite browser such as Internet Explorer and Firefox.

TIP

Let us see how the toolbar can be used. Let us suppose that you wish to visit a gaming site on the Internet and you have already indicated gaming as one of your areas of interest while registering. After launching your browser, when you click on the "Stumble" button on the toolbar, you will be taken to a gaming site recommended by other StumbleUpon users.

If you like the Website, click the "Thumbs Up" button. Otherwise, click the "Thumbs Down" button. The site remembers your preferences and will take you to the sites you like when you use the toolbar to browse in the future.

Digg

If you are a technology enthusiast, this site, located at **http://www.digg.com** is the right one for you. However, the site lists other topics as well. The six topics are Technology, Science, World & Business, Sports, Entertainment and Gaming. Each main topic has several sub-topics listed under it. Digg was founded by Kevin Rose in 2004.

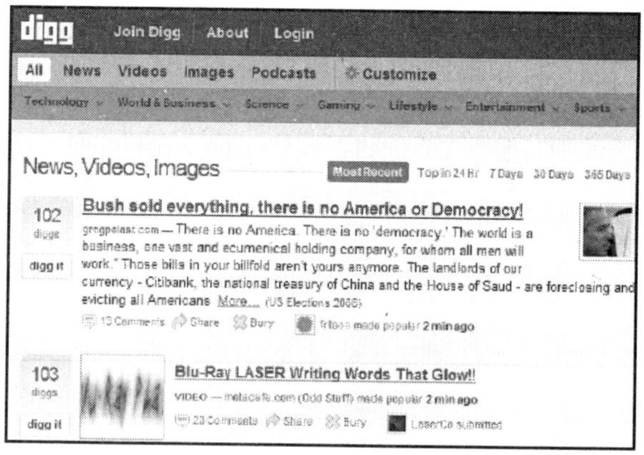

Fig 9.08 – Digg Main Page

Digg has the usual tools to integrate it with your favourite browser. After registering, you can submit stories or comments about stories posted by other users. Apart from being a source of bookmarks, Digg contains videos, news articles and pod-casts (collection of media files on the Internet) submitted by other registered users. You can view them and post comments.

There are very many more such Bookmarking sites. Often, the best way of finding out the ones that are most useful to you is to visit them and try out their features.

Caution

For all Websites including social networking ones, it is good to remember that popular Websites attract malicious programmers and spammers. Therefore, be careful while browsing them. In *Chapter 11 – Virus, Spam and Other Perils* later in this book, we will discuss in detail how you can virus-proof your PC and how you can get rid of virus if they do slip through your defences.

If you visit many new and sometimes exotic Websites, you do increase the risk of infection. Therefore, make it a habit to regularly scan your computer with one or two good anti-virus software.

10. Sharks in the Ocean

In this chapter:

- We look at the dark side of the Internet. We examine Websites that contain excessive violence, sex or objectionable racial content, clearly unsuitable for children and indeed for many of us.
- You are shown how to use the Content Advisor, a part of your Internet Explorer Web browser. We show you how to configure it to block sites, restrict access or otherwise limit what any user of your computer can see on the Internet.
- You are shown how to protect your supervisory privileges by using a password so that your settings may not be changed by other users of your computer.
- There is special software available to block access to undesirable Websites. We discuss four popular ones and show you how to download and use them.
- We discuss why these protections are not completely foolproof in the final analysis. Therefore, we suggest that to prevent unauthorised access to your computer, the best way is to use password protection.

The Dark Side

So far, we have been surfing on the sunny side of the Internet, the side that is filled with knowledge, beauty, music and laughter. If there is a sunny side to surfing, it follows that there is a dark side as well. Just as you need to know where to look for particular information, a special video clip or a well-loved song you want to hear, you must also know what you must do to protect yourself and those who may use your computer, from darkness and ugliness. If you have children at home, such protection becomes even more necessary. We shall devote this chapter to protection techniques and special filtering and blocking software.

The Content Advisor

Your Web browser, the Internet Explorer, has a built-in safety feature called the Content Advisor. Its purpose is to give you the ability to block some or all the inappropriate Internet contents you may encounter. For example, you may wish to protect other users of your computer, especially your children, from visiting Websites that deal with excessive violence or have contents of an explicit sexual nature. Here, the Contents Advisor aids you.

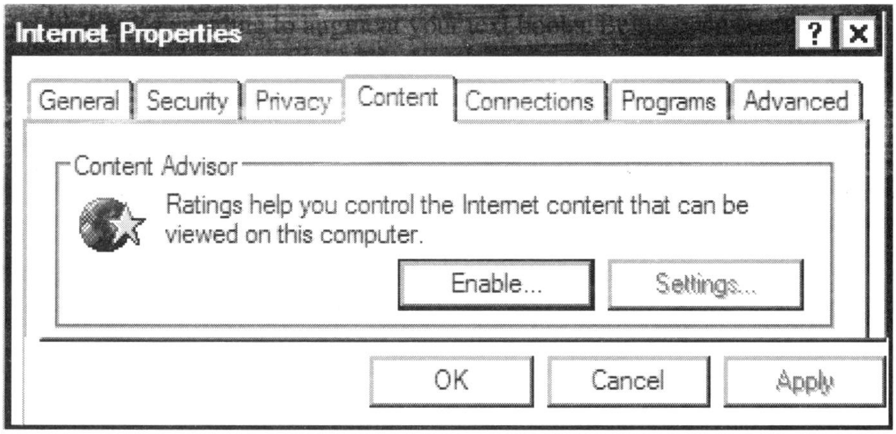

Fig 10.01 – The Content Advisor

Controlling Access

Content Advisor provides a way to help you control the types of Websites that a Web surfer can visit using your Web browser. First, you have to set the limits you want on your Content Advisor. You protect the settings using a password. Then, you turn Content Advisor on. Now, the Web browser will not allow prohibited pages to be seen until the settings are changed by someone with the supervisory password. Here is a more detailed list of what you can do with Content Advisor:

- You can control access to Content Advisor settings. You turn Content Advisor on, and view the settings, through the use of a password. You will need this password to change any Content Advisor settings, so you might want to write it down for future reference.

- You can view and adjust the "Ratings" settings to reflect what you think is appropriate content in each of four areas: language, nudity, sex, and violence. Under the "Ratings" tab, move the slider to select allowed rating for your selection.
- You can adjust what types of content other people will view, with or without your permission. You can override content settings on a case-by-case basis, selecting the ratings for each log-in name.
- You can set up a list of Websites that other people can never view, regardless of how the sites' contents are rated. Alternatively, you can set up a list of Websites that other people can always view, regardless of the sites' contents rating.
- View and change the ratings systems and bureaus you use.

NOTE

Content Advisor is set to the most conservative (least likely to offend) settings when you first turn it on. You can adjust these settings to match your own preferences.

Not all Internet content is rated. If you choose to allow other people to view unrated sites on your computer, some of those sites could contain inappropriate material.

In the paragraphs that follow, you will find procedures for setting the ratings and limits of what can be viewed. In all cases, it is assumed that you have already enabled the Content Advisor. If you have not, do so as follows:

1. In Control Panel, open **Internet Options** by clicking on its icon.
2. On the **Content** tab, under **Content Advisor**, click **Enable**.

TIP

You can also open Internet Options by clicking the **Tools** menu in Internet Explorer, and then clicking **Internet Options**.

You should create a **supervisory password** for your use and write it down at this time. You will need the password to change any Content Advisor setting.

Setting Limits

Here are the steps you need to follow to set the limits in each category such as language or sex:

1. Click a **category** in the list, and then move the slider to set the limits you want to use.
2. Repeat this process for each category you want to limit, and then click **OK**.
3. To prevent others from visiting objectionable Websites that do not use ratings labels, click the **Approved Sites** tab, and change the settings as appropriate.

Restrictions for Others

Follow these steps to set the restrictions for other users of your computer:

1. In Control Panel, open **Internet Options** by clicking on its icon.
2. On the **Content** tab, under **Content Advisor**, click **Enable**.
3. Type your **password**.

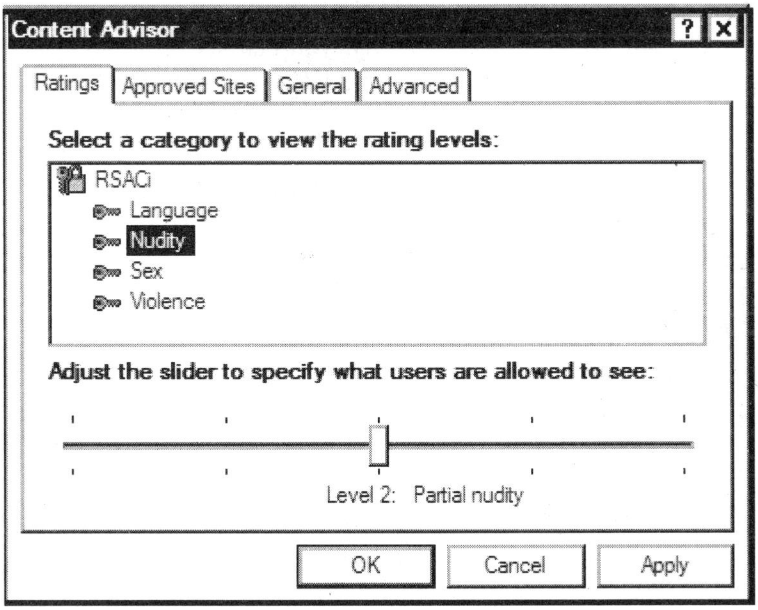

Fig 10.02 – Set Ratings for Each Category

4. To allow others to view restricted content, click the **General** tab, and then select the following check box: **Supervisor can type a password to allow users to view restricted content**. To allow others to view unrated content, select the following check box: **Users can see sites that have no rating**.
5. Click **OK**.

Rate Websites

To allow or to restrict the Websites that others using your computer may see, proceed as follows:

1. In Control Panel, open **Internet Options** by clicking on its icon.
2. On the **Content** tab, under **Content Advisor**, click **Enable**.
3. Click **Settings**, and then type the supervisor **password**.
4. Click the **Approved Sites** tab, type the Internet address (URL) of the Website you want to rate and then choose whether you want others to always or never have access to this site.
5. Repeat this process for each Website that you want to set access for.

Warning Messages

You may come across certain questionable Websites while surfing the Internet yourself. Many Websites will warn you concerning the content and give you the option to exit the Website or to continue viewing.

In most cases, there will be clearly marked "EXIT" and "ENTER" command buttons on the Website along with a declaration that you are an adult and wish to proceed of your own free will. You can exit such Websites quite easily.

Fig 10.03 – Typical Warning Message

Special Software

When you surf to Websites with questionable content, in many cases, you will find that the sites themselves will warn you about the nature of their contents and give you the option of blocking the site by invoking special blocking software available on these sites. "Cyber Patrol", "Net Nanny", "Cyber Sitter" and "Surf Watch" are amongst the most popular blocking software available. Blocking is an effective option if you wish to stop just a few Websites. Since new sites appear all the time, you will probably need to repeat the site blocking exercise at regular intervals to renew the protection.

Fig 10.04 – The Net Nanny Home Page

Of the four filtering software mentioned here, the most popular is Net Nanny. It has many options and is quite effective. You can reach its home page at **http://www.netnanny.com**. The other well-regarded blocking software is Cyber Patrol. You can reach its home page at the following Website **http://www.microsys.com/cyber**. Regretfully, neither Net Nanny nor Cyber Patrol is free.

Quality of Protection

We have discussed protection in detail, both what is built into Internet Explorer and what can be installed by downloading commercial software. However, it must be admitted that there is no foolproof way to eliminate the risk that undesirable content will be found by children or others who you may wish to protect.

You will probably need to combine several strategies. You may block some Web pages using Internet Explorer's Content Adviser. Other sites may be best stopped using Net Nanny, Cyber Patrol or some other commercial software.

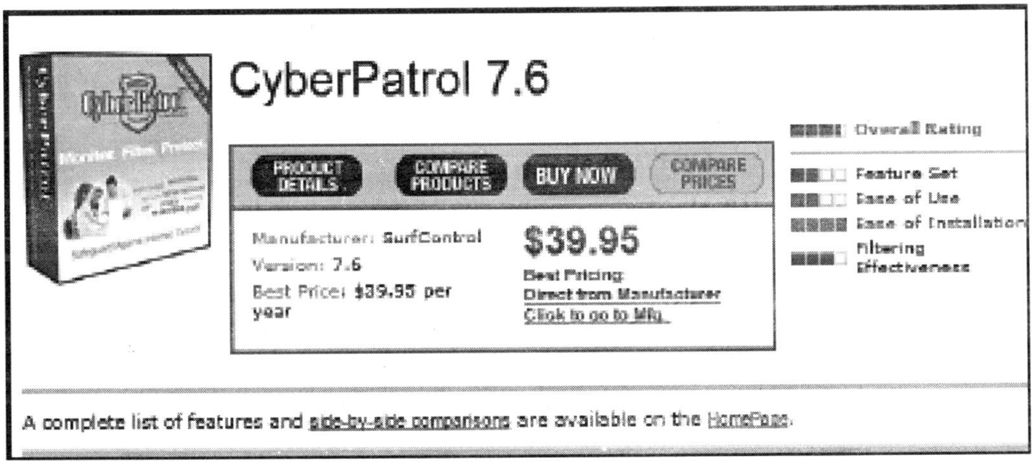

Fig 10.05 – The Cyber Patrol Home Page

TIP

In addition to all that we have discussed, it may be necessary to restrict access to your computer by using a password. Though rather drastic, this may be the only effective way to curb the curiosity of other users of your computer. You have to remember that children are more adept at handling computers than their parents these days and we must acknowledge their ingenuity in circumventing the barriers that we may put in their way!

11. Virus, Spam and Other Perils

In this chapter:

- We discuss the threats of virus, worms and other malicious infections (collectively called malware) that can enter your computer from the Internet, local networks or even from borrowed floppy disks or CD-ROMs.
- We study different defence techniques in depth. They include precautions, preventions and if infected, methods of virus or other malware removal.
- We examine how to install and configure firewalls. We look at anti-virus software and specialised software to protect you from malicious programmes that damage your computer's programmes or steal confidential information from your computer such as e-mail identity or your credit card details.
- We examine the threat from unwanted e-mails, often called spam and study ways to protect mailboxes from undesirable, malicious or simply annoying e-mail that can choke your computer's hard drive.
- We examine techniques and protective software, some of which is free to download from the Internet that makes sure that you can e-mail and surf the Internet safely.

Internet Invaders

It is not surprising that operating systems (such as Windows 98 or Windows XP) account for the largest number of computer software sold in the world. After all, each computer must have at least one operating system installed. The surprise however is that anti-virus software is a close second, although they do nothing else except protect your computer! The popularity of anti-virus programmes is solely due to the fact that today, protecting your computer from malicious attack has become the number one priority for computer users.

In *Chapter 10 – Sharks in the Ocean*, we saw that there are many websites containing objectionable material such as sex, violence or racial slurs. We saw how to filter or block such Websites. However, apart from offending us, objectionable content in itself, will not damage your computer. The threat is passive. In this chapter, we deal with a much more dangerous, active threat. We look at the Internet invaders. These are malicious programmes that attack your computer causing data loss, invasion of privacy and even prevent your computer from carrying out your commands.

NOTE

We can broadly classify these invaders into two groups, Malware and Spam. Malware or malicious software includes computer virus, Internet worms, Trojan Horses, Logic Bombs and Spyware or Adware. All of them have a sinister purpose, to invade your computer and damage software, wipe out data and steal information such as your password or even your credit card details. Malware may reach your computer through the Internet, through a local network, as e-mail or even from a shared floppy disk, CD-ROM, or a flash memory stick.

ALERT

Spam, on the other hand, is unwanted e-mail. Some spam may only be commercial advertisement. They will annoy, but they are not malicious. Others may indeed do harm. For instance, an unsolicited e-mail with gross sexual content can harm your reputation, sowing suspicion about your character. As the rapidly soaring sale of anti-virus software will testify, the harmful capabilities of these Internet invaders have become a matter of very serious concern for computer users today.

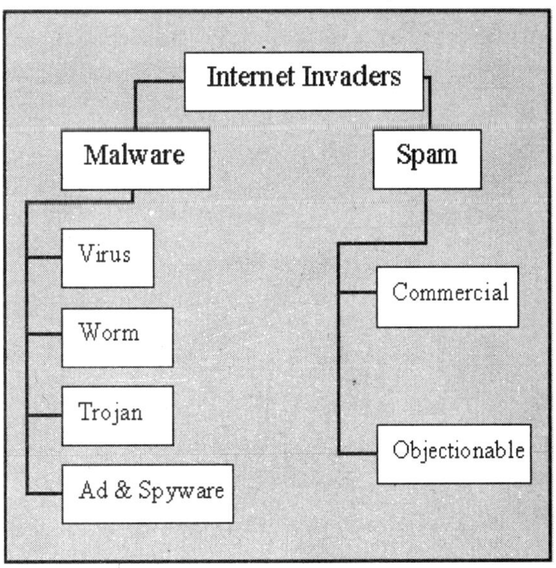

Fig 11.01 – Internet Invaders

Although there are over 100,000 known viruses and the list is growing daily, 90% of the damage is done by about 200 or so malware. So, protection against a limited number of attacking malware may be all that you really need to protect yourself. Therefore, the task is not as hopeless at it may seem at first glance. To install and configure effective defences however, the first thing you need is a clear understanding of the nature of the threat. So, we will devote the rest of this section to an understanding of the nature and characteristics of malware and spam.

All malware are often loosely referred to as viruses. However, to select the correct Internet settings and to select the best strategy to block or remove the malware, we have to be more precise. Therefore, we will look at viruses, worms, Trojans and spyware individually. In addition, we will study spam as a separate problem. See Fig 11.01.

Viruses

A computer virus is a software programme deliberately created to infect and cause damage or annoyance to an unsuspecting computer user. When a computer is infected, the virus attaches itself to one or more legitimate programmes in the computer. The virus runs whenever the infected programme (such as Microsoft Windows or Microsoft Word) is run. Milder viruses will reproduce themselves, using up the computer's memory and disk space. More virulent viruses will also damage the software and the data stored in the computer, often causing the computer to crash and become unusable. Viruses, therefore, are serious threats indeed. Viruses and other malware account for 80% of data loss in computers worldwide. Unlike other malware such as Worms, viruses almost always travel from an infected computer to others through shared files.

You may come across three basic types of viruses. The System (or boot) Sector Virus attaches itself to the system files (part of your operating system) in the system or boot sector of your hard disk. The system files run every time you start your computer. The File Virus, on the other hand, infects programme files in your computer. It reproduces, infecting even more programme files. If there are other computers connected to the infected one on a network, then the file virus will spread over the entire network, causing severe damage to all the connected computers. File viruses are the most common of all viruses. Finally, there is the Macro Virus that attacks data files containing macros. A macro is a short code written to automate some action on a data sheet. For example, you can create an Excel spreadsheet containing a macro to automatically calculate totals. A macro virus attacks your computer through the script used to write the macro. All the viruses we have discussed will make copies of themselves, using up your computer's memory and disk space thus slowing down your computer. In addition, many of the viruses will corrupt your operating system, your programme files or your data files.

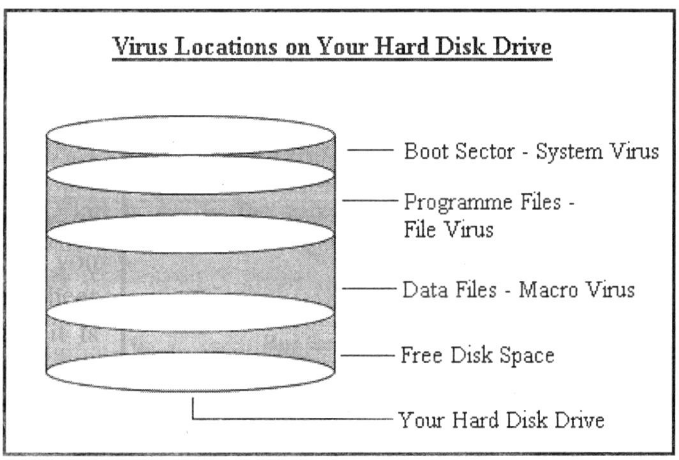

Fig 11.02 – Viruses and where they attack

Worms

Worms are almost always picked up by a healthy computer while surfing the Internet or downloading files from an infected Website, whereas Viruses propagate through shared floppy disks or CD-ROMS. Both can travel through a local network. A Worm is more deadly because it requires no trigger to begin its destructive work on the computer or network that it infects. When a worm enters a computer it launches a programme which searches for other computers on a local network. All connected computers are infected unless they are protected against the worm. At no time does the worm need any particular programme or macro to be launched in order to do damage. Once the worm discovers an Internet or local Intranet connection, it automatically sends a copy of itself to connected computers so that they too become infected and suffer damage to programmes, data or both.

Trojan Horses

According to legend, the Greeks won the Trojan War by hiding inside a huge, hollow wooden horse. Thinking that the Greeks had left, the unsuspecting Trojans dragged the horse into the fortified city of Troy thereby letting the Greeks into the city and losing the war! In today's computer world, a Trojan horse is defined as a "malicious, security-breaking programme that is disguised as something harmless". For example, you download what appears to be a movie or music file, but when you click on it, you unleash a dangerous Trojan horse programme that erases your hard disk and sends your credit card numbers and passwords to a malicious stranger.

As we have seen in case of worms, once you are "infected", Trojans are just as dangerous as viruses and can spread to hurt others just as easily. Trojans can spread in the guise of literally anything people find desirable, such as a free games, movies, songs, screensavers, etc. Trojans are typically downloaded from a WWW website or a File Transfer Protocol (FTP) archive on the Internet. Trojans usually do their damage silently. The first sign of trouble is often when others tell you that you are attacking them or trying to infect them!

Trojans are executable programmes, which means that when you open the file, it will perform some action or actions. In Windows, executable programmes have file extensions like "exe", "vbs", "com", "bat", etc. Trojans too have similar file extensions. Some actual Trojan filenames include "dmsetup.exe" and "LOVE-LETTER-FOR-YOU.vbs". You may pick up a Trojan from a malicious e-mail like the second example we just saw. Therefore, unless you know the sender and trust that person, never open an e-mail attachment which has an executable file extension like "exe", "vbs", etc.

Spyware

Spywares are even more insidious than Trojans. You may pick up spyware just by browsing an Internet website that contains hidden spyware programmes. Unlike Trojans, however, spyware does not attempt to damage your computer. Instead, it tries to find private information on your hard disk such as your usernames, passwords and credit card information for transmitting them back to the host website. The information may be used to bombard you with unwanted e-mail (spam) or to use your credit card information for fraud. Spyware can be detected by monitoring any attempt that your computer makes on its own (with no commands from you) to access the Internet as the Spyware tries to send information back.

Adware

Some free computer programmes display advertisements when you use them on the Internet. A very popular file download manager called "Download Accelerator Plus" will display banner advertisements in the top part of its window as you download files. Apart from the annoyance that unwanted advertisements may cause and a small loss of speed used to download the advertisements, Adwares will not damage your computer. Adware may rightly be called "Annoyance-ware" rather than Malware.

Spam

Spam is unsolicited, worthless or junk e-mail sent to large numbers of people to promote products or services. While they are not harmful in themselves, they can certainly be annoying. They may choke your mailbox, causing a jam and not letting you use of your e-mail facility. Objectionable spam such as sexually explicit unsolicited e-mail, sometimes called "porn spam" is more damaging.

Apart from personal spam, directed at an individual's mailbox, spam may also refer to inappropriate promotional or commercial postings to news groups, discussion groups or bulletin boards on the Internet. The common factor in all cases of spam, whether objectionable or not, is that spam is unsolicited e-mail and a violation of your privacy. According to e-mail security leaders, in the United States, Spam may account for almost 60 to 70% of all e-mails in 2008. At first glance, therefore, though you may not think of spam as being as great a threat, it may end up by choking your Internet-based communications!

Symptoms of Malware

How do you know that your computer has been infected? To help you find out, we look at symptoms of a malware infection in this section.

It is easy to know when you get spam. Your inbox will be full. There will be so many junk mails that you will find it difficult to find the ones that are important. Many users get so impatient that they delete the entire lot, throwing the baby out with the bath water! Patience and a few simple rules will help you out of this situation. We will discuss the cures a little later.

Malware has some common symptoms. In addition, some other symptoms are unique to a particular infection. Since the cure for different types of malware are different, it is important to identify the problem by studying the tell-tale signs. Here are some of them:

- Look for erratic behaviour such as sudden shutdowns, strange messages on your monitor's screen, very slow start-up or slow running of programmes as a first sign of trouble.
- Slow start-ups or unexpected reboots usually mean a boot (or system) sector virus. If the computer behaves erratically after a particular programme has been launched, you should suspect a file virus. A macro virus will be triggered only after a particular data file (containing a macro) has been used by your computer.
- If your Internet connection appears much slower than usual or if you find that your programmes are often running out of memory, you may have a spyware in your computer downloaded without your knowledge. If you see some random pop-up advertisements on your browser while surfing, then a rogue Website may be trying to take control of your computer. Spyware may also change the opening page of your Web browser or install dialler software that will automatically dial a rogue Website as soon as your computer is connected to the modem.

If your computer attempts to access the Internet on its own, it is a sure sign of a spyware infection. You will see the dial up dialogue box appear on your monitor's screen even though you have not asked for it. The spyware is trying to connect to the Internet in order to send some confidential information from your computer to its parent Website. The information may contain passwords or credit card information, harmful to you if the spyware can send it to its parent Website for fraudulent use.

Many malware lies dormant, showing no symptoms until a triggering event sets it off. The trigger may be a date, a particular event (such as the 100th time you switch on your computer) or the use of a specific programme or data file. Therefore, scan your computer periodically using good, updated anti-virus software.

Fig 11.03 – An Infected Computer

Protecting Yourself

Introduction

Not so long ago, before malware and spam became so numerous, it was enough if you installed reasonably good anti-virus software (AVS) on your computer. The software protected your computer from viruses and filtered your e-mail to keep malware out. Today, attacks are more sophisticated and more intense. A simple AVS is no longer enough. You have to consider protecting your computer at five different levels. We recommend that you use:

- A Firewall.
- One or two good anti-virus software.
- Special software to detect and block Spyware and Adware.
- Higher security settings on your Internet browser.
- Mail filter settings on your e-mail software such as Outlook Express.

Before we examine each of the recommendations in detail, here are some simple precautions.

Precautions

- New malware are being released every day. To make sure that your operating system has the latest security patches or software updates installed, visit its home page to download and install at least the critical patches. Microsoft Windows has a built in "Windows Update" feature for this purpose. See Fig 11.04. Make sure, however, that Microsoft still supports the Windows version you are using. At the time of writing this book, Microsoft no longer supports Windows 95 and Windows 98.

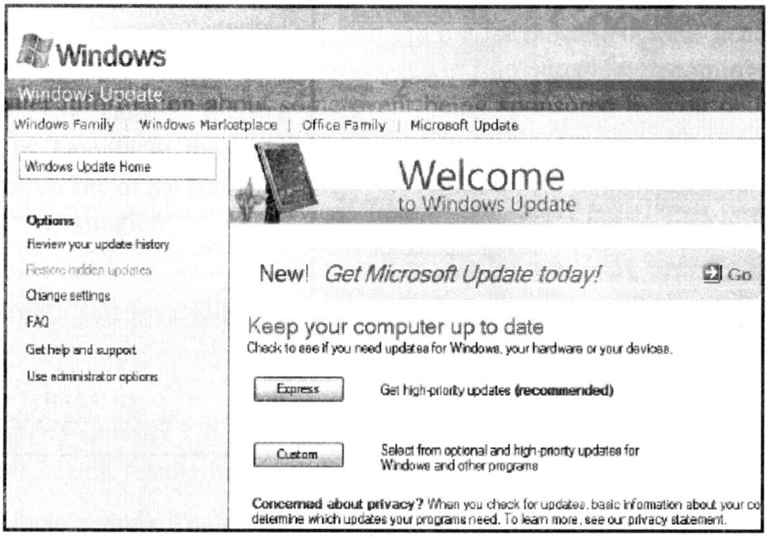

Fig 11.04 – The Windows Update Page

- Never open an e-mail attachment. That is right, never! Although it may appear to be from a friend, it need not be the case. Instead of opening the attachment, right click and select 'save as' to save the attachment on the hard disk of your computer. Now scan it for viruses using your anti-virus software. Open it only if you get a "clean" report.
- Since you have to depend so much on your anti-virus software for protection, make sure that you keep it up-to-date by downloading its latest updates. All good anti-virus software has its home page on the Internet from where you can download what you need.
- Keep a rescue floppy disk handy. When things go bad, a boot or rescue disk is your first step to recovery. The rescue disk contains the basic elements of your operating system. It is very easy to make. Insert a blank, formatted floppy disk and go to **Control Panel → Add-Remove Programs** and click the **Start-up Disk** tab. Insert a floppy disk, open **My Computer**, right click on that **drive** (usually A:) and select **Format**. In the Format options choose "Create a MS-DOS Start-up disk". Label it with a date and store it near your computer where you can find it easily.
- Back up your important data on CD-ROMs, Zip disks or some other removable media. Keep backing up regularly.

NOTE

You can also use your installed anti-virus (AVS) programmes to create a rescue disk for use if your system gets infected. We shall discuss the procedure for creating a rescue disk from your AVS a little later in this chapter.

Start-up Disk for Windows XP

You can make a start-up disk as follows:

1. Insert a floppy disk into your computer's floppy drive.
2. Open **My Computer**, and then click the **floppy disk drive** to select it.
3. On the **File** menu, point to the **name** of the floppy drive, and then click **Format**.
4. Under Format options, click "Create an MS-DOS start-up disk".
5. Click **Start**.

ALERT

If due to a catastrophic virus attack you have to reformat you hard disk, while you will be able to reinstall your operating system or programmes from their original CD-ROMS, your personal data files will be irretrievably lost. Therefore, backing up your important personal data is very important.

Install a Firewall

A firewall is specialised software that you can install on your machine. Like a doorkeeper for your computer, it checks every attempt to exchange information between your computer and the network. A firewall will work equally well for Internet or local network connections. The firewall will not let anything in or out until you allow it. Therefore, a malicious attacker, (often called a "hacker") can not steal personal information from your hard drive. Similarly, a Trojan horse that steals your keystrokes over the Internet can not read your passwords. If an attempt is made to send or receive information, the firewall stops the transfer and displays a warning message to alert you.

We recommend two good free firewall programmes, the Sygate Personal Firewall (see Fig 11.05) and Kerio Personal Firewall. At their websites, you can select the free versions for download. If you are a corporate user, you can opt for their more powerful corporate versions for a fee. The website addresses are:

- **http://www.sygate.com**
- **http://www.kerio.com**

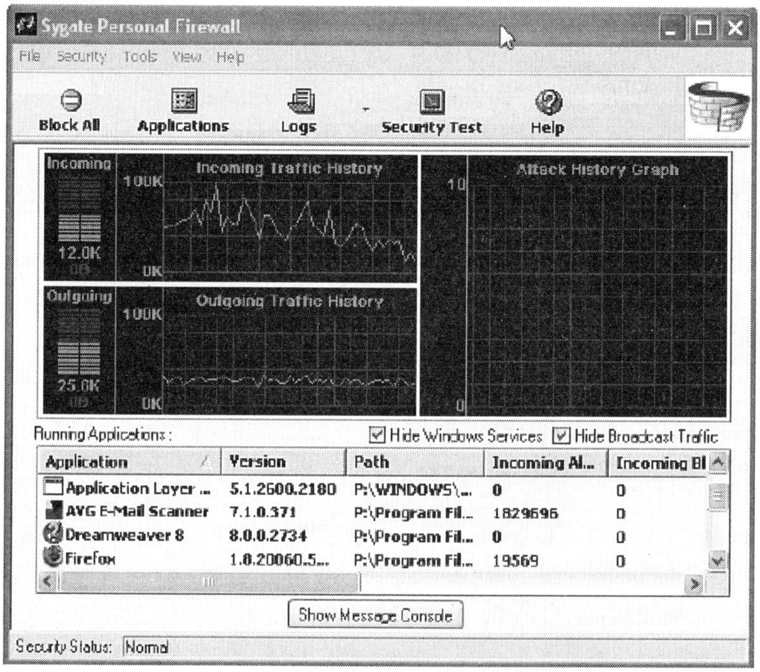

Fig 11.05 – Sygate Personal Firewall

Windows XP Professional has its own built-in firewall. You can activate it as follows:

1. Click **Start**, click **Control Panel**, and then double-click **Network Connections**.
2. Click the Dial-up, LAN or High-Speed **Internet connection** that you want to protect, and then, under **Network Tasks**, click "Change settings of this connection".
3. On the **Advanced** tab, under **Internet Connection Firewall**, select one of the following:
   - To enable Internet Connection Firewall (ICF), select the "Protect my computer and network by limiting or preventing access to this computer from the Internet" check box.

- To disable Internet Connection Firewall, clear the "Protect my computer and network by limiting or preventing access to this computer from the Internet" check box.

ALERT

The built-in firewall is adequate if you use the Internet occasionally. For heavier users and users with an "always on" cable or DSL Internet connection, you may wish to use one of the third party firewalls we have just recommended. Do not use two different firewalls at the same time. They will probably interfere and cause your computer to behave erratically.

NOTE

Some anti-virus software packages such as McAffee or Norton contain both firewalls and anti-virus software. For really top class protection, one of these two packages is recommended for installation on your computer. Both are available in India and may be purchased from your local software supplier. Both come on CD-ROMs and with instruction manuals. All you have to do is to insert the CD-ROM and follow the simple instructions on your monitor's screen to install and configure the software.

The McAffee Firewall's home (or opening) page is shown in Fig 11.06.

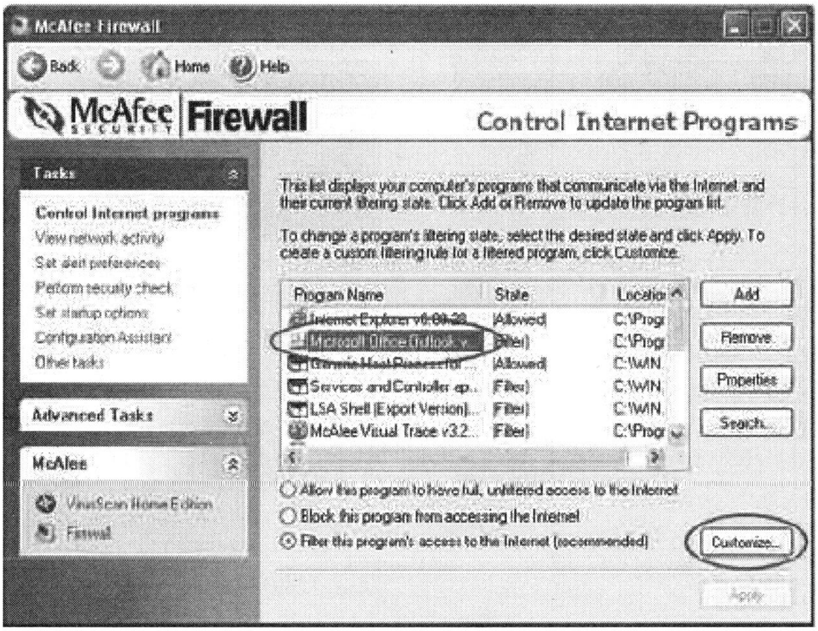

Fig 11.06 – The McAffee Firewall Home Page

Anti-virus Software

Viruses come in a great many different forms, but their method of attack is quite similar. They attack in two phases, first they infect the computer and then they attack the infected computer. When the virus runs, it infects other programmes. Some may infect each time they are executed, while other viruses infect only when a certain triggering event occurs. The event may be a date or time, a programme launch or a counter within the virus.

In the infection phase, a virus may become resident in the memory of your computer. It behaves just like a "terminate and stay resident" (TSR) programme such as Sidekick or Quicken. The TSR virus waits for some external event such as inserting a diskette, copying a file, or executing a programme to actually infect another programme. Such viruses are very difficult to detect. TSR viruses frequently corrupt the system software on your computer to hide their existence. You get the first indication of trouble when your computer takes too long to start or fails to start at all.

NOTE

In the attack phase, viruses do unpleasant things such as deleting files or changing random data on your disk. Often they will slow your computer down. Some viruses do less harmful things such as playing music or creating messages or animation on your screen. Just as some event triggers the virus's infection phase, the attack phase also has its own trigger. Therefore, the attack may be delayed for a long time after the initial infection. All viruses do not have an attack phase. Many viruses simply reproduce. However, they too write themselves on your hard disk stealing disk storage space and slow your computer down.

Like firewalls, there is a large number of anti-virus software available. Some are free such as the Avast! 4 while others such as McAffee and Norton have to be paid for. See Fig 11.07. All these three are very good if they are configured correctly and updated regularly so that their virus detection abilities remain current. See Fig 11.07.

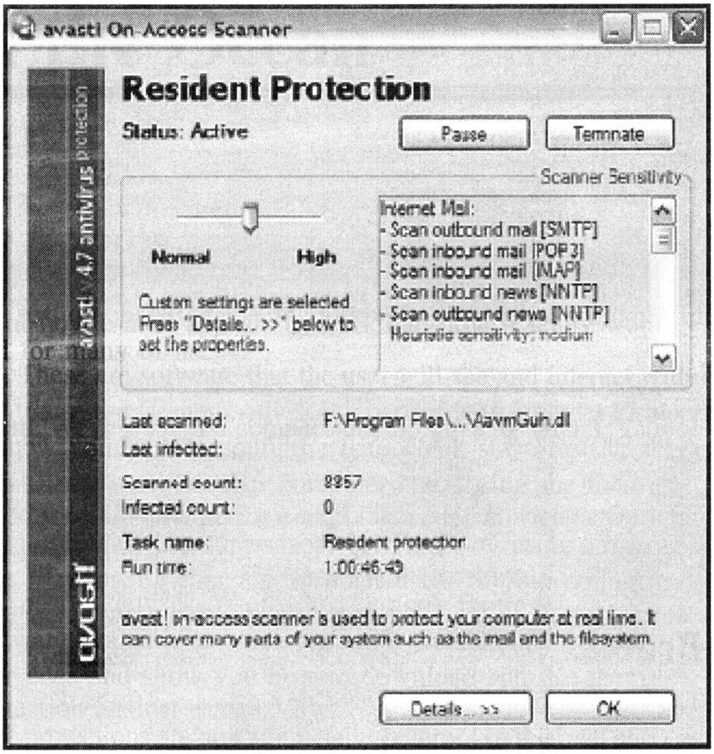

Fig 11.07 – The Avast! 4 Anti-virus Software

Specialised Software

In addition to firewalls and anti-virus software, there is a special class of software that deal, with adware and spyware. Firewalls do indeed try to block spyware but some do get through. Therefore, you should occasionally scan your computer using good specialised software such as Zone Alarm or Spybot Search and Destroy. Fortunately, both are very effective programmes and are free for personal use.

You can download the free version of Zone Alarm from **http://www.zonelabs**.com and Spybot Search and Destroy is available free at **http://security.kolla.de/**. The downloaded programmes can be installed and configured quite easily. In case of Zone Alarm, it is best not to change any of the default settings. In both cases, it is very important to periodically update the software by connecting to the Internet and clicking the update button on the opening page. In Fig 11.08, you can see the home page of Spybot Search and Destroy, a good anti-spyware programme.

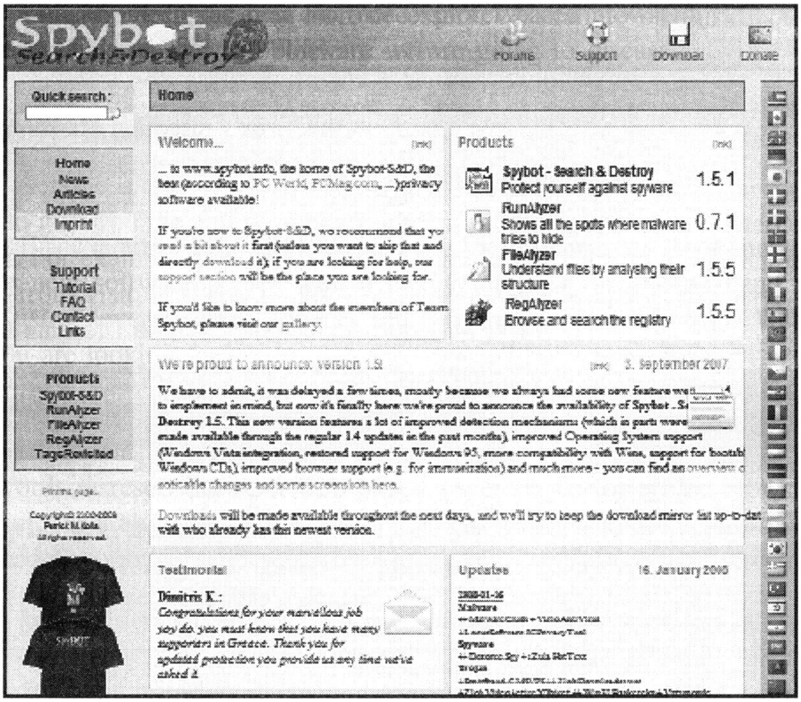

Fig 11.08 – Spybot Search and Destroy

Browser Settings

The software you use for browsing the Internet is your Web browser. If you are using Windows as your operating system, you will have some version of the Internet Explorer installed in your computer as your default browser. While the instructions here are for the Microsoft Internet Explorer, you can also use them with Netscape or Opera and set the desired level of security (protection) of your browser.

NOTE

If you have Windows 98 or Windows 2000 as your operating system, you may have Internet Explorer version 5.0 or 5.5 installed. Upgrade your browser to Internet Explorer (IE) 6.0. You can do so by connecting to Microsoft's Windows Update Site (See Fig 11.05) and downloading the IE 6.0 upgrade pack. The upgrade is free but will take a long time on a dial-up connection since the package is rather large, running to 11.0 to 22.0 Megabytes (MB). If you have Windows XP installed, then you will have IE 6.0 already.

To set the desired level of Internet security on your browser, proceed as follows:

1. Click on the **Start** button, go to **Settings** and click on **Control Panel**.
2. Double-click on **Internet Options**. The dialogue box opens. See Fig 11.09.
3. Click on the **Security** tab.
4. Click once on the **Internet** icon (to highlight it).
5. Check your security level: Under the words "Security level for this zone" the word "Medium" should appear in bold letters. This is the default setting and the one we recommend. If your security level is not Medium, click on the **Default Level bar** near the bottom right side of this dialogue box and shift it up or down till the word "Medium" appears. Now click on the **Apply** button and then on the **OK** button. See Fig 11.09.
6. Close the **Control Panel**.

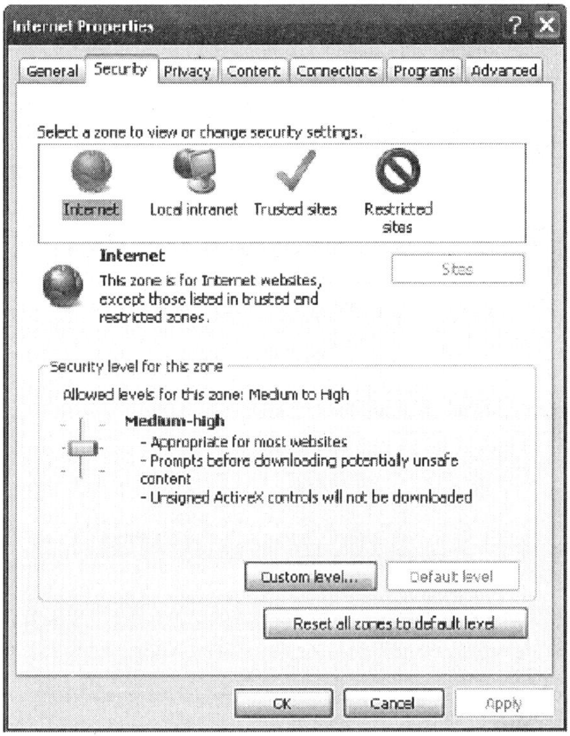

Fig 11.09 – The Security Tab on Internet Options

If you set your security level high, you may not be able to view some Web pages that require JavaScript for its display. However, if your main concern is protection from Internet malware attack, we recommend a high security level setting.

To do so proceed as follows:

1. Click on and drag the **slider** (left side of dialogue box) up to **High**.
2. Click the **Apply** button and then on the **OK** button.
3. Close the **Control Panel**.

Disinfecting Your Computer

Virus Removal

In spite your best efforts, a malware such as a virus, a worm, a Trojan or a spyware may gain entry into your computer. You may become aware of an infection in two ways. If you have good, regularly updated anti-virus software (AVS) always running in the background on your computer, the AVS will display a warning message on your monitor's screen. Usually, an audible beep will also sound, warning you that some malware has been detected. If your AVS does detect the intruder, it will also quarantine the malware to prevent it from spreading. You can then ask your AVS to try to disinfect the infected file. That is, remove the intruder without damaging the file itself. If the AVS fails to remove the virus, it will be necessary to delete the file and reinstall a fresh copy from the source programme's CD-ROM.

Sometimes, however, the AVS is unable to detect the intruder. This may be because you have not set your AVS to start automatically as Windows is started and then run in the background. It may also be because the AVS has not been updated regularly and does not have the latest virus signature files. The AVS needs these signatures to detect a malware. Whatever is the reason, if a malware enters, you will experience slowing down of your computer, strange messages or even computer crashes. If you suspect a virus infection, follow these steps:

1. Shut down your computer. Remove all floppy disks and CD-ROMs from their drives. If you have an Internet and/or a local network connection, disconnect your computer from both.

2. Reboot your computer using the DOS based rescue disk or emergency disk that you have prepared when the AVS was installed. In the following section, we will explain how to make an emergency disk. If you do not have a rescue disk, use the DOS start-up disk that was made when you installed your Windows operating system. See *Protecting Yourself* earlier in this chapter.

3. After rebooting with the DOS start-up disk, change to the drive where the AVS is located. Use DOS commands appropriate for your AVS to start scanning your computer for virus. For more details, consult the documentation that came with your AVS. Follow instructions on your monitor's screen to try to disinfect the affected files. If that is not possible, the AVS should prompt you do delete the file. You can replace the deleted file later from the CD-ROM of the affected programme.

TIP

We advise you to run your AVS in the DOS mode instead of running it normally in Windows. This is because when you start Windows, the virus will launch itself and reside in your computer's memory. If that happens, it may corrupt your AVS and/or mask itself so that it escapes detection. By running your AVS, in the DOS mode therefore, you improve your chances of detecting and removing the virus.

Create an Emergency Disk

We will now show you how to create an emergency disk with McAfee AVS. The procedure is roughly the same with other well-known AVS such as PC-cillin, Norton AVS, etc. Each AVS contains documentation and on-line help files describing their specific procedures. To create an emergency disk with McAffee AVS, proceed as follows:

1. Click **Start** in the Windows taskbar; point to **Programs**, then to **McAfee VirusScan**. Next, choose "Pick a Task" on the main panel and then choose "Create Emergency Disk" from the list that appears. The first panel of the wizard will appear. See Fig 11.10.

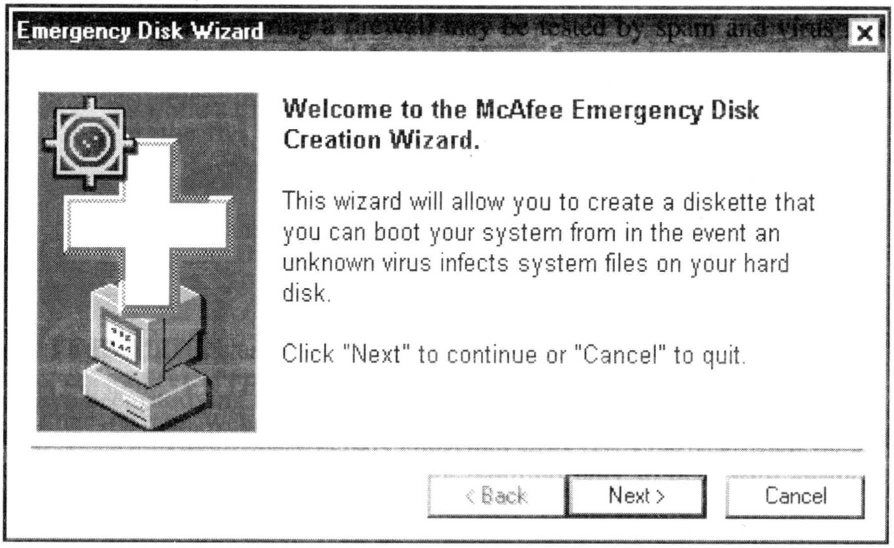

Fig 11.10 – The Emergency Disk Creation Wizard

2. Click **Next** to continue. Choose one of the following depending on the operating system you have on your computer:
   - If your computer runs Windows NT Workstation v4.0 or Windows 2000 Professional, the wizard will tell you that you must format your Emergency Disk with the proprietary NAI operating system (OS). Click **Next** to continue and then skip to Step 3.
   - If your computer runs Windows 95 or Windows 98, the wizard will offer to format your Emergency Disk either with the NAI-OS or with Windows start-up files. Choose the operating system files that you want to use and then click **Next** to continue.
3. Insert a new and unformatted 1.44MB floppy disk into your floppy drive. McAfee recommends that you use a completely new disk that you have never previously formatted to prevent the possibility of an earlier virus infection on your Emergency Disk.
4. Click **Next** to continue. The Emergency Disk wizard will copy its files from a disk image stored in the VirusScan programme directory. As it does so, it will display its progress in a wizard panel.
5. Click **Finish** to quit the wizard after it has created your disk. Next, remove the disk from your floppy drive, write protect it, label it "McAfee Emergency Boot Disk" and store it in a safe place.

NOTE

You may write protect the floppy disk by sliding the tab in the write protect window downwards. This will protect the floppy disk from virus infection as well as accidental erasure.

Removing Trojans

As we have seen earlier in this chapter, Trojan Horses (or simply Trojans) may sneak into your computer without your knowledge. Trojans contain a harmful payload (or component) that behaves very much like a virus. It may replicate itself in your computer or try to infect other computers connected to yours through a network.

When you suspect that you have a Trojan on your machine, you can detect it by looking for any unfamiliar programme that starts up automatically every time you start (boot up) your computer.

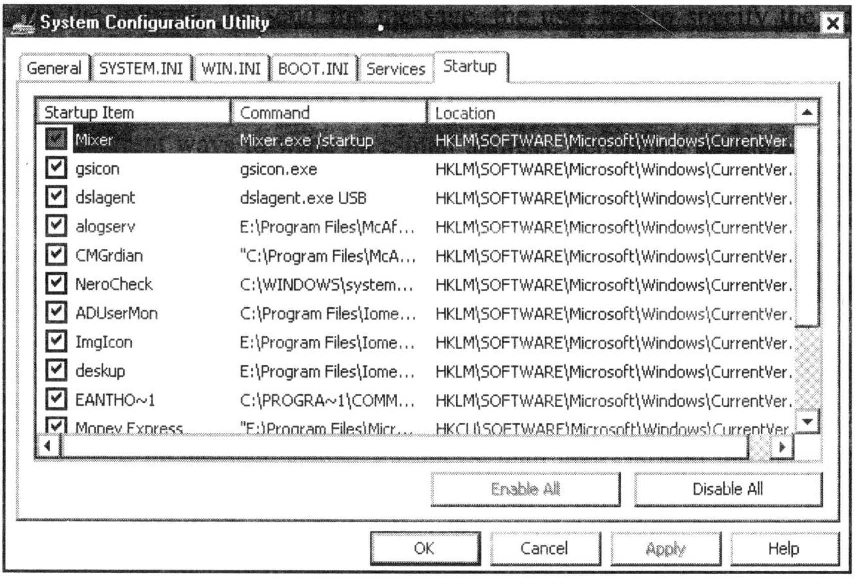

Fig 11.11 – The Start-up Tab on System Configuration Utility

To look for any suspicious programmes in your start-up set, you can use the system configuration utility "msconfig" in Windows 98 or Windows XP and the Services Manager in Windows 2000 or NT. In Windows 98 or XP, you can use msconfig as follows:

For Windows 98 and XP

1. At the opening screen click **Start** → **Run** and then type **<msconfig>** in the edit box that appears. Click **OK**.

2. The System Configuration Utility appears. Select the **Start-up** tab. Under this tab, a list of programmes will be displayed that are automatically launched every time your computer starts. Note closely any programme that is not connected with Windows or any of the programmes you have installed on your computer. The Trojan should appear on this list as an unknown programme. Note the programme name and close the msconfig utility. See Fig 11.11.

3. Locate the suspicious programme by using the "Search" option you see when you click the Start button on your opening screen. The search result will show the location of the unknown programme. Navigate to this location and delete the programme.

Be very careful before deleting a programme. If it is a legitimate one, you will lose its function. It is especially dangerous if you delete a programme or dynamic link library (DLL) required by Windows since your computer may crash! Carefully note the file name and its location before you delete anything.

For Windows 2000

In Windows 2000, many start-up processes run as Services. To check the services which start when Windows starts, you have to display the "Services" page on the Microsoft Management Console (MMC). To do this, click **Start** ➔ **Run** then type **<services.msc>** or, type **Start** ➔ **Programs** ➔ **Control Panel.** The control panel opens. Click on **Administrative Tools** ➔ **Services** to display the "Services" page.

As before, on the services page, look for unfamiliar or suspicious items in the list. To prevent a suspicious service from starting automatically, right click it and choose **Properties**. Then from the Start-up type box, choose either **Manual** or **Disabled**. "Manual" will stop the service from starting automatically and will allow you to start it manually by clicking **Start** from the console. "Disabled" will prevent the service from starting at all until the setting is changed back.

Be very careful about the services that you stop. Some of them are critical for Windows operation. We suggest that you begin by setting the start-up of any suspected service to "manual" to see what impact it has. If no problems occur after several start-ups, then set the service to "disabled" to turn it off permanently.

Because of the risk involved in manually removing a Trojan from your computer, you may wish to use one of many special software available on the Internet. In Fig 11.12, you can see a number of free anti-Trojan software. In addition to the free software, a good anti-Trojan called "Cleaner" is available from **http://www.moosoft.com**. Unfortunately, it is not free.

Anti-Trojan Category	Downloads	Size
Anti-Trojan 5.5.420 Anti-Trojan is a fast and reliable trojan remover **Requirements:** Windows 95/98/Me/NT/2000XP	4247	4.9 Mb
Iparmor 5.39 Anti trojan virus protect your PC from trojan virus and worm **Requirements:** Windows 95/98/Me/NT/2000/XP	644	2.2 Mb
PC DoorGuard 2.9 This is a full-featured professional anti-trojan fighter **Requirements:** Windows 95/98/Me/NT/2000	790	2.6 Mb

Fig 11.12 – Some Anti-Trojan Software

Removing Worms

A worm is not always easy to detect. In some cases you may detect nothing unusual even though your computer is already infected. On the other hand, an initial worm attack may produce infection-like symptoms even before the worm has actually entered your computer.

Suspicious computer behaviour may include frequent rebooting of your system if you are using Windows XP or Windows 2003 Server. If you have Windows 2000 or NT installed, you may find that your computer has become sluggish and takes much longer to respond than before. With all versions of Windows, you may see the "Shutdown Error" message if your computer has been infected by a worm.

If you do suspect a worm infection or even a worm attack (prior to actual infection), take the following action immediately, to prevent the worm from succeeding in its attack, or from spreading if it is already in your computer:

1. Shut your computer down.
2. Disconnect your computer's Internet connection and/or local network connection.
3. Make sure that you have the worm removing tools provided by one of the following Anti-virus software vendors:
   - Network Associates
   - Trend Micro
   - Symantec
   - Computer Associates

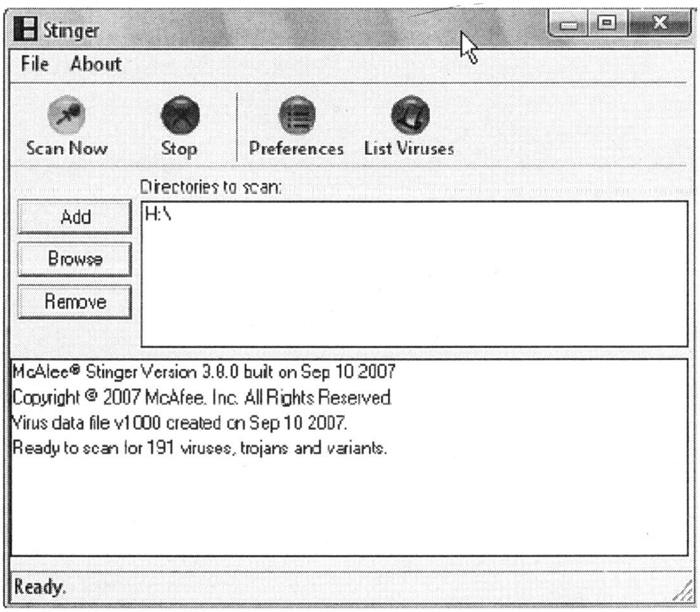

Fig 11.13 – The McAffee Stinger Anti-Worm Tool

4. The tools usually fit on a floppy disk. Keep the disk handy, restart your computer with Internet and network connections removed and run the tools from the floppy disk to clean your machine. See Fig 11.13.

Removing Spyware

Since most spyware are programmed to auto-launch when you start your computer or when you launch your Internet browser, they will either be listed in your start-up set and/or, have entries in your Windows registry. While discussing Trojans earlier in this chapter, we have seen how you can use "msconfig" to examine your start-up set. You can use the "regedit" command in a similar way to examine your Windows registry entries to detect unwanted entries. You can launch "regedit" by typing **Start ➜ Run** and then typing **<regedit>** in the edit box and clicking **OK**.

ALERT

Altering Windows registry is a job best left to the experts. If you make an error, you may find it impossible to restart Windows. If you must experiment, make sure that you save a copy of the registry before attempting any changes. To do so, click **File ➜ Export** while the registry editor is open and then save the current registry in a drive or folder of your choice. You can then use the **File ➜ Import** command to restore a malfunctioning registry with the version you had saved earlier.

Specialised Software

If you do not wish to use "msconfig" or "regedit" to tackle your spyware problem, you can download and install some excellent and free, software programmes to do the job for you. We discuss two great favourites below.

Spybot Search&Destroy (Spybot S&D) has one of the most complete spyware detection lists that you will find. Lavasoft AD-aware is a free Windows utility that detects and removes many adware products. Both can be easily updated by visiting their respective home Websites.

As in the case of any anti-virus programme, the efficiency of anti-spyware programmes also depends on how current their detection lists are. Therefore, make sure that you check for, download and install updates at least once a week to keep your programmes fighting fit.

ALERT

These two programmes (and others of a similar nature) will detect and remove both spyware and adware. While spyware should be always removed, in case of adware, note that there are many free utilities that require their adware to remain in operation. Otherwise, the utility too will stop working.

This completes our round-up of Malware and Adware. We have examined how they attack and the precautions that you can take to avoid them. We have also discussed the steps you can take to get rid of the malware that have slipped through your defences.

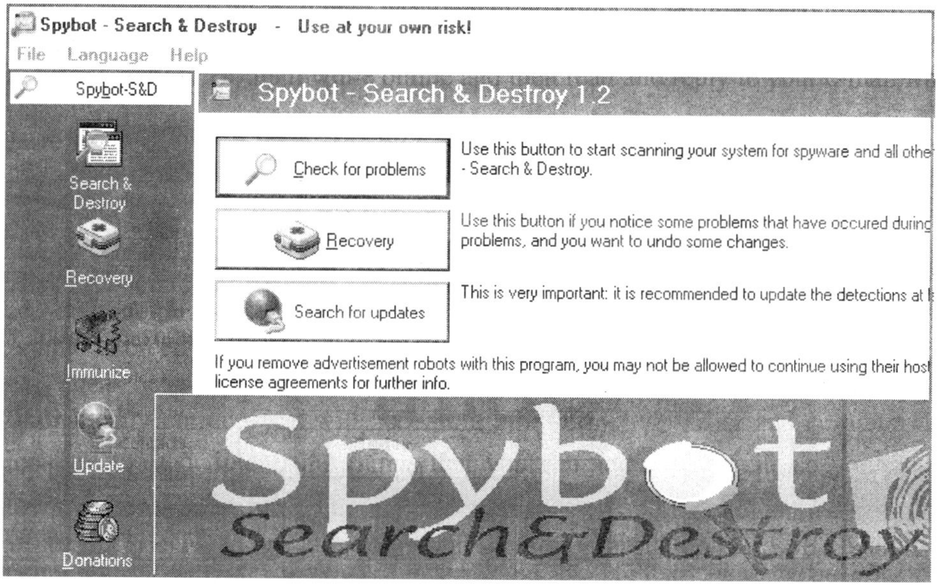

Fig 11.14 – The Spybot S&D opening Screen

TIP

We repeat a very important message here. Make sure that you keep your Windows operation system and the anti-Malware products installed in your computer always up-to-date. A weekly visit to the Windows Update site and similar visits to your anti-virus supplier's home page for updating your software is the most important thing you can do to keep your defences sharp and active. Remember that there are literally hundreds of new malwares being released every day. On the Internet, out-of-date protection is no protection at all!

Spam

In Internet language, "spam" means being deluged with unwanted e-mails. Spam actually means a type of ham. However, the American TV personality Monty Python popularised an advertisement in which customers at a restaurant were only offered unwanted spam regardless of what they ordered! Since then, deluging someone's mail box with very large numbers of unwanted and even offensive e-mails is called "spamming". Spam may fall into three categories such as commercial, offensive or virus ridden.

NOTE

Mail Filter

Commercial spam is very annoying. It can choke your mail inbox and make it difficult for you to find the important e-mails that you really want to read. To ensure that e-mail from important people such as your boss or close friend is never lost in the clutter, use the sorting ability of Outlook Express to send selected mail to a separate folder.

To do so, proceed as follows:

- Open Outlook Express and go to the Inbox
- Click **Tools** → **Message Rules** → **Mail**
- The New Mail Rule dialogue box appears.

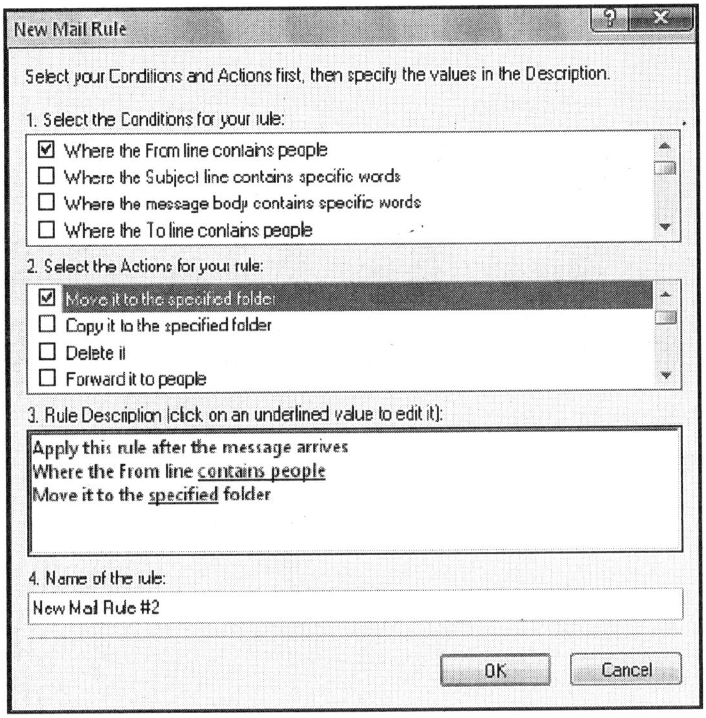

Fig 11.15 – New Mail Rule Dialogue Box

- Click the following check boxes:
  1. **Where the From line contains people**
  2. **Move to the specified folder**
- Now click on **contains people** in the lowest window. The Select People dialogue box appears. Type in the name of the sender whose mail you wish to segregate.
- Click on **specified folder** in the lowest window. The Move dialogue box appears. Either create a new folder by clicking on the **New Folder** button on the right of this dialogue box, or select an existing folder for storing e-mails from the selected sender.
- Click **OK** till all dialogue boxes are closed.

Henceforth, all e-mails received from the selected sender will be automatically removed from your inbox and stored in the folder you have selected.

Blocking Spam

TIP

You can use message rules to automatically delete spam as well. If you are being annoyed by persistent spam mail form a specific person or company, or you know from past experience that mail from a specific source contains virus or otherwise offensive material, then use the New Mail Rule dialogue box as before to identify the offensive sender and then click on the **Delete it** checkbox before closing all dialogue boxes. Henceforth, all mail sent by the selected sender will be automatically deleted.

ALERT

The most harmful e-mails however are the ones that contain a virus, usually as an attachment. After peaking in 2005, there appears to be a decline in e-mail borne viruses subsequently. However, there are still enough infected e-mails on the Internet to take their virus threats seriously. Unfortunately, mail rules are not adequate to protect your computer. To protect yourself, you need good Anti-virus software (AVS).

TIP

A good AVS should scan both incoming and outgoing e-mails. The incoming scan protects you while the outgoing scan is for the protection of your friends and colleagues. Any warning message on an outgoing scan is also a warning to you that your computer is probably infected by a virus. You can then begin a virus scan using your AVS and prevent further damage to yourself or to people receiving e-mails from you.

E-Mail Anti-Spam and Antiviral Action

Incoming Mail	Action taken by AVS	Output to E-mail Client
Clean and useful E-mail from Internet	Mail is filtered. No action	Clean E-mail
Commercial spam	Spam filtered out	No output
Mail from Objectionable site	Block the Sender	No output
Mail with virus	Delete virus or Delete mail	Clean E-mail No output

Fig 11.16 – E-mail Protection

E-mail Viruses

E-mail viruses have become increasingly common and virulent. Usually, one has to open an attachment containing a virus before being harmed by it. The Melissa worm, the Sircam and the Iloveyou virus all exploit the curiosity of the e-mail recipient by adding a provocative subject line such as "I love you" or "Free gifts for you" tempting you to open the attachment. When released, the virus sends a copy of the rogue e-mail to every e-mail address in your computer's address book, thus flooding your friends with copies. We recommend, therefore, that you should not open even e-mails, not just attachments, unless you trust the sender completely.

There are other, even more dangerous viruses that do not even require you to open the e-mail. It is enough if it is displayed in your preview pane of Microsoft Outlook or Outlook Express!

One such e-mail virus, called the "Nimda" virus does so by hiding a malicious visual basic script in the e-mail. Microsoft Outlook or Outlook Express uses visual basic script (VBS) for displaying its preview pane. The process of displaying the e-mail header is enough to trigger the malicious script in Nimda to do its dirty work!

In Fig 11.15, you can see how the anti-spam and the anti-viral components of good anti-virus software work. Its job is to deliver clean and safe e-mails to your e-mail client such as Outlook or Outlook Express. It will filter spam and disinfect infected e-mail. If an e-mail cannot be cleaned, the AVS will help you to delete it.

Anti-virus Software for E-mails

To filter out plain spam, message rules are generally sufficient. However, you require special software to deal with virus in the e-mail. See Fig 11.16 for a view of the McAffee anti-virus. The page shows the e-mail scan settings.

Most e-mail AVS use an internal programme (called a mail proxy) to filter, clean or remove virus before passing safe e-mails to your computer's e-mail client software. The proxy sits between your e-mail service provider (such as VSNL) and your e-mail software (such as Outlook Express). Let us take a specific example to see how the proxy works. For the purpose of this illustration, we will assume the following parameters:

The e-mail software you use	Outlook Express
Your Internet service provider (ISP):	VSNL
Mail server's post office protocol (POP3) address:	pop.vsnl.com
Your login name:	jlneogy
Your password:	youdontknow

If you use no AVS and connect directly to VSNL, while configuring Outlook Express, you would use the settings exactly as they are shown above. However, if you use an AVS that installs a mail proxy, two of the parameters will require to be changed as follows:

Mail server's POP3 address:
localhost (or 127.0.0.1)

Your login name:
jlneogy#pop.vsnl.com

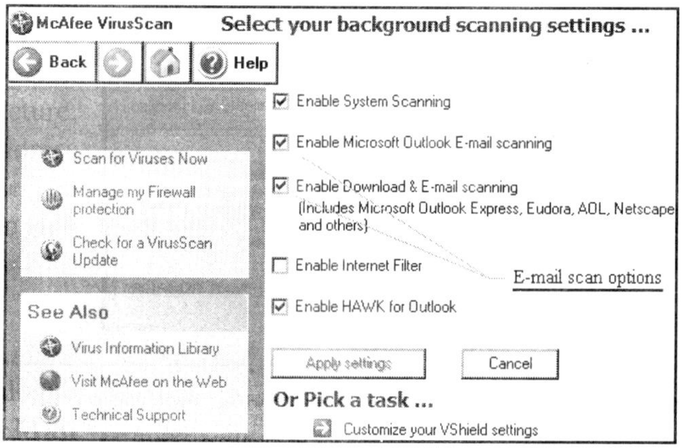

Fig 11.17 – E-mail Scan Settings

The # shown in the login name is a separator character. The actual character depends on the AVS you use. Thus '#' changes to '/' if you use Norton Anti-virus instead of McAffee.

The outcome of all this is that e-mails will be downloaded from VSNL into the mail proxy of your AVS. The e-mails will then be scanned for virus. If any virus is found, the software will attempt to remove it. Failing that, it will delete the e-mail. After the scan, safe e-mails will be passed on to Outlook Express and will appear in its inbox and preview pane as usual.

Some of the recommended e-mail anti-virus software (AVS) and their Websites are given below:

AVG Antivirus	**http://www.grisoft.com**
McAffee Virusscan	**http://www.mcaffee.com**
Norton Antivirus	**http://www.symantec.com**
Panda Antivirus	**http://www.pandasoftware.com**
Pc-cillin	**http://www.antivirus.com**
ZoneAlarm	**http://www.zonelabs.com**

Of the above, ZoneAlarm and AVG are both free for personal users. Others such as Norton have evaluation versions that you can use before deciding which AVS to buy.

We have now covered a wide variety of strategies and anti-virus software to protect your computer from harm while surfing the Internet or communicating through e-mails. Protection has become an integral part of computer use today, especially if you happen to have fast Internet connections such as cable Internet or DSL connections. Protection is vital even if you are just connected to a local network since malware has become so common.

Although the threat is real and the potential for data loss and programme corruption is so great, we believe that in this chapter you have learned enough to effectively protect yourself from harm and enjoy the knowledge and joy of the Internet without fear.

12. Student's Resources

As we have seen throughout this book, there is simply no limit to the information that you may get from the Internet. In fact, the problem is usually too much rather than too little information. Apart from the problem of finding relevant information, the student must be absolutely sure of the reliability of the information. In other words, for academic use, your information must not only be authoritative but also authentic.

In this chapter:

- We provide you with reliable and well-respected Websites on all the important topics you will come across as a student, no matter what your subject may be.
- We cover all the important educational streams – Science, Arts, Commerce and Engineering.
- Each stream is further sub-divided into topics. For example, under Science, we cover Physics, Chemistry, Biology, Mathematics and Statistics.
- For each topic, we recommend two excellent Websites that contain valuable information.
- At some Websites, you will be able to download complete text books for free, a very valuable resource indeed.

We trust that no matter what your subject may be, this chapter will arm you to face your examinations so very much better prepared.

Coverage

We cover the following streams and topics in this chapter:

Science	Commerce	Arts	Engineering
Physics	Accountancy	History	General Engineering
Chemistry	Taxation	Geography	Open Courseware
Biology	Economics	Civics	Online Training
Mathematics	Business Organisation	Sociology	Free Computer Books
Statistics		Psychology	
		Political Science	
		Anthropology	
		Literature	

For each topic, we recommend two Websites and give you a brief description of what you may expect at the Website.

ALERT

A word of caution, do remember that Websites are not permanent. So, if a site cannot be accessed, the reason may be anything from the site being very busy to the site being discontinued. For guidance on how to download information and save the data on your hard disk, refer to *Chapter 4 – Web Surfing*.

Let us now begin with the websites.

Science Stream

For many of us Science subjects are challenging, perhaps second only to Mathematics. While looking at the information available at each Website, focus on finding answers to the queries you have, or to supplement the information in your text book.

Physics

Many of the sites in this topic use flash animation, Java applets and movies to supplement text. Make sure that your Web browser is capable of supporting these so that you can get the full benefit of the Website's capabilities.

Glenbrook South Physics Home Page

Created by Physics tutors at Glenbrook South High School, topics are presented in a very interesting manner. In addition to text, pictures and animation, a section has quiz questions for a student to test his or her knowledge. A multimedia section contains movies on experiments in physics, carried out by the school students.

Website: **http://www.glenbrook.k12.il.us/gbssci/phys/phys.html**

You can access the Physics 1 online course by clicking on the link on the right sidebar. Important topics such as the Laws of Motion are covered in this course.

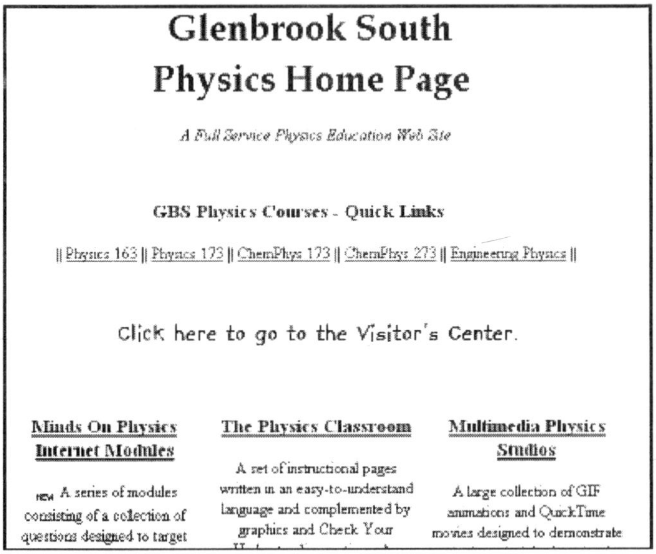

Fig 12.01 – Glenbrook South

MIT Department of Physics Open Courseware

High quality educational material is available at this site organised by the justly famous Massachusetts Institute of Technology. The consortium providing the courseware includes several well-known institutions. The contents are indeed of very high quality.

Website: **http://ocw.mit.edu/ocwweb/physics**

The contents are not divided into chapters as in text books, but include lecture notes, video recordings of lectures and screen shots of blackboards. Therefore, you may have to look a little patiently for the precise information you need.

Fig 12.02 – Open Courseware, MIT

Chemistry

With Biotechnology making giant strides in today's world, Chemistry is again a sought after subject. Whether you are a regular student, or working on the next great chemical discovery, the Websites we describe below will be of interest to you.

An Introduction to Chemistry

This Website is an online version of the well known book of the same name by Mark Bishop. The Website is maintained and regularly updated by the author and contains excellent multimedia materials in addition to regular text.

NOTE

You may select the "chemistry first" version form the two viewing options. If you do so, then the mathematics related topics will be found pushed back in the book, from chapter 8 onwards. In the other "early conversion" version, the mathematics related topics appear earlier.

Each chapter text can be downloaded as PDF files. In addition, there are concept maps that summarise each chapter in one page each, convenient for revisions. Lessons can also be viewed as PowerPoint presentations.

Website: **http://prepatorychemistry.com**

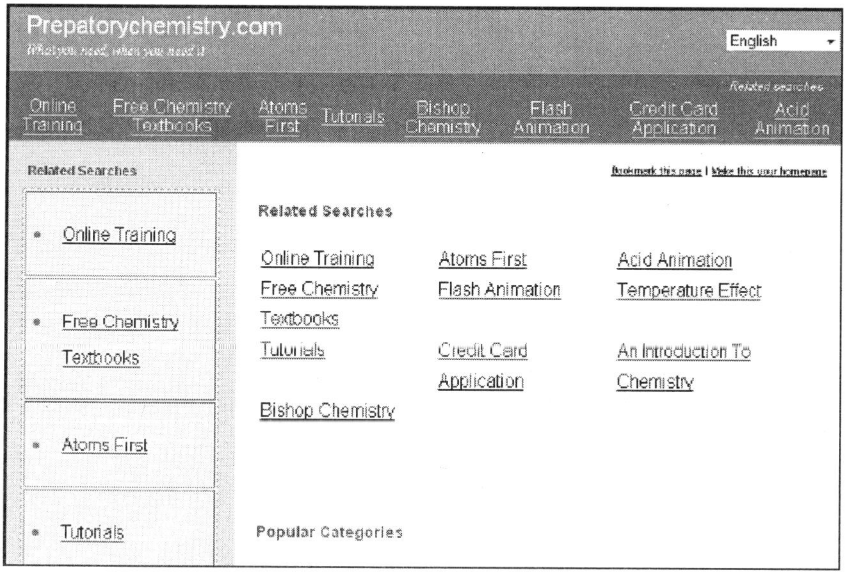

Fig 12.03 – An Introduction to Chemistry

World of Chemistry

In addition to the usual course text books, students often need to consult a reference guide in order to refresh some concepts or clarify others that may not have been dealt with very clearly in the prescribed text book.

The World of Chemistry is an encyclopaedia-type Website where information is organised under the usual sections under general chemistry. By clicking on any main topic, you can display a list of sub-topics. Further clicking will take you down into sub-layers of details.

Website: **http://scienceworld.wolfram.com/chemistry**

Biology

The sites we discuss in the field of Biology are meant to supplement your regular text books prescribed in your own institute. They are supplementary sources of information, to be read alongside your regular text books. However, they provide you with valuable supplementary information.

An Online Biology Book

The Online Biology Book is based on the lectures given by Professor M J Farabee of the Estrella Mountain Community College. The book is meant for college students and covers topics as diverse as the inner construction of cells, bio-diversity and the causes of periodic extinction of species on earth. The information provided is both clear and self-explanatory.

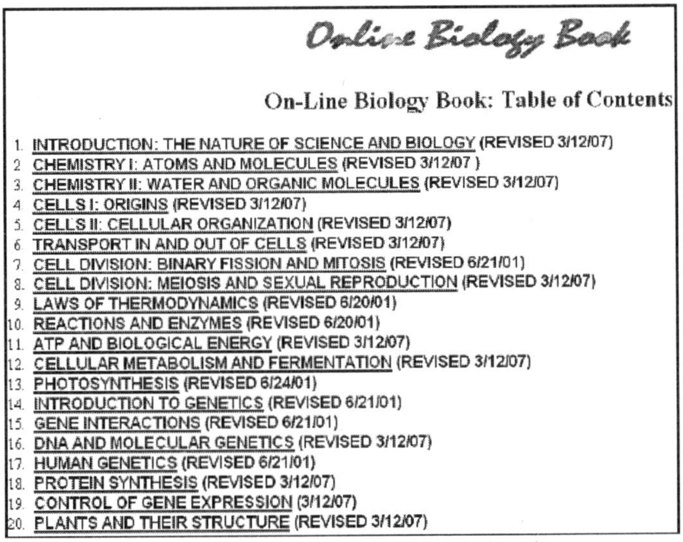

Online Biology Book

On-Line Biology Book: Table of Contents

1. INTRODUCTION: THE NATURE OF SCIENCE AND BIOLOGY (REVISED 3/12/07)
2. CHEMISTRY I: ATOMS AND MOLECULES (REVISED 3/12/07)
3. CHEMISTRY II: WATER AND ORGANIC MOLECULES (REVISED 3/12/07)
4. CELLS I: ORIGINS (REVISED 3/12/07)
5. CELLS II: CELLULAR ORGANIZATION (REVISED 3/12/07)
6. TRANSPORT IN AND OUT OF CELLS (REVISED 3/12/07)
7. CELL DIVISION: BINARY FISSION AND MITOSIS (REVISED 6/21/01)
8. CELL DIVISION: MEIOSIS AND SEXUAL REPRODUCTION (REVISED 3/12/07)
9. LAWS OF THERMODYNAMICS (REVISED 6/20/01)
10. REACTIONS AND ENZYMES (REVISED 6/20/01)
11. ATP AND BIOLOGICAL ENERGY (REVISED 3/12/07)
12. CELLULAR METABOLISM AND FERMENTATION (REVISED 3/12/07)
13. PHOTOSYNTHESIS (REVISED 6/24/01)
14. INTRODUCTION TO GENETICS (REVISED 6/21/01)
15. GENE INTERACTIONS (REVISED 6/21/01)
16. DNA AND MOLECULAR GENETICS (REVISED 3/12/07)
17. HUMAN GENETICS (REVISED 6/21/01)
18. PROTEIN SYNTHESIS (REVISED 3/12/07)
19. CONTROL OF GENE EXPRESSION (3/12/07)
20. PLANTS AND THEIR STRUCTURE (REVISED 3/12/07)

Fig 12.04 – Online Biology Book

Website: **http://www.estrellamountain.edu/faculty/farabee/biobk/biobooktoc.html**

The MIT Biology Hypertext Book

For advanced students, this Website provides information on Introductory Biology as well as Molecular Biology. While some of the material goes beyond the normal syllabus of college level biology as taught in India, the site is an excellent source if you wish to prepare an MIT programme.

Website: **http://web.mit.edu/esgbio/www**

Mathematics

Mathematics is one of the most difficult subjects that we encounter in school and college. Therefore, any help that you can get through online education materials in this field is always welcome. The sites we review will provide you with information to supplement your regular class work and school or college text books.

Webmath.com

This Website provides you with problem-solving help in several categories such as Trigonometry, Algebra, Calculus, etc. From any of these categories, you can navigate to a particular sub-topic by clicking on the topic and selecting the sub-topic you want in the drop down menu that appears. For instance, from the main topic "calculus", you can jump to such sub-topics as "derivatives", "integration", "solved integrals", "quotient rules" etc.

You can also use the tabs to navigate to different sections on the Website such as "General Math", "Math for everyone", "Algebra", "Trigonometry and Calculus", etc. Overall, it is a good source of basic level information.

Website: **http://www.webmath.com**

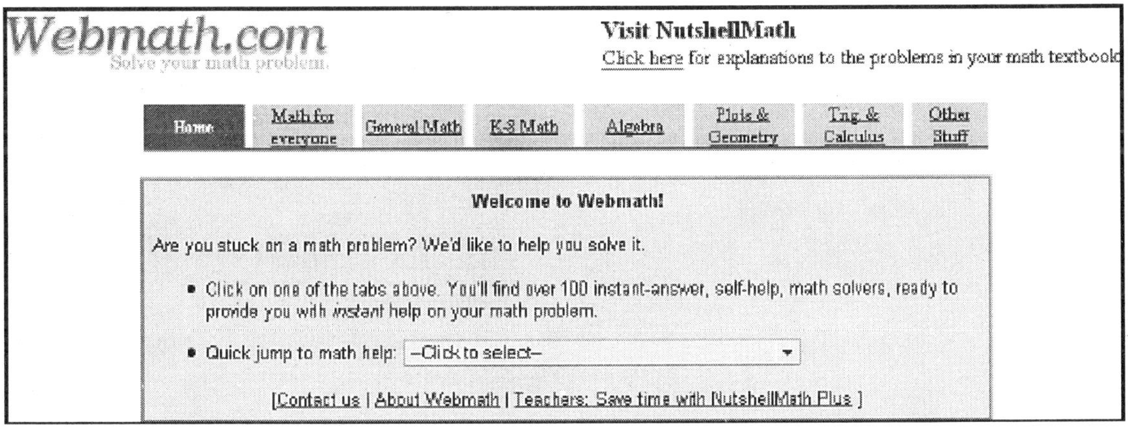

Fig 12.05 – Webmath.com

Wolfram MathWorld

TIP

This Website is perhaps the most comprehensive of them all, containing very large volumes of information on different branches of mathematics. However, because of its very size, it is somewhat difficult to navigate and you may have to wade through a great deal of information to find what you want.

The effort is still worthwhile since whatever you need in mathematics is probably available at this Website.

Website: **http://mathworld.wolfram.com**

Statistics

Though a part of Mathematics, you are likely to encounter Statistics as part of your Commerce curriculum. The subject is also very important in higher studies as in business colleges and in advanced studies such as Econometrics.

For the purpose of classification in this chapter, we consider it a part of the Science stream.

Richard Lowry's Page

Richard Lowry is a professor of Vassar College, USA. His on-line textbook is a free and full length inferential statistical handbook that covers topics of interest to graduate or college level students. The site is somewhat overloaded with text and the layout could have been more attractive.

Website: **http://faculty.vassar.edu/lowry/intro.html**

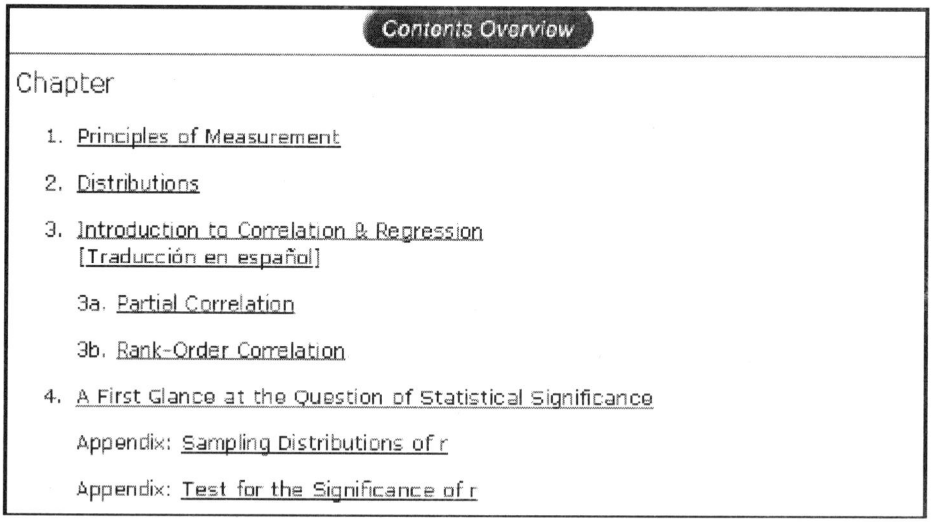

12.06 – Richard Lowry's Page

Elementary Statistics

This is the best Website for Elementary Statistics. The layout is attractive and it is easy to navigate through the Website. The contents however, are meant mainly for pre-college level statistics. There are video presentations also available to supplement the text and the topics are simply yet comprehensively dealt with.

Website: **http://sofia.fhda.edu/gallery/statistics/index.html**

Commerce Stream

Accounting

Although names change, the function of an accountant remains the same. While in India an accountant may be called a Chartered Accountant, the same function is carried out by a Certified Public Accountant in the US. The Websites that follow, though of foreign origin, have information relevant to Indian college curriculums as well.

Principles of Accounting

The information available on this Website is very useful to students of Financial Accounting and Managerial Accounting. The data is available as an online text book where each accounting principle is dealt with in a separate chapter.

The Website provides quizzes and fill-in-the-blanks type of questionnaires so that a reader can test comprehension during study. The language is easy to understand and the presentation is very good.

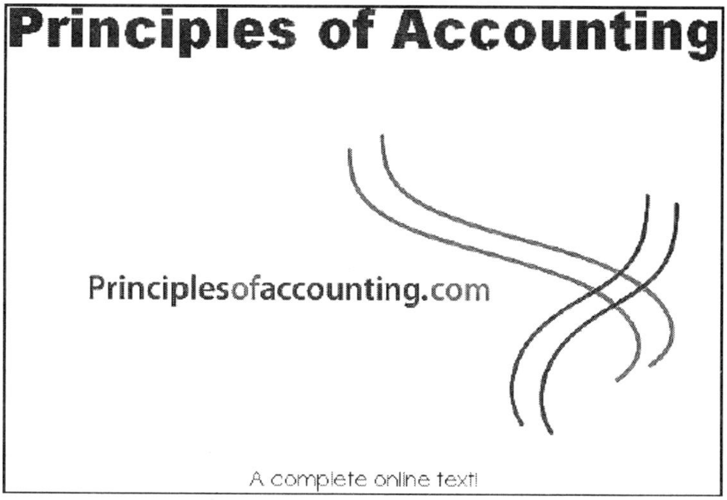

12.07 – Principles of Accounting

Website: **http://www.principlesofaccounting.com**

Future Accountant

This is a well designed Website providing a step-by-step guide to become a Chartered Accountant (CA), a Cost and Works Accountant (CWA) or a Company secretary (CS). Each topic in accounting is explained in detail, beginning with definitions and moving on to illustrations that explain the application of the accounting principle under discussion.

Website: **http://www.futureaccountant.com**

A valuable resource at this site is a collection of examination question papers that a reader may look at and use for practice. In most cases, model answers are also provided.

Taxation

Taxation laws and their study is country specific. Therefore, we deal with Websites that are based on Indian laws on taxation.

Website of Income Tax Department

A good place to start is at the National Website of the Income Tax Department of India. By clicking on the Tax Laws and Rules link, you can see drop down lists containing Acts, Rules, Circulars, Notifications and Forms. By clicking on one of the options, you can display additional options. Thus, under Rules, you will see Income Tax Rules, Wealth Tax Rule, Gift Tax Rules, and Expenditure Tax Rules, etc.

Website: **http://www.incometaxindia.gov.in**

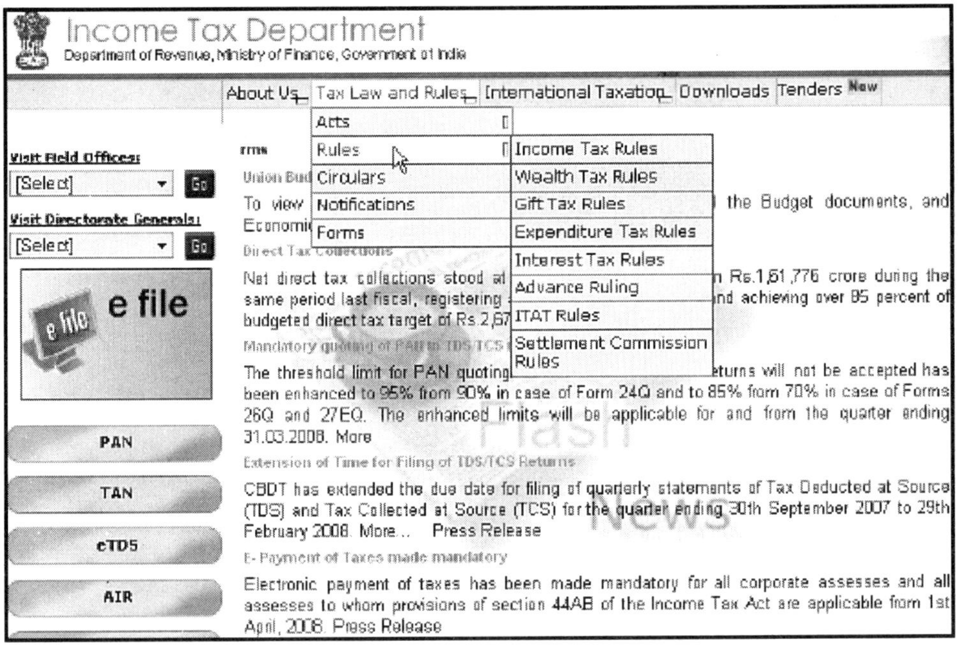

Fig 12.08 – Income Tax Department

Do not be put off by the legal jargon and the rather heavy usage of specialised Tax parlance. Inside all that is authentic information on government rules and circulars, essential for any serious student of Income Tax Laws.

India Mart – Taxation

This site is of great interest to anyone studying Tax laws or planning to file income tax returns after a self-assessment of income and expenditure. The site has information on income tax returns, filing of income tax, the forms to be used as well as legal procedures involved. You can also find information on income tax administration and procedures here.

Website: **http://finance.indiamart.com/taxation**

Economics

Economics is a subject in all courses on Commerce in Indian colleges. The information in the Websites we recommend is not limited to the Indian context, but have wider implications. You can browse these sites, picking up information of interest to you, ranging from the basic to the advanced.

The Library of Economics and Liberty

This site is truly encyclopaedic, containing books, articles, topics and links to further information from all around the world. Some famous online books include works by Alfred Marshall,

John Milton, etc. The books are completely free. Use the search function available at the Website to search for specific books or authors.

Website: **http://www.econlib.org/**

Fig 12.09 – Library of Economics

This Website is a very valuable library of articles and even text books, very useful to any student of Economics or Commerce.

Business Organisation

While Business Organisation (BO) as a topic is included in Commerce courses, there is a great deal of similarity between the contents of Business Organisation courses and Management courses. Therefore, for both BO and Management students can benefit from visiting Websites that specialise on both the topics.

Managerial Marketing

NOTE

In some colleges at graduate level, you can select marketing as an option in Commerce instead of Accounting. If you want information on marketing, this is an excellent site, dedicated to the subject of marketing management. You can select topics from the right hand sidebar and reach sub-topics on your selected subject. It is a very good site for the basics of Marketing Management.

Fig 12.10 – Marketing Management

Website: **http://www.marketingmanagement.com/**

Online Book on Marketing

This online book by Gemmy Allen contains useful study guides and notes.

Website: **http://telecollege.dcccd.edu/mrkt2370/book/mrktbook.htm**

You can browse outline of topics covered, definition of important terms and browse through objective and discussion questions. The site is very useful for checking progress of your studies.

Arts Stream

Arts stream has a very large number of courses. We will try to cover as many topics as possible, but limit ourselves to just one Website per topic.

History

TIP

History is one subject where you will see more disagreements amongst books written by experts than in any other topic. If you surf the Web, you will notice differences amongst historians in Websites as well. However, for a balanced view of history, it is a good idea to be exposed to differing points of views and draw up your own.

Indian History

In this Website, information is grouped under three links arranged along the top. They include Ancient India, Medieval India and Modern India. While some of the links will open rather longish texts, others have relatively little information. However, almost all presentations are good and are well illustrated.

Website: **http://www.indhistory.com**

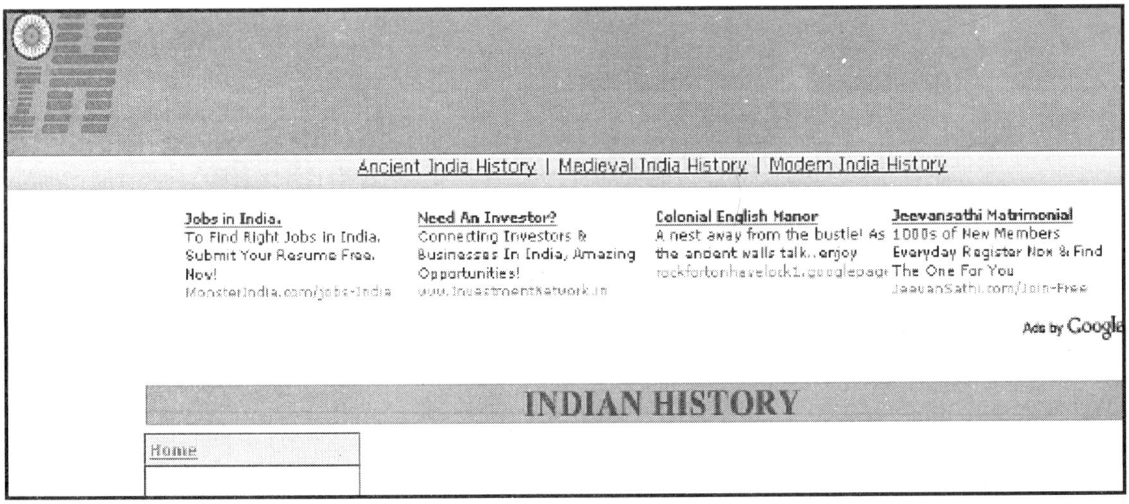

Fig 12.11 – Indian History

One feature of real interest is the timeline available for each period of Indian history. Clicking on the timeline is a convenient way to gather information about a particular period in Indian history.

For similar information on World history, you may want to visit The Encyclopaedia of World History at: **http://www.bartleby.com/67/**

Geography

We recommend sites that contain much more than just tables and statistics about countries.

The World Fact Book

NOTE

This site is a very comprehensive source of information about countries of the world. Instead of searching information on countries only, you can widen your search to include regions. For example, Indian Ocean or Antarctica will throw up information about the entire region you select. You can also use the search feature to zero in on a single town or a small country.

Website: **http://www.cia.gov/cia/publications/factbook/index.html**

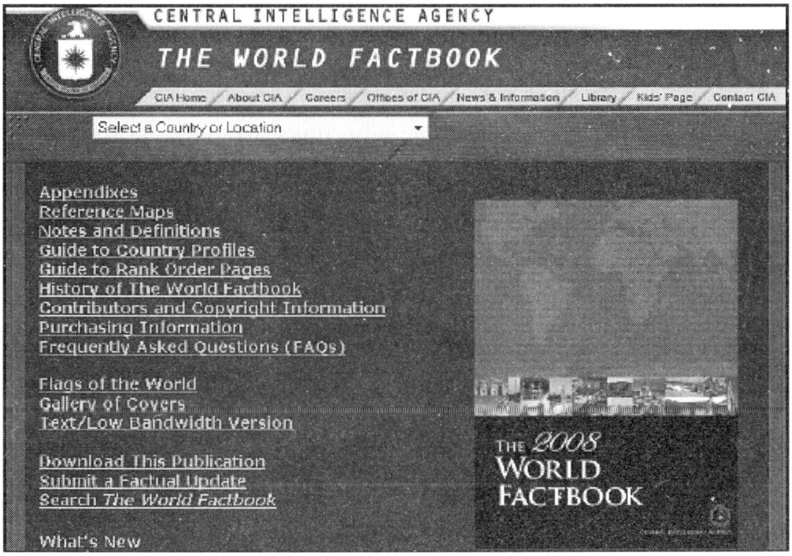

Fig 12.12 – World Fact Book

Civics

An excellent source for information on Indian laws is found at the US Library of Congress Website. Amongst the links available on the India Research Guide page is the one titled "Legal Research Guide India". In addition, you can find information on the Indian Constitution, the Executive, Legislature and Judiciary as well as a number of links to general sources.

Website: **http://www.loc.gov/law/help/guide/nations/india.html**

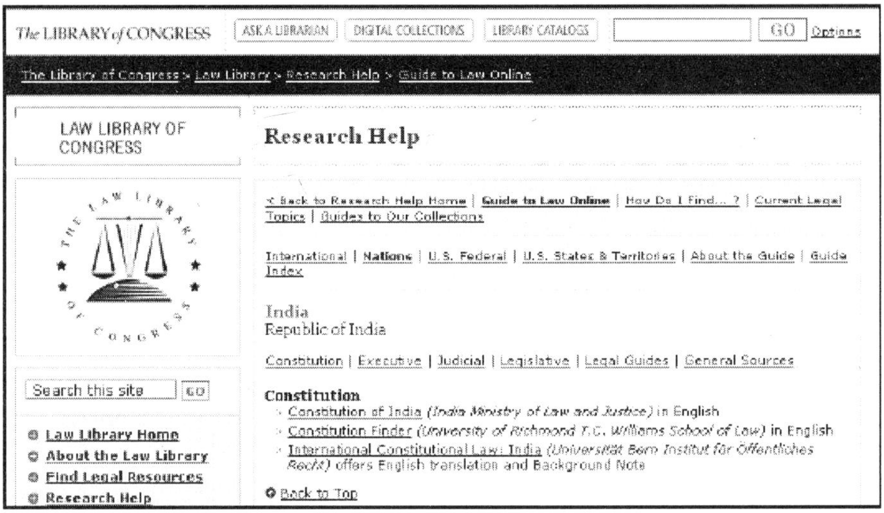

Fig 12.13 – Library of Congress Website

Sociology

Much information and much of the standard course material on this subject can be found on the Web. Information on some elective courses is also available.

Sociology Central

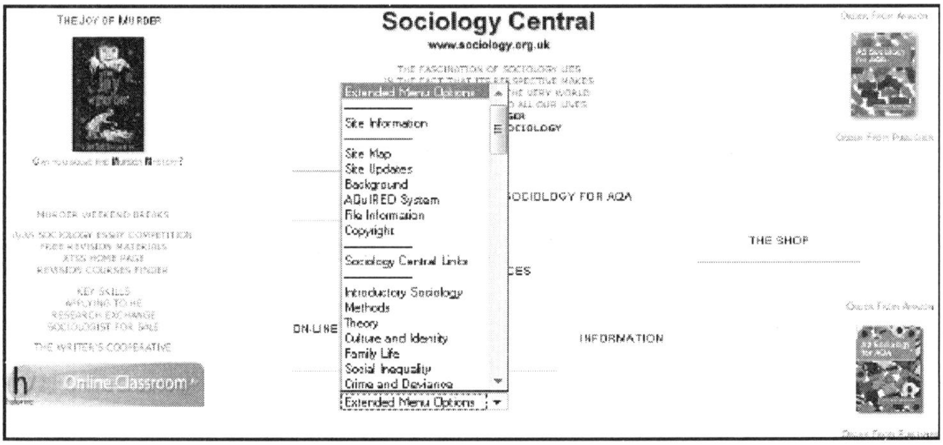

Fig 12.14 – Sociology Central

TIP

Being a United Kingdom (UK) Website, the site is designed for use by "A" level students in UK. However, much of the material is useful to first and second year Sociology students in India. Begin by browsing the Resources section and clicking on Teaching Notes for more information on various topics such as Cultural Identity, Education and Religion.

Website: **http://www.sociology.org.uk/index.htm**

Psychology

Substantial information is available on the Internet for undergraduate studies in Psychology. You may have to search a little longer for postgraduate study material. For Psychology and related subjects, you may want to visit the website at the Highear Education Academy, UK.

Higher Education Academy Psychology Network

A comprehensive Website, it is updated almost every day. You can use the top line of main menus or the links provided on the left hand sidebar. While there is a paid membership option, there is enough "free" data to make a visit to the site very worthwhile.

On the left hand sidebar, there is a very useful link for graduating school students who are thinking of taking up Psychology in college. Here you can get replies concerning the study of Psychology to decide if this subject is for you.

Website: **http://www.psychology.heacademy.ac.uk/**

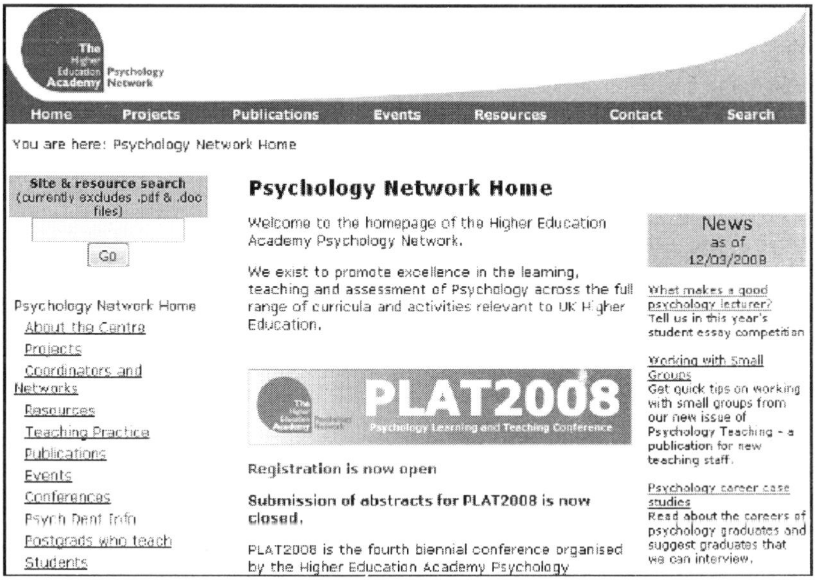

Fig 12.15 – H E Academy

Another Website containing a great deal of material on Psychology, but with a rather strange name is Alley Dog at **http://www.alleydog.com**. It contains a glossary, forums and hints on how to improve your marks (grades) in college.

Political Science

ALERT

As in the case of History and Geography, much of the information you can get on the Internet on Political Science will only apply to the country that hosts the Website. However, there are general principles regarding Political Science in other countries that will also interest students in India.

For information specific to India, you may visit the Website of the Ministry of Law and Justice, Government of India.

Ministry of Law and Justice

ALERT

While this site is a mine of information for students of Political Science, it is difficult to navigate. In fact, for casual visitors without a background of the subject, the Website can actually look confusing. On the other hand, the information is completely authentic and is updated regularly so that any change in the Indian legislative system is soon reflected in the Website.

A very useful source of information on legislation past and present can be accessed by clicking on the "India Code" text link. Here you can find all legislation passed by the government since 1834.

Website: **http://lawmin.nic.in/**

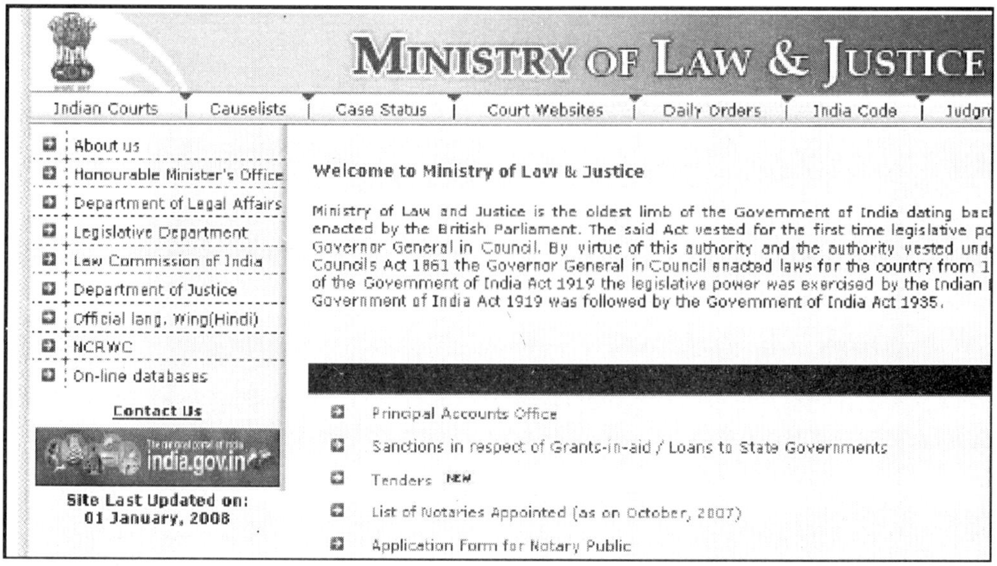

Fig 12.16 – Ministry of Law and Justice

For international material you can also visit the Central Library of Political Science, Vanderbilt University at **http://www.library.vanderbilt.edu/romans/polsci/**

Anthropology

As in the case of Sociology, the Web contains a great deal of information on Anthropology useful to both first and second year college students as well as to students pursuing higher studies in the subject. You may wish to visit the Virtual Library of Anthropology which has information on almost all anthropological and related subjects.

Virtual Library of Anthropology

In order to explore the entire site, it is necessary to register yourself in a simple and free procedure. To do so, click on the "Create Account" link located at the top right hand corner of the Website. Thereafter, you can log in with your username and password. The site is maintained by an organisation called Anthrotech.

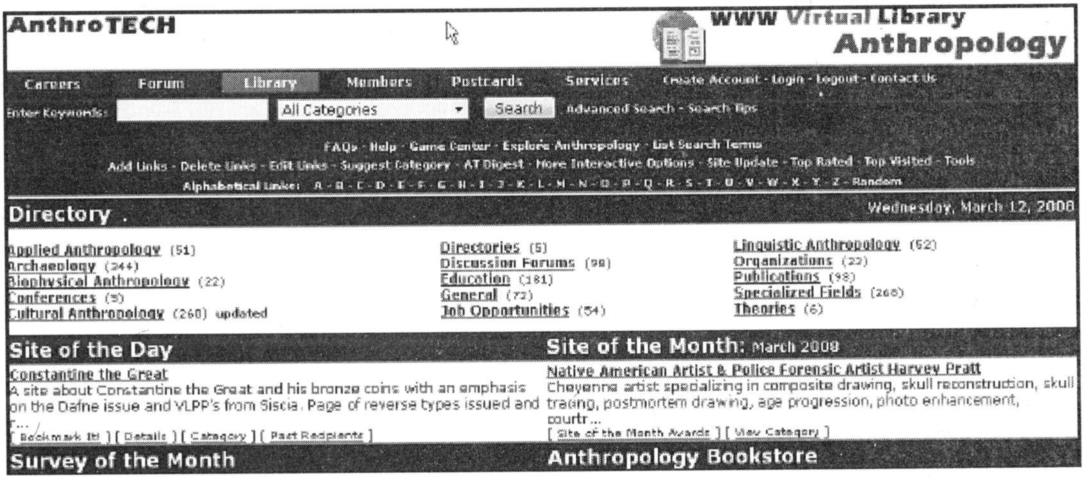

Fig 12.17 – Anthrotech

The really attractive feature of the Website is its directory that gives you access to hundreds of links to topics and issues related to Anthropology. Check the links for last updates since some are rather old, although most of the links are recent.

Website: **http://vlib.anthrotech.com/**

A somewhat less comprehensive but simply designed Website on Anthropology is available at the Palomar College Anthropology Programme Website. The homepage of the Website has a brief introduction to the subject as well as a list of useful links. Amongst these, there is a link to take you to a Website that gives students career options in the field of Anthropology.

Website is: **http://www.palomar.edu/anthropology**.

There is an excellent section at the main Website that contains links to Anthropology tutorials. There are links to both Biological and Cultural Anthropology.

Literature

In this section, we confine ourselves to Websites dealing with English literature. While there are no common guidelines prescribed by the University Grants Commission (UGC), the sites mentioned here will provide you with the commonly taught principles and courses.

The Internet Public Library

Hosted by the School of Information at the University of Michigan, this site is well known for the literary criticism that is available here, covering different writers and their works. The site is well designed and navigation is simple.

You can browse the collection of criticisms using different classifications. You will notice that the coverage of Indian literature is not as complete as that of US literature. However, several Indian writers writing in English have been covered.

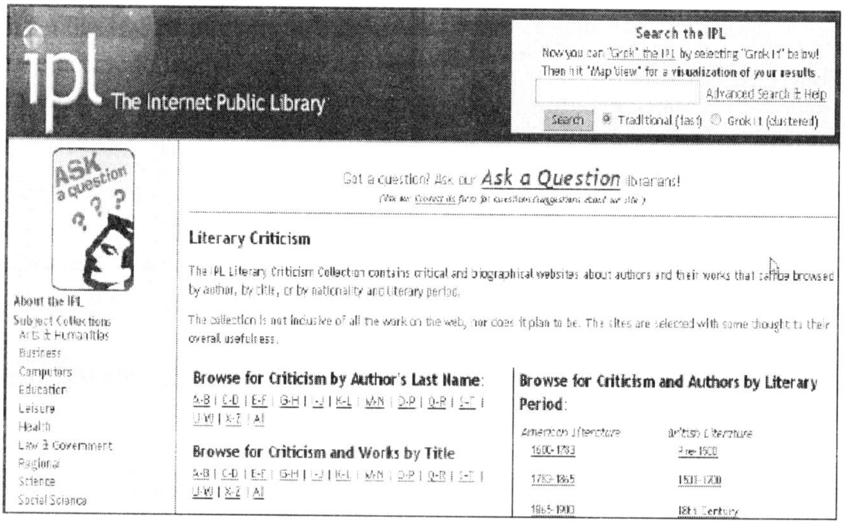

Fig 12.18 – The Internet Public Library

A good place to start on the site is to go to the Literary Criticism Guide and look through the links provided that will lead you to other relevant sites.

Website is located at: **http://www.ipl.org/div/litcrit**

Engineering

General

NOTE

Engineering consists of a vast collection of disciplines. It is virtually impossible to even cover the outlines in a book of the nature that you are holding in your hands. In this section, we will try to only point you towards some appreciation of the width of engineering disciplines and to Websites that may help you select an appropriate engineering course for yourself.

To give you a feel for the different branches of engineering, we suggest that you may visit the Wikipedia Entries Website. At this site, you can get a broad overview by reading through the articles on the main page at **http://en.wikipedia.org/wiki/Main_Page**. You can also jump to the Engineering portal to view details on specific engineering disciplines.

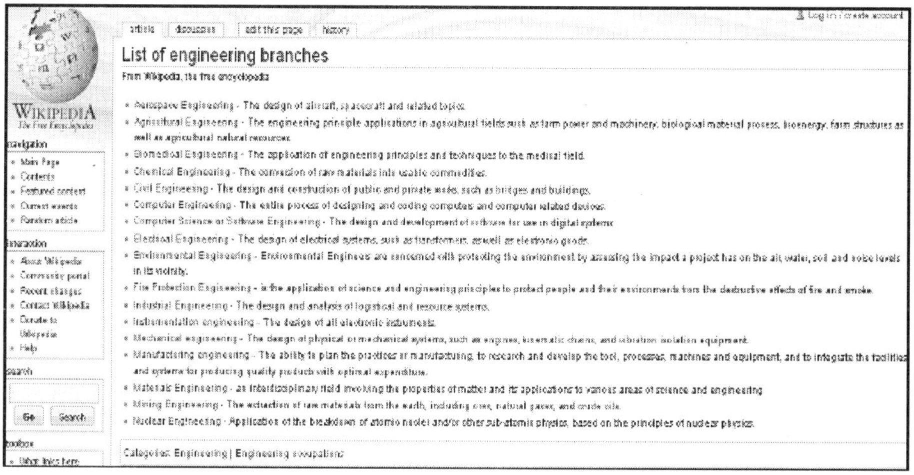

Fig 12.19 – List of Engineering Branches - Wikipedia

Open Courseware

TIP

Open source courseware in different branches of Engineering is very useful for supplementary reading to augment your text books. Being open source, the courseware is free and all you need is a fast broadband Internet connection to download what you need. Some sites may require that you register yourself. However, registration is usually free and quite straightforward.

An excellent site is the Open Courseware site of the Massachusetts Institute of Technology (MIT). Through the Open courseware (OCW) programme, MIT has made teaching syllabus, lecture notes, and even digital textbooks available free for public use over the Internet.

Visit MIT's OCW programme at: **http://ocw.mit.edu**

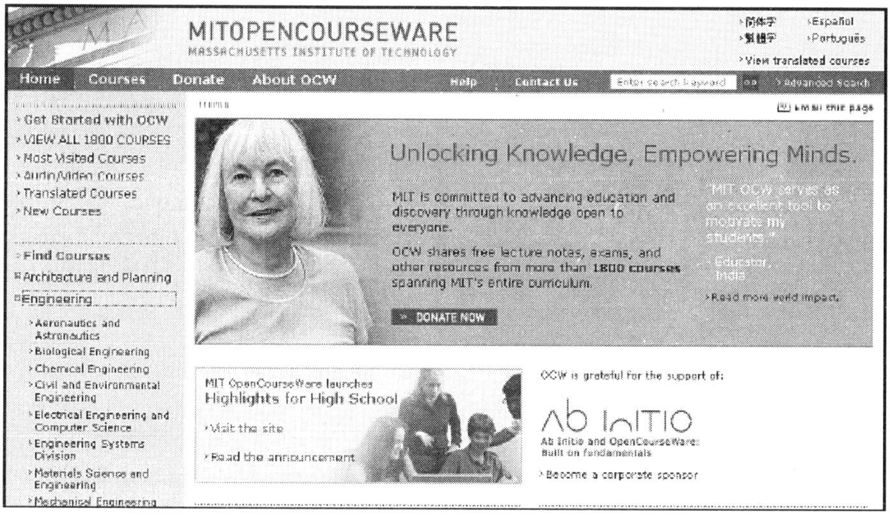

12.20 – MIT's Open Courseware

Another very good source of open courseware is the Open Courseware Finder, located at: **http://opencontent.org/ocwfinder.** As the name implies, the site is useful for finding open courseware on the Internet by entering a topic and then narrowing down the search by inserting appropriate filters (up to four levels).

Free Online Training Courses

Hewlett Packard has a number of popular online courses available that include both Engineering topics and other topics such as Digital Photography, Security Solutions and the Home Office. The language is designed to suit hobbyists and is not really academic. However, the information is very reliable and useful.

You have to register with and username and password and select a course. Thereafter, lessons are sent to you by e-mail.

The site is at:
http://www.hp.com/co/learningcenter

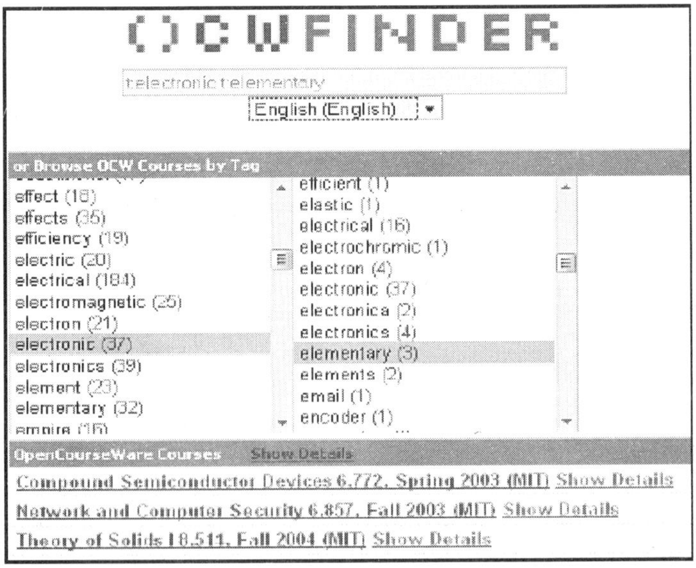

Fig 12.21 – Open Courseware Finder

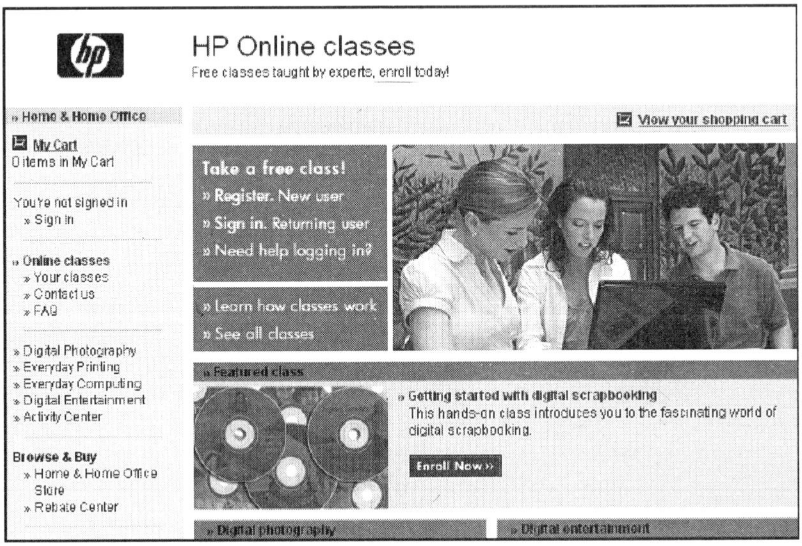

Fig 12.22 – HP Online Classes

Another useful site for online classes is at the E-Learning Centre, which specialises mainly in Computer-related teaching such as C ++, MCSE course, Microsoft Office subjects, etc.

The site is at: **http://www.e-learningcenter.com/free.htm**.

Free Books, Tutorials and Lecture Notes

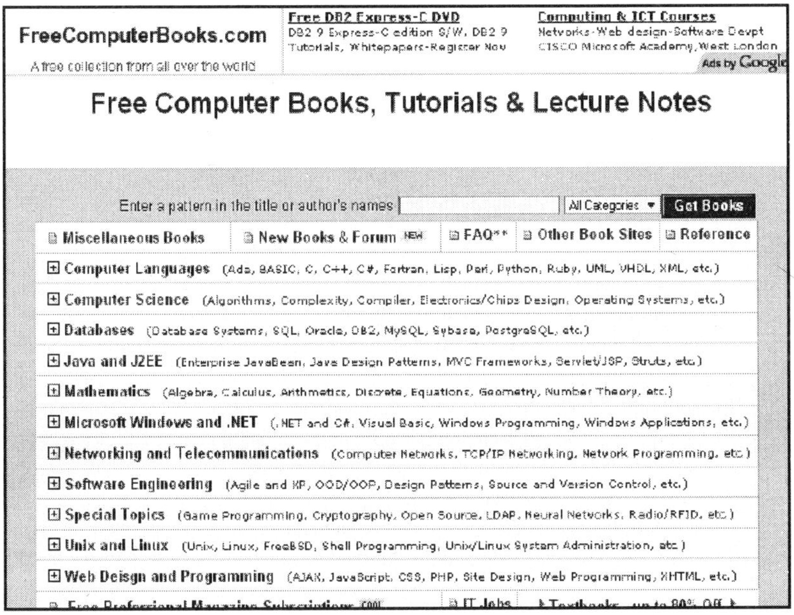

Fig 12.23 – Free Computer Books

The material available is directed towards Computer courses. There are a large number of computer books, tutorials and lecture notes available at the FreeComputerBooks.com. There are some eight computer sciences topics covered here in addition to links to many other sites. These links will lead to free electronic books, list of trade magazines, some of which is free and forums you can join to exchange information on topics that interest you.

Visit this website at: **http://freecomputerbooks.com/**

Skim, Scan, Scroll

A Quick Guide to Web Writing

— Jyotsna Atre

Writing is an art, but writing for the web can be quite a scientific experience. Especially, if you plan to capture the eyeballs of the fickle readership of this neo-medium! This book deals with the what, why and how of writing for the web. Not necessarily in that order or in those words.

Whether you are creating content for Corporate websites, writing promotional copy for Sales pages, developing your Personal websites, or updating your Blog, this practical guide aims to help you write effective web content that will make your visitors want to read.

You will get quick tips about how to cater to specific audiences, how to make sure that your content is the attention grabber that you want it to be, and how to get good search engine rankings for your web page.

You will also learn about the:

- ✔ Importance of hyperlinks
- ✔ Technicalities of a style guide
- ✔ Style rules for visual design and layout

And lots more...

Demy Size • Pages: 92
Price: Rs. 125/- • Postage: Rs. 20/-

Make Computers Speak Your Language

Computing in Your Own Language

— Barun Kumar Sahu

If you are working in a non-English speaking environment anywhere in the world, and want to work on computers — this book is a must.

This book will aid interested persons to work on computer in any language such as Hindi, Telugu, Kannada, Sanskrit, Persian, Tamil, Greek, Gujarati, Chinese, Urdu, Spanish, French and many more...you can use any of them to surf the Internet, or to send and receive mails and documents using a Desktop, Laptop, or a Palmtop.

Now computers can be made (instructed) to read and write your language. No technical knowledge is required and anybody can work on it. This book starts with the popular way of using computer, and then goes step-by-step to explain how to write text and data in a chosen language. Explanations have been given in simple manner. There are plenty of illustrations in the form of screenshots. Many concepts have been provided in Hindi. Other Indian languages have also received their due. Chinese, Japanese and Korean have also been touched upon.

Apart from Microsoft Windows, detailed guidelines have also been provided to setup your computer to work in Microsoft Office, Open Office or Linux environments etc.

Following this book you can:

✔ Search Internet in your language ✔ Sort text and search in your preferred language ✔ Write e-mail in any language ✔ Hindi e-mail will appear in Hindi

And yes, you do not need any extra software to do all this. Not even pirated ones!

Big Size • Pages: 208
Price: Rs. 175/- • Postage: Rs. 20/-

Rapidex® Computer Course

Windows 98/Me/XP Edition

Get FREE CD, Mouse Pad & Google User Guide
Also available in Hindi

Big Size • Pages: 560 (approx.)
Price: Rs. 275/- • Postage: Rs. 25/-

The new millennium has seen major changes in Information Technology. To be in tune with all that has happened in the world of computers, software and the Internet, the Rapidex Computer Course — with over a million copies in print — has been completely revised and updated. This edition is based on Windows 98 or Windows Me as the operating system and the Office 2000 suite as the basic software package. **A new chapter on Windows XP (in colour) has been added at the end of the book.**

This book covers all aspects of computers, the Internet and software suites. It begins with instructions for setting up and switching on your computer. Then it guides you through the Disk Operating System (DOS) and the Windows operating system (Windows 98 and Windows Me). You move on to the highly popular Microsoft Office 2000 software suite. You gain knowledge of the Internet, e-mails, and anti-virus software along the way.

The mission of this book is to provide a step-by-step teaching aid for self-learners and students of computer courses. Full of practical examples, it stands out from a host of other "teach yourself" books. While the contents have been thoroughly revised and updated, the style is the same friendly and familiar one.

To provide a richer, more interactive learning experience, the book comes with a free CD-ROM containing multimedia learning courses that complement what you read in the book.

Unicorn Bestsellers

9376 C • Rs.296/-

9703 C • Rs.125/-

9717 K • Rs.150/-

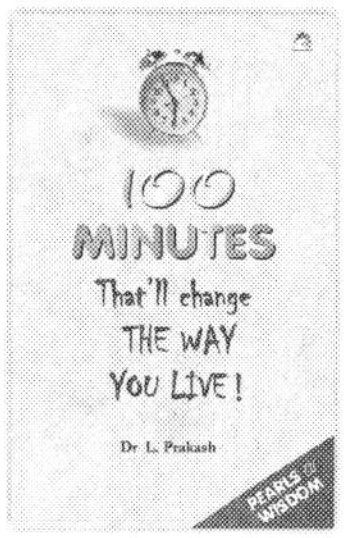

9336 B • Rs. 135/-

9376 B • Rs. 150/-

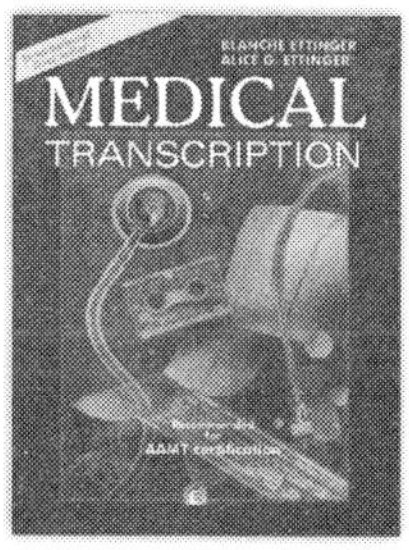

9207 D • Rs. 450/-

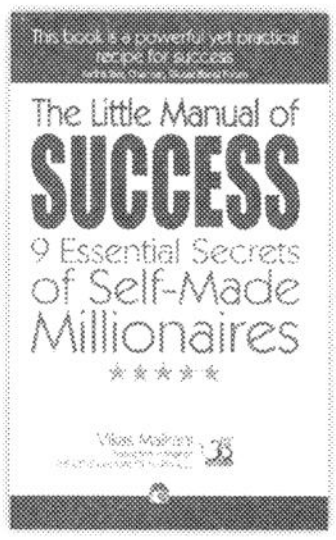

9351 D • Rs. 150/-

5625 D • Rs. 110/-

9272 A • Rs. 150/-

7795 E • Rs. 150/-

9324 E • Rs.60/-

9369 D • Rs. 150/-

9213 F • Rs. 88/-

9333 D • Rs. 96/-

9355 D • Rs. 150/-

9971 C • Rs. 80/-